THE EVOLUTION OF PROPERTY

AND

SOCIAL AND PHILOSOPHICAL
STUDIES

PAUL LAFARGUE

The
Evolution of Property
from
Savagery to Civilization

AND

Social and Philosophical
Studies

NEW PARK PUBLICATIONS LTD

Published by New Park Publications Ltd.,
186a Clapham High Street, London SW4 7UG

This edition: 1975

Set up, printed and bound by trade union labour

Distributed in the United States by:
Labor Publications Inc.,
135 West 14 Street, New York
New York 10011

ISBN 0 902030 69 8

Printed in Great Britain by
Grafton Litho Ltd. (T.U.)
150 Stonhouse Street, London SW4

CONTENTS

THE EVOLUTION OF PROPERTY

SOCIAL AND PHILOSOPHICAL STUDIES

CONTENTS

Publishers' Foreword

'A mere property career is not the final destiny of mankind, if progress is to be the law of the future as it has been of the past. The time which has passed away since civilisation began is but a fragment of the ages yet to come. The dissolution of society bids fair to become the termination of a career of which property is the end and aim; because such a career contains the elements of self-destruction. Democracy in government, brotherhood in society, equality in rights and privileges and universal education, foreshadow the next higher plane of society to which experience, intelligence and knowledge are steadily tending. It will be a revival, in a higher form, of the liberty, equality and fraternity of the ancient gentes.'

THESE WORDS, near the close of Lewis Henry Morgan's classic *Ancient Society*, are the inspiration of Paul Lafargue's *Evolution of Property from Savagery to Civilisation*. Already Marx and Engels had seen Morgan's work on primitive society as an independent confirmation of the materialist conception of history [see Engels *Origin of the Family, Private Property and the State*]. Lafargue, like Engels, explicitly started from what Morgan could only dimly perceive, the revolutionary role of the working class in ending the reign of private property. Lafargue's purpose is to demonstrate, from existing knowledge of pre-capitalist societies, that the forms of private property at the foundation of modern capitalism have evolved historically out of the original form of primitive communism. Tribal communism broke down because the growth of productive forces within it came into conflict with the existing communal property. For centuries, joint ownership by members of extended families or lineage groups — collective property — served as the social framework for the utilisation of the world-historical inventions of agriculture and stock breeding, together with the handicrafts whose development could be provided for on this new basis of food production. The many hundreds of scattered human societies, living in widely different geographical conditions and encountering each other at uneven stages of their development, provide many different forms of the break-up of primitive communism, and of the later replacement of collective property by patriarchal family property. In some cases the latter transition followed relatively soon after the dissolution of tribal communism, in others only after thousands of years. The study of the economic basis of these transitions still remains to be carried out. Lafargue wrote near the end of the 19th century, and brought together many of the accounts of pre-capitalist societies which had become available since Morgan sketched out the evolution of property in the short final chapters of *Ancient Society*. Engels had already filled out, from his knowledge of Greek, Roman and West European history, the different forms of development of property and the state in these areas. Since Lafargue's day, ethnology or 'social anthropology', as it is called in Britain, has accumulated a considerable body of new data, particularly on African societies with patriarchal family property. But this material not only remains unanalysed from any historical point of view, it is often unsuitable for any such analysis. The work of social anthropologists has been carried out from a very reactionary ideological standpoint, that of 'functionalism'. Claiming to have dispensed with Morgan as a practitioner of historical guesswork, the functionalists have devoted themselves to isolated field-work monographs on particular 'communities'. The different studies are then linked together only abstractly—by Raddcliffe-Brown's mystical 'structural principles', according to which societies organise themselves so as to function smoothly, or by Malinowski's 'basic biological needs' which it is the function of all social behaviour to satisfy. It is fashionable for these anthropologists to reject the social evolutionism of Morgan on the grounds that he assumed an inevitable series of stages through which all societies must pass. This 'unilinearism' as it is called, is condemned as metaphysics. It is of course a caricature of the views of Morgan, and of Lafargue and other Marxists who learned from Morgan. Marx's writings of 1857-1858 on the different paths of break-up of primitive communism, a remarkably accurate general framework in view of the limited material available, are now available in translation in the *Grundrisse*.

Morgan specifically warned *against* oversimplified conclusions from his views on social evolution; for example: 'In speaking thus positively of the several forms of the family in their relative order, there is danger of being misunderstood. I do not mean to imply that one form rises complete in a certain status of society, flourishes universally and exclusively wherever tribes are found in the same status, and then disappears in another, which is the next higher form. . . ' And when Lafargue, in this book, speaks of reconstructing the life of a nation by 'piecing together the scattered data which we possess respecting the different peoples of the globe' he is correct in asserting the historically lawful connection between property forms and the evolution of society as a whole, without being tied to some vulgar 'unilinearism'.

What the anti-evolutionists really object to in Morgan, Engels and Lafargue is hidden by their concentration on 'unilinearism'. They are above all hostile to what Marx and Engels recognised had been independently discovered by Morgan, the source of historical development in the mode of production of material life. Lafargue's book was in its time a major contribution to the development of this evolutionist conception. It showed that all notions of the eternal nature of private property were completely without historical foundation, and it showed that capitalist property was only the latest form in a long evolution of property, a form containing the seeds of its own destruction, and preparing its own replacement, through proletarian revolution, with socialist society. Only a generation after the first publication of Lafargue's book, the Bolshevik Party led the working class of Tsarist Russia to the overthrow of capitalism. The first workers' state expropriated the landlords and capitalists, and nationalised state property, the first economic step in the transition to socialism, was brought into existence for the first time. What bourgeois critics had dismissed as a dream, an impossibility, when Marxists like Lafargue deduced its historical necessity, became reality.

In the accompanying essays in this volume (*Social and Philosophical Studies*), Lafargue sets out to demonstrate in several fields the truth of Marx's materialist conception of history: 'The mode of production of the material means of life dominate in general the development of the social, political and intellectual life.'

Lafargue shows that in earlier historical periods, men had grasped in a general and inexact way the material origins of certain abstract ideas, but that in the evolution of class society this truth had been ideologically obscured time and again. In particular, the bourgeoisie's boldest thinkers, prior to the French Revolution, had rejected belief in God. But for the bourgeoisie as a class, the uncontrollability of capitalist social relations replaced the earlier incomprehensibility and unpredictability of nature as the source of religious belief. These brief essays may be supplemented by Marx's writings on 'commodity fetishism' in Chapter 1, Volume I of *Capital* on the characteristic illusions of the capitalist in Volume III of *Capital* (especially the chapter 'The Trinity Formula').

In 'The Origin of Abstract Ideas', Lafargue quotes many examples from the history of language to show that the words for abstract concepts have the same source as do those for certain material objects or qualities of objects; and this is evidence for the materialist tenet that ideas are reflections of the material world. This evidence cannot be explained by the idealists, who see abstract ideas as having a separate origin from 'ordinary' material objects and their names and qualities, or indeed as prior to those objects.

On the questions of the historical origins of the idea of justice and the idea of the good, Lafargue brilliantly utilises the historical, literary and ethnographic evidence available at the time to show that, here again, these spring not from some abstract independent ideal which somehow 'manifests' itself as history, but in the changes in the economic structure of society. Vengeance and feud are the mode of justice of self-acting groups of persons of common descent, under economic conditions where equality must prevail and enjoin corporate responsibility upon the members. With the growth of productivity and a limited amount of material wealth, the law of retaliation ('life for life, an eye for an eye, a tooth for a tooth. . .') was replaced by forms of compensation and settlement. But later property became a source of even greater conflict, and perverted 'justice' into something else. 'The barbarian had substituted property for the shedding of blood. Property substituted itself for man, who in civilized societies possesses no rights but those conferred on him by his property.'

Finally Lafargue exposes the 'heroic ideal' to a similar analysis. He traces the hypocrisy and insoluble contradiction in the social relations of class society, as well as, in its elaborated forms, modern capitalism. The hero of early human society was the man of courage, integrity, unity of purpose. The first noblemen, the patricians of the city states of the Eastern Mediterranean, Phoenicia and Greece, could fight their wars with this integral ideal. But the growth of class divisions brought a separation between the parasitic man of wealth on the one hand

and the warrior and slave on the other. A man encouraged in bravery and strength of will and purpose on the battlefield might not be so easily changed back into the meek and humble helot! The classical philosophers of Athenian slave society, as Lafargue notes, were often honest observers and analysts of these contradictions in a way which modern bourgeois 'moral philosophers' cannot be. Hence Socrates:

'When the rich and the poor find themselves together in the army on land or sea and observe each other continually in circumstances of danger, the rich then have no reason to despise the poor; on the contrary, when the poor man, wiry and sunburned, posted on the battlefield by the side of the rich man, brought up in the shade and weighted down by superfluous flesh, sees him all out of breath and troubled with his body — what thought do you think comes to him at that moment? Does he not say to himself that these people owe their riches only to the cowardice of the poor, and when they are by themselves, do they not say to each other, "Of a truth, these rich are not good for too much".'

Following in the footsteps of Frederick Engels, Paul Lafargue was one of those few writers who took the teachings of Marx and used them to explore new fields of history in order to educate the many thousands of workers who have read his work in many languages. This edition will make it available for the first time in two generations.

Biographical Note

PAUL LAFARGUE, the author of this book, was one of the leading figures in the French socialist movement in the period of the First and the Second Internationals. A friend and collaborator of Marx and Engels, he acquired an international reputation as a writer and propagandist. Speaking at his graveside Lenin said that the workers and Social Democrats of Russia had 'learned profound respect for Lafargue as one of the most gifted and profound disseminators of the ideas of Marxism, ideas that were so brilliantly confirmed by the class struggle during the Russian revolution and counter-revolution' (of 1905).

Lafargue was born to a family of Cuban planters, who also had property in the United States, in Santiago da Cuba in 1842. He numbered among his immediate ancestors a refugee from the French Revolution, a French Jew, a Mulatress and a Caribbean Indian. In 1851 the family came to France and he was enrolled in French schools, going on to the university to study medicine. He first met Marx in 1865 and in the same year was in trouble with the authorities for organizing an international students' conference at Liege. Marked out as an opponent of the regime of Napoleon III he was forced to leave France three years later, resuming his medical studies in London.

At this time Lafargue's intellectual outlook was that of the French radical democrats and to Marx's distaste he was much under the influence of Proudhonism and the positivists. A regular visitor to the Marx household, he had already become engaged to Marx's youngest daughter, Laura, in 1866, and they were married in April 1868. A somewhat jealous father, Marx had some doubts about his prospective son-in-law and insisted on proof that he would be able to support his daughter. Moreover he had frequent occasion to complain about his obstinacy, suspecting him of a lingering regard for the ideas of Proudhon. Despite the rough way in which Lafargue is treated in some of Marx's letters they seem to have got on well and he became a special favourite of Engels, who treated him almost as a son.

After the fall of the Second Empire the Lafargues returned to Paris, but later left for Bordeaux where Paul edited a newspaper favourable to the Commune. They were then forced to flee to Spain where efforts by the French government to extradite them failed. During this period the couple lost three children in infancy, which impelled Lafargue to lose confidence in medical science and he ceased to practice as a doctor.

While in Spain he re-established contact with the International Working Mens' Association (the First International), acting as one of the Spanish representatives at the Hague congress of September 1872. He did battle with the Bakunists, who were particularly strong in that country, on behalf of the Marxists whose paper he helped to set up.

After the congress the Lafargues came to London, where Paul took a leading part in the struggle with the Bakuninists in the International, translated *Anti-Duhring* into French and closely followed developments in France. He seems to have made no impact on the workers' movement in England.

With the amnesty for the supporters of the Commune in 1880 the Lafargues could have returned to France, but in fact they remained in London for a further two years. In the meantime Lafargue had established contact with Jules Guesde, and in May 1880, in collaboration with Marx and Engels, they drew up the programme for the Parti Ouvrier Francais (POF), the first French Marxist party. On his return to France in April 1882 Lafargue was rapidly to take his place as the outstanding leader of this party alongside Guesde. Already known for his articles and pamphlets, he was now able to establish contact with the working class as a lecturer and speaker and became a popular figure.

During the 1880s and 1890s Lafargue took part in hundreds of workers' meetings in the industrial and mining areas, which were the strongholds of the POF, lecturing and speaking on Marxist theory. His activities resulted on two occasions in his arrest and imprisonment: In April 1883 he was jailed for six months for using subversive language, and in 1891 he was put on trial for 'incitement to murder', after troops had fired on a May Day demonstration of workers in a region of France where he had been speaking. He was sentenced to a year's imprisonment, but was elected to parliament while still in jail and was then released.

Lafargue not only possessed the advantage of having had close contact with the founders of Marxism, but Engels continued to correspond regularly with him and Laura until his death. This correspondence gives a vivid picture of the development of the workers' movement in both Britain and France during the period, as well as providing revealing glimpses of the personal and political life of the two men.

Although Lafargue wrote prolifically on Marxist theory for the French socialist press as well as for *Der Neue Zeit*, the leading journal of Marxist studies at this time, there is no doubt that he interpreted it in a dogmatic and somewhat mechanical fashion after the style of Karl Kautsky. Thus, he saw historical materialism too narrowly as a form of economic determinism and never understood the dialectical side of Marxist philosophy. He assumed, for example, that contact with modern industrial techniques drove the working class irresistably to break with religion and thus there was no need for atheist propaganda.

As the correspondence with Engels shows, the older man had constantly to keep him on the rails and at times he committed serious tactical mistakes. In 1888, at the time of the bid for dictatorship by the demogogue, General Boulanger, Lafargue took up an ambiguous position towards the Boulangist movement. On the other hand, when Guesde refused to commit the POF to support the Dreyfusards in their campaign against the reactionaries and anti-semites Lafargue felt that this abstentionism was a mistake which tended to isolate the party.

When the POF fused with the Blanquists to form the Parti Socialiste de France, Lafargue continued in the leadership, with his reputation growing as a result of his writings. A book on *The American Trusts* published in 1903 was a study of the early stages in the development of monopoly capitalism, which anticipated some of the points in Lenin's *Imperialism*. He also wrote on the materialist conception of history and the Marxist theory of knowledge in articles which were later republished as pamphlets.

For all his weaknesses Lafargue kept aloft the banner of Marxism at a time when, despite the numerical growth of the socialist movement in France, theoretical interest was at a low ebb. In fact he was virtually the only French socialist at this time who made any contribution to theory, and that mainly in a propagandist defence of Marxist principles as he understood them. Like Lafargue himself, his writings remain undeservedly neglected and a number of them, including the present works, have more than a merely historical interest, as representing a stage in the development of Marxist theory.

Reaching the age of 70 Lafargue apparently came to the conclusion that he could not face the decline of old age. He and his wife took poison and died on November 26, 1911. Their funeral was attended by socialist leaders from all over Europe including Keir Hardie, Karl Kautsky and Lenin, whose tribute is to be found in his *Collected Works*, Vol. XVII, pp. 304-5.

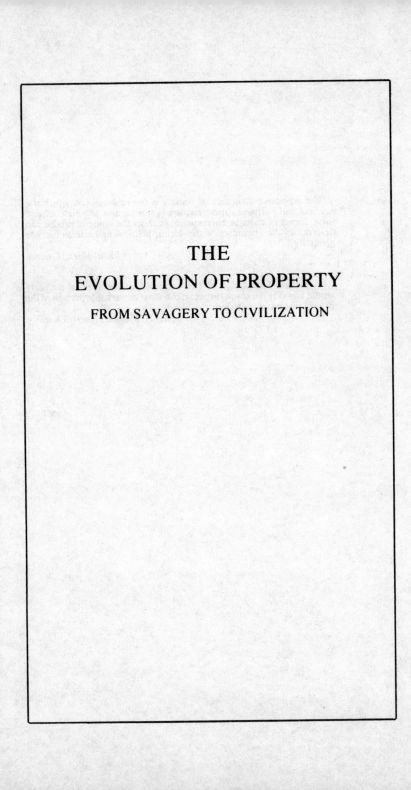

THE
EVOLUTION OF PROPERTY
FROM SAVAGERY TO CIVILIZATION

'The economic structure of society is the real basis on which the juridical and political superstructure is raised, and to which definite social forms of thought correspond: in short the mode of production determines the character of the social, political and intellectual life generally.'

Karl Marx, *Capital.*

'A critical knowledge of the evolution of the idea of property would embody, in some respects, the most remarkable portion of the mental history of mankind.'

Lewis H. Morgan, *Ancient Society..*

1

Forms of Contemporaneous Property

POLITICAL economists have laid it down as an axiom that capital, the form of property at present predominant, is eternal; they have tasked their brains to show that capital is coeval with the world, and that as it has had no beginning, so it can have no end.[1] In proof of which astounding assertion all the manuals of political economy repeat with much complacency the story of the savage who, having in his possession a couple of bows, lends one of them to a brother savage, for a share in the produce of his chase.

So great were the zeal and ardour which economists brought to bear on their search for capitalistic property in prehistoric times, that they succeeded, in the course of their investigations, in discovering the existence of property outside the human species, to wit, among the invertebrates: for the ant, in her foresight, is a hoarder of provisions. It is a pity that they should not have gone a step further, and affirmed that, if the ant lays up stores, she does so with a view to selling the same and realising a profit by the circulation of her capital.

But there is a gap in the economists' theory of the eternity of capital. They have omitted to show that the term capital likewise

---

[1] By capital is meant anything which produces interest: a sum of money lent, which at the end of months or years, yields a profit: land that is cultivated, or any instrument of labour that is set in action not by its proprietor, but by salaried workmen; but the land which is cultivated by the peasant and his family, the gun of the poacher, the plane or hammer of the carpenter, albeit property, is not capitalistic property, because the owner utilizes it himself instead of using it to extract surplus value from others. The notion of profit without labour sticks like a Nessus-shirt to the term capital.

exists from all time. In a ship every rope has its appropriate name, with the exception of the bell rope. It is inadmissible that in the domain of political economy the terminology should have been so inadequate as not to furnish a name for so useful and all-important a thing as capital; yet it is a matter of ɪact that the term capital, in the modern sense, dates no further back than the 18th century. This is the case also with the word philanthropy (the humanitarian hypocrisy proper to the capitalistic régime). And it was in the 18th century that capitalist property began to assert itself, and to acquire a preponderating influence in society. This social predominance of capital led to the French Revolution, which, although one of the most considerable events of modern history, was, after all, but a bourgeois revolution accomplished with those catchwords of liberty, fraternity, equality, justice and patriotism which the bourgeoisie were, later on, to employ in puffing their political and financial enterprises. At the time of the Revolution the capitalists were cattle so newly raised by society that in his *Dictionnaire de Mots Nouveaux,* published in 1802, Sébastien Mercier thought it necessary to insert the word *capitaliste,* and to append the following curious definition:—`Capitaliste:` this word is well nigh unknown out of Paris. It designates a monster of wealth, a man who has a heart of iron, and no affections save metallic ones. Talk to him of the land tax — and he laughs at you; he does not own an inch of land, how should you tax him? Like the Arabs of the desert who have plundered a caravan, and who bury their gold out of fear of other brigands, the capitalists have hidden away our money.`

In 1802 mankind had not as yet acquired the feeling of profound respect which in our day is inspired by the capitalist.

The term capital, though of Latin origin, has no equivalent in the Greek and Latin tongues. The non-existence of the word in two such rich languages affords a proof that capitalist property did not exist in ancient times, at least not as an economical and social phenomenon.

The form of property which corresponds to the term capital was developed and acquired social importance only after the establishment of commercial production which crowned the economical and political movement agitating Europe after the 12th century. This commercial production was stimulated by the discovery of America and the route to India by the Cape of Good

Hope, by the importation of precious metals from America, the taking of Constantinople, the invention of printing, the family alliances among the sovereigns of Europe, and the organization of the great feudal states, with the relative and general pacification which resulted therefrom. All these and other collateral causes co-operated to create a rapid development of capital, the most perfect of all forms of private property, and, it may be averred, the last. The comparatively recent appearance of capital is the best proof adducible that property is not immutable and always the same, but that, on the contrary, it, like all material and intellectual phenomena, incessantly evolves and passes through a series of forms which differ, but are derived, from one another.

So far indeed is property from being always identical that in our own society it affects divers forms, capable of being reduced to two principal ones.

I. FORMS OF COMMON PROPERTY

a. Common property of ancient origin, the type of which are the communal lands, exposed for centuries past to the encroachments of the nobility and *bourgeoisie.*

b. Common property of modern origin, administered by the State, comprised under the term Public Services, (the Mint, Post Office, Public Roads, National Libraries, Museums, etc.)

II. FORMS OF PRIVATE PROPERTY

a. Property of personal appropriation.

b. Property. — Instruments of labour.

c. Property. — Capital.

(a). Property of personal appropriation begins with the food one eats, and extends to the articles of clothing and objects of luxury (rings, jewels, etc.), with which one covers and decks oneself. Time was when the house, too, was included in this branch of personal property; a man possessed his dwelling, a marble palace or a hut of straw, like the tortoise his shell. If by the application of machinery to industry, civilisation has placed

numberless objects of luxury within the reach of the poor which
hitherto have been purchasable by the rich alone, it has on the
other hand deprived the bulk of the nation of their
dwelling-houses. It constrains them to live in hired apartments and
furnished lodgings; and in the midst of unprecedented wealth it has
reduced the producer to a strict minimum of property of personal
appropriation.

Capitalist civilization condemns the proletarian to vegetate in
conditions of existence inferior to those of the savage. To waive
the important fact that the savage does not labour for others, and
to confine ourselves wholly to the question of food, it is
indisputable that the barbarians who invaded and peopled
Europe, and who, possessing as they did, herds of swine and
other animals, and having within their reach all the resources of
the chase in richly stocked forests, and of fishing in the seas and
rivers—if ill-clad with the skins of wild beasts and
coarsely-woven materials—partook of more animal food than do
our proletarians, whose shoddy clothing, excellently woven by
perfected machinery, is a very poor protection against the
inclemencies of the weather. The condition of the proletarian is
the harder in that his constitution is less robust and less inured to
the rigour of the climate than was the body of the savage. The
following fact affords an idea of the robustness of uncivilized
man. In the prehistoric tombs of Europe skulls have been
discovered bearing traces of perforations suggestive of
trepanning. Anthropologists at first took these skulls for amulets
or ornaments, and concluded that they had been perforated after
death, until Broca showed that the operation could not have been
performed on corpses by producing a number of skulls in which a
process of cicatrization was observable, that could not have taken
place unless the trepanned person had survived the operation. It
was objected that it must have been impossible for ignorant
savages, with their rude instruments of bronze and silex, to
practise so delicate an operation, considered dangerous by
modern doctors, despite their learning and the excellence of their
surgical instruments. But all doubts have been removed by the
positive knowledge that this kind of operation is practised by
savages with perfect success. Among the Berbers of the present
day the operation is performed in the open air, and after the lapse
of a few days, to the infinite astonishment of European witnesses,

the trepanned man is on his legs again and resuming his occupations just as if a portion of his skull had not been scraped away, for the operation is performed by scraping. Skull wounds, which entail such grave complications in civilized persons, heal with extraordinary quickness and ease in primitive peoples. Notwithstanding the frantic enthusiasm with which civilization inspires the philistine, the physical, and maybe the mental, inferiority of the civilized man, allowing, of course, for exceptions, must be conceded. It will require an education beginning at the cradle and prolonged throughout life and continued for several generations to restore to the human being of future society the vigour and perfection of the senses which characterize the savage and the barbarian.[1] Morgan, one of the rare anthropologists who do not share the imbecile disdain professed for the savage and the barbarian by the philistine, was also the first to classify in logical order the abundant and often contradictory materials that have accumulated respecting savage races, and to trace the first outlines of the evolution of prehistoric man. He observes, 'It may be suggested as not improbable of ultimate recognition that the progress of mankind in the period of savagery, in its relation to the sum of human progress, was greater in degree than in the three sub-periods of barbarism, and that the progress made in the whole period of barbarism was, in like manner, greater in degree than it has been since in the entire period of civilization.'[2] The savage or barbarian transplanted into civilized society cuts a sorry figure: he loses his native good qualities, while he contracts the diseases and acquires the vices of civilized man; but the history of the Greeks and the Egyptians shows us how marvellous a degree of material and intellectual development a barbarous people is capable of attaining when placed in the requisite conditions and evolving freely.

---

[1]   Caesar, to whom the panegyrists of our society allow certain powers of observation, never wearied of admiring the strength and skill in bodily exercises of the German barbarians whom he was forced to combat. So great was his admiration for them, that in order to overcome the heroic resistance of the Gauls, commanded by Vercingetorix, he sent across the Rhine into Germany for cavalry and light-armed infantry, who were used to engage among them; and as they were mounted on bad horses he took those of the military tribunes, the knights and veterans, and distributed them among the Germans.— *De Bello Gallico*, vii 65.

[2]   Lewis Morgan. *Ancient Society*, Part I, chap. iii. 'Ratio of Human Progress'.

The civilized producer is reduced to the minimum of personal property necessary for the satisfaction of his most urgent wants merely because the capitalist possesses means and to spare for the indulgence of his most extravagant fancies. The capitalist should have a hundred heads and a hundred feet, like the Hecatonchiri of Greek mythology, if he would utilize the hats and boots that encumber his wardrobe. If the proletarians suffer from the want of personal property, the capitalists end by becoming the martyrs of a superfluity thereof. The ennui which oppresses them, and the maladies which prey on them, deteriorating and undermining the race, are the consequences of an excess of the means of enjoyment.

(b.) Private property in the instruments of labour.

Man, according to Franklin's definition, is a *tool-making animal*. It is the manufacture of tools which distinguishes man from the brutes, his ancestors. Monkeys make use of sticks and stones, man is the only animal that has wrought silex for the manufacture of arms and tools, so that the discovery of a stone implement in a cavern or geological stratum is proof as positive of the presence of a human being as the human skeleton itself. The instrument of labour, the silex knife of the savage, the plane of the carpenter, the bistouri of the surgeon, the microscope of the physiologist, or the plough of the peasant, is an addition to man's organs which facilitates the satisfaction of his wants.

So long as petty manual industry prevails, the free producer is the proprietor of his instruments of labour. In the middle ages the journeyman travelled with his bag of tools, which never left him; the yeoman, even before the constitution of private property, temporarily possessed the patch of land which was allotted to him in the territorial partition; the mediaeval serf was so closely connected with the soil he cultivated as to be inseparable therefrom.

There remain many vestiges of this private property in the instruments of labour, but they are fast disappearing. In all the industries which have been seized on by machinery, the individual implement has been torn out of the worker's hand and replaced by the machine tool — a collective instrument of labour which can no longer be the property of the producer. Capitalism divests man of his personal property, the tool; and the first perfect instruments he had manufactured for himself, his weapons of defence, were the first to be wrested from him. The savage is the proprietor of his bow and arrows, which constitute at one and the same time his arms and his tools, historically the most perfected. The soldier was the first proletarian who was stripped of his tools, i.e., his arms, which, belong to the government that enrols him.

Capitalistic society has reduced to a minimum the personal property of the proletarian. It was impossible to go further without causing the death of the producer — the capitalist's goose that lays the golden eggs. It tends to dispossess him altogether of his instruments of labour, a spoliation which is already an accomplished fact for the great bulk of workers.

(c) *Property Capital.*

The capital form of property is the truly typical form of property in modern society. In no other society has it existed as a universal or dominant fact.

The essential condition of this form of property is the exploitation of the free producer, who is robbed hourly of a fraction of the value he creates; a fact which Marx has demonstrated beyond refutation. Capital is based on the production of commodities, on a form of production, that is, in which a man produces in view, not of the consumption of the labourer, or of that of his feudal lord or slave-owning master, but in view of the market. In other societies, also, men bought and sold, but it was the surplus articles alone that were exchanged. In those societies the labourer, slave, or serf, was exploited, it is true, but the proprietor had at least certain obligations towards him; *e.g.*, the slaveholder was bound to feed his human beast of burden whether he worked or not. The capitalist has been released from all charges, which now rest upon the free labourer. It roused the indignation of the good natured Plutarch that Cato, the sour moralist, rid himself of slaves grown old and decrepit in his service. What would he have said of the modern capitalist, who allows the workers that have enriched him to starve or to die in the workhouse? In emancipating the slave and bondman, it was not the liberty of the producer that the capitalist sought to compass but the liberty of capital, which had to be discharged of all obligations towards the workmen. It is only when the capital

form of property is in force that the proprietor can exercise in all
its stringency the right to use and abuse.

These are the extant forms of property in modern society. Even
a superficial view thereof will convince us that these forms are
themselves undergoing change; *e.g.*, while communal property of
ancient origin is being converted into private property, private
capitalistic property is being turned into common property
administered by the State; but before attaining this ultimate form,
capital dispossesses the producer of his individual tool and
creates the collective instrument of labour.

Now having convinced ourselves that the existent forms of
property are in a state of flux and evolution, we must be blind
indeed if we refuse to admit that in the past also property was
unstable, and that it has passed through different phases before
arriving at the present forms, which must, in their turn, resolve
themselves and be replaced by other novel forms.

*   *   *   *   *

In this essay I propose to treat of the various forms of property
anterior to its assumption of the capital form. Before entering on
my subject I would premise a few particulars touching the method
employed by me in this attempt at a partial reconstruction of
history.

All men, without distinction of race or colour, from the cradle
to the grave, pass through the same phases of development. They
experience at ages, which vary within narrow limits, according to
race, climate, and conditions of existence, the same crises of
growth, maturity, and decay. In like manner human societies
traverse analogous social, religious, and political forms, with the
ideas which correspond thereto. To Vico, who has been styled
'the father of the philosophy of history,' is due the honour of
having been the first to apprehend the great law of historical
development.

In his *Scienza Nouva* he speaks of 'an ideal, eternal history,
in accordance with which are successively developed the
histories of all nations, from what state so ever of savagery,
ferocity, or barbarism men progress towards domestication.'[1]

---

[1] Una storia ideal, eterna, sopra la quale corrono in tempo le storie di tutti le
nazioni: ch'ovumque da tempi selvaggi, feroci e fieri comminciarno gli uomini ad
addimesticarsi. (G. Vico, *Principi di Scienza Nuova.* De' Principi Libero secondo.
Section V. ed. di Ferrari, Milano, 1837.)

If we could ascertain the history of a people from the state of savagery to that of civilization, we should have the typical history of each of the peoples that have inhabited the globe. It is out of our power to reconstruct that history, for it is impossible for us to reascend the successive stages travelled by a people in their course of progress. But if we cannot cut out this history, all of a piece, of the life of a nation or a race, we can, at any rate, reconstruct it by piecing together the scattered data which we possess respecting the different peoples of the globe. It is in this wise that humanity, as it grows older, learns to decipher the story of its infancy.

The manners and usages of the forefathers of civilized nations survive in those of the savage peoples whom civilization has not wholly exterminated. The investigations of the customs, social and political institutions, religious and mental conceptions of barbarians, made by men of learning and research in both hemispheres, enable us to evoke a past which we had come to consider as irrevocably lost. Among savage peoples, we can detect the beginnings of property: by gleaning facts in all parts of the globe, and by co-ordinating them into a logical series, we may succeed in following the different phases of the evolution of property.

2

Primitive Communism

I

IF political economists so confidently refer capital to the childhood of humanity, it is because they indulge themselves in a convenient ignorance of the customs of primitive peoples.[1]

There are savages at present in existence who have no conception of landed property, whether private or collective, and who have barely arrived at a notion of individual ownership of the objects which they personally appropriate. Certain Australians possess, for all personal property, the objects attached to their persons, such as arms, ornaments inserted in their ears, lips, and noses; or skins of beasts for clothing; human fat, wherewith to cure their rheumatism; stones laid up in baskets, woven of bark, fastened to the body of the owner. Personally appropriated by them, so to say incorporated with them, these objects are not taken away from them at their death, but are burned or buried with their corpses. Names are among the primary individual property we meet with. The savage never reveals his name to a stranger; it is a precious thing of which he will make a present to a friend: so completely is his name identified with his person, that

---

[1] In his recent and notorious discussion with Mr. Herbert Spencer, the learned Professor Huxley, who acts as a champion of capital, and who calls Rousseau an ignoramus, has given a remarkable proof of his ignorance of the customs of savages which he discusses with such assurance. 'The confident assertions,' wrote the learned professor in the *Nineteenth Century* of January, 1890, 'that the land was originally held in common by the whole nation are singularly ill-founded. 'Land was held as private or several property, and not as the property of the public or general body of the nation.'

after his death his tribe ceases to pronounce it. For an object to become individual property, it must be really or fictitiously incorporated with the person of the proprietor: when the savage desires to intimate that an object belongs to him, he will simulate the appropriation of it by licking it with his tongue; the Eskimo after buying any article, if but a needle, immediately applies it to his mouth, or he will consecrate the object by a symbolical act, significative of his intention to keep the same for his personal use: this is the origin of *taboo*.

Manufactured articles are, in like manner, owned only if they have been appropriated; thus, an Eskimo cannot possess more than two canoes; the third is at the disposal of the clan: whatsoever the proprietor does not use is considered as property without an owner. A savage never holds himself responsible for the loss of a canoe or any other borrowed implement for hunting or fishing, and never dreams of restoring it.

If the savage is incapable of conceiving the idea of individual possession of objects not incorporated with his person, it is because he has no conception of his individuality as distinct from the consanguine group in which he lives. The savage is environed by such perpetual material danger, and compassed round with such constant imaginary terrors that he cannot exist in a state of isolation; he cannot even form a notion of the possibility of such a thing. To expel a savage from his clan, his horde, is tantamount to condemning him to death; among the pre-historic Greeks, as among all barbarians, a murder intentional or by accident of one of the members of the clan was punished by exile. Orestes, after the assassination of his mother, was compelled to expatriate himself to appease the public indignation; in very advanced civilizations, like those of Greece and Italy in historic times, exile was considered the worst of penalties. 'The exile,' says the Greek poet Theognis, 'has neither friends nor faithful comrades, the most doleful thing in exile.' To be divided from his companions, to live alone, seemed a fearful thing to primeval man, accustomed to live in troops.

Savages, even though individually completer beings, seeing that they are self-sufficing, than are civilized persons, are so thoroughly identified with their hordes and clans that their individuality does not make itself felt either in the family or in property.[1]

The clan was all in all; the clan was the family; it was the clan that married; it was the clan, again, that was the owner of property. In the clan all things are in common: the bushman of Africa who receives a present divides it among all the members of his horde; when he has captured an animal or found any object he shares his booty with his comrades, frequently reserving for himself the smallest portion. In times of famine, the young Fuegians explore the coast, and if they chance to light upon any cetaceous animal (a favourite dainty) they hasten, before touching it, to inform their comrades of their find. These at once hurry to the spot; whereupon the oldest member of the party proceeds to portion out equal shares to all.

Hunting and fishing, those two primitive modes of production, are practised jointly, and the produce is shared in common. According to Martius, the Botocudos, those dauntless tribes of Brazil, organize their hunt in concert and never abandon the spot on which an animal has been captured until they have devoured it. The same fact is reported of the Dakotas and the Australians. Even among those tribes in which the chase in common is in abeyance, this ancient mode of consuming the prey holds good: the successful hunter invited to a feast all the members of his clan, of his village, and occasionally of his tribe, to partake of his chase: they are, so to say, national feasts. At Svarietie, in the Caucasus, whenever a family slaughters an ox, a cow, or a dozen sheep, it is the occasion of a village feast; the villagers eat and drink together in memory of the relations that have died in the course of the year. The feasts of the dead are reminiscences of these common repasts.

---

[1] In savage hordes there exists no private family, not even the matriarchal one. The children belong to the entire horde, and they call mother, indifferently their own mother, the sisters of their mother and the women of the same age as their mother. When, in process of time, the sexual relations, at first promiscuous, began to be restricted, prior to the appearance of the 'pairing family,' there obtained the common marriage of the clan. All the women of one clan were the wives of the men of another clan, and, reciprocally, all the men of that clan were the joint husbands of the women; when they met, it was only necessary for them to recognize each other in order to legitimate a conjugal union. This curious form of communist marriage has been observed in Australia by Messrs. Fison and Howitt. Traces of it are discoverable in the mythological legends of Greece.

Morgan, who has so minutely studied the primitive communist manners, in his last and important work[1] describes the methods of hunting and fishing practised among the Redskins of North America: — 'The tribes of the plain, who subsist almost exclusively upon animal food, show in their usages in hunt the same tendency to communism. The Blackfeet, during the buffalo hunt, follow the herd on horseback, in large parties, composed of men, women, and children.

'When the active pursuit of the herd commences, the hunters leave the dead animal in the track of the chase, to be appropriated by the first persons who come up behind. This method of distribution is continued until all are supplied. . . . They cut up the beef into strings, and either dry it in the air or smoke it over a fire. Some make part of the capture into *pemmican*, which consists of dried and pulverized meat, mixed with melted buffalo fat, which is boiled in the hide of the animal. During the fishing season in the Columbia river, where fish is more abundant than in any other river on the earth, all the members of the tribe encamp together and make a common stock of the fish obtained. They are divided each day according to the number of women, giving to each an equal share. The fishes are split open, scarified and dried on scaffolds, after which they are packed in baskets and removed to the villages.

When the savage ceases to lead a nomadic existence, and when he settles and builds himself a dwellinghouse, the house is not a private but a common one, even after the family has begun to assume a matriarchal form. The communal houses resemble those that La Pérouse discovered in Polynesia; they are 10 feet high, 110 feet in length, and 10 feet in width, having the shape of an inverted pirogue; the entrance was by doors situated at both extremities, and they afforded shelter for a clan of upwards of 100 persons. The *long houses* of the Iroquois, which, according to Morgan, disappeared before the commencement of the present century, were 100 feet long by 30 broad, and 20 feet in height; they were traversed by a longitudinal passage having an opening at both ends; into this passage, like the alveoles of a hive, opened a series of small rooms, 7 feet in width, in which dwelt the married women of the clan. Each habitation bore the totem of the clan,

[1] Lewis H. Morgan, *Houses and House Life of the American Aborigines*. Washington, 1881.

i.e., the animal supposed to be its ancestor. The houses of the Dyaks of Borneo are similar, with the difference that they are raised from 15 to 20 feet from the ground on posts of hard timber; they recall the lake cities, built upon piles, discovered in the Swiss lakes. Herodotus says that the Paeonians dwelt in houses of this description in Lake Prasias (V., sec 16). The *casas grandes* of the Redskins of Mexico presented the appearance of an enormous stairway, with super-imposed storeys, sub-divided into cells for the married people: not improbably it is in such like communist dwellings that the prehistoric Greeks lived, as may be inferred from the palace brought to light in Argolis by the excavations of Dr Schliemann. In these communist dwelling-houses the provisions are in common and the repasts are common.

We must turn to Morgan for a description of the life of the inhabitants of these communal houses. His researches were confined, it is true, to the American Redskins, and principally the Iroquois, amongst whom he had lived; but as he says, 'when any usage is found among the Iroquois in a definite or positive form, it renders probable the existence of the same usage in other tribes in the same condition, because their necessities were the same.'

'The Iroquois who formed a household, cultivated gardens, gathered harvest, and stored it in their dwellings as a common store. There was more or less of individual ownership of these products and of their possession by different families. For example, the corn, after stripping back the husk, was braided by the husk in bunches and hung up in the different apartments; but when one family had exhausted its supply, their wants were supplied by other families so long as any remained; each hunting or fishing party made a common stock of the capture, of which the surplus on their return was divided among the several families of each household, and, having been cured, were kept for winter use.' In these Indian villages we note the singular phenomenon of individual ownership combined with common usage. 'There is nothing in the Indian house and family without its particular owner,' remarks Heckewelder, in treating of the Delawares and the Munsees; 'every individual knows what belongs to him, from the horse or cow to the dog, cat, or kitten and little chicken. . . . For a litter of kittens or a brood of chickens there are often as many owners as there are individual animals. In purchasing a hen with her brood one frequently has to deal for it with several children. Thus while the principle of community of goods prevails in the state, the rights of property are acknowledged among the members of the family.'[1]

The Indians of Laguna village (New Mexico) had common stores. 'Their women, generally, have the control of the granary,' wrote the Rev. Sam Gorman to Morgan in 1869, 'and they are more provident than their Spanish neighbours about the future; they try to have a year's provision on hand. It is only when two years of scarcity succeed each other that Pueblos, as a community, suffer hunger.'

Among the Maya Indians food is prepared in a hut, and every family sends for a portion. Stephen saw a procession of women and children, each carrying an earthen bowl containing a quantity of smoking hot broth, all coming down the same road and disappearing among the different houses.[2]

But among the Iroquois each household prepared the food of its members. A matron made the division from the kettle to each family according to their needs; it was served warm to each person in earthern or wooden bowls. They had neither tables, chairs, nor plates, in our sense, nor any room in the nature of a kitchen or a dining-room, but ate each by himself, sitting or standing where was most convenient to the person, the men eating first and by themselves, and the women and children afterwards and by themselves. That which remained was reserved for any member of the household when hungry. Towards evening the women cooked *hominy*, the maize having been pounded into bits the size of a grain of rice, which was boiled and put aside to be used cold as a lunch in the morning and evening and for entertainment of visitors; they had neither formal breakfast nor supper; each person, when hungry, ate whatever food the house contained. They were moderate eaters. This, adds Morgan, is a fair picture of Indian life in general in America, when discovered.

Similar manners obtained in pre-historic Greece, and the syssitia (common repasts) of historic times were but a

---

[1] Heckewelder. — *History. Manners and Customs of Indian Nations who once inhabited Pennsylvania and the Neighbouring States.* Reprinted in 1876. — Heckewelder lived as a missionary among the American Indians for fifteen years,' from 1771 to 1786, and was conversant with their language.

[2] Stephen, 'Incidents of travel in Yucatan', II.

reminiscence of the primitive communist repasts. Heraclides of Pontus, the disciple of Plato, has preserved for us a description of the communistic repasts of Creta, where the primitive manners prevailed during a long period of time. At the *andreies* (repasts of men) every adult citizen received an equal share, except the *Archon*, member of the council of the ancients *(geronia)*, who received a fourfold portion—one in his quality of simple citizen, another in that of president of the table, and two additional portions for the care of the hall and furniture. All the tables were under the supervision of a matriarch, who distributed the food and ostensibly set aside the choicest bits for the men who had distinguished themselves in the council or on the battlefield. Strangers were served first, even before the archon. A vessel with wine and water was handed round from guest to guest; at the end of the repast it was replenished. Heraclides mentions common repasts of the men only, but Hoeck assumes that in the Dorian cities there were also repasts of women and children. Our knowledge of the constant separation of the sexes among savages and barbarians renders probable the assumption of the learned historian of Creta.

According to Aristotle the provisions for these repasts were furnished by the harvests, the flocks and herds, and the tributes of the serfs belonging to the community; hence we may infer that men, women, and children, in Creta, were maintained at the expense of the state. He asserts that these repasts may be traced back to a very remote antiquity; that it was Minos who established them in Creta and Italus among the Oenotrians, whom he taught agriculture; and as Aristotle finds these common repasts still prevalent in Italy, he concludes that they originated there, ignoring the fact that they occur among all primitive peoples. [1]

Plutarch informs us that at these common repasts no one person was considered as superior to the other, wherefore he styles them aristocratic assemblies *(sunedria aristokratika)*. The persons who sat down at the same table were probably members of the same family. In Sparta the members of a syssitia were formed into corresponding military divisions, and fought

---

[1] Aristotle, *Politics*. Book II. chap. iii, section 4. Book IV, chap. ix, sections 2, 3, 4. French ed., B. St. Hilaire, 1848.

together. Savages and barbarians, accustomed at all times to act in common, in battle always range themselves according to families, clans and tribes.

It was of such imperative necessity that every member of the clan should get his share of the aliments, that in the Greek language the word *moira*, which signifies the portion of a guest at a repast, came to signify Destiny, the supreme Goddess to whom men and gods are alike submitted and who deals out to everyone his portion of existence, just as the matriarch of the Cretan syssitia apportions to each guest his share of food. It should be remarked that in Greek mythology Destiny is personified by women—*Moira*, *Aissa*, and the *Keres*—and that their names signify the portion to which each person is entitled in the division of victuals or spoils.

When the common dwelling house, sheltering an entire clan, came to be sub-divided into private houses, containing a single family, the repasts ceased to be held in common, save on occasions of religious and national solemnities, such as the Greek syssities, which were celebrated in order to preserve the memory of the past; the provisions, although individually possessed by each private family, continue, practically, at the disposal of the members of the tribe. 'Every man, woman, or child, in Indian communities,' says Catlin, 'is allowed to enter anyone's lodge, and even that of the chief of the nation, and eat when they are hungry. Even so can the poorest and most worthless drone of the nation; if he is too lazy to supply himself or to hunt, he can walk into any lodge, and everyone will share with him as long as there is anything to eat. He, however, who thus begs when he is able to hunt, pays dear for his meat, for he is stigmatized with the disgraceful epithet of poltroon or beggar.'

In the Caroline Isles, when an indigene sets out on a journey, he carries with him no provisions. When he is hungry he enters a lodge without any kind of ceremony, and without waiting for permission he plunges his hand into the tub containing the *popoi* (a paste of the fruit of the bread tree) and when his hunger is satisfied he departs without so much as thanking anybody. He has but exercised a right.

These communistic habits, which had once been general, were maintained in Lacedaemonia long after the Spartans had issued out of barbarism; private property in objects of personal appropriation was extremely vague and precarious. Plutarch says that Lycurgus, the mythical personage to whom the Spartans refer all their institutions, forbade the closing of the house doors in order that everybody might walk in and help himself to the food and utensils he wanted, even in the absence of the owner: a citizen of Sparta was entitled, without permission, to ride the horses, use the dogs, and even dispose of the slaves of any other Spartan.

Very gradually did the idea of private property, which is so ingrained in, and appears so natural to, the philistine, dawn upon the human mind. The earliest reflections of man, on the contrary, led him to think that all things should be common to all. 'The Indians,' says Heckewelder, 'think that the Great Spirit has made the earth, and all that it contains, for the common good of mankind; when he stocked the country and gave them plenty of game, it was not for the good of a few, but of all. Everything is given in common to the sons of men. Whatever liveth on the land, whatever groweth out of the earth, and all that is in the rivers and waters, was given jointly to all, and everyone is entitled to his share. Hospitality with them is not a virtue, but a strict duty . . . They would lie down on an empty stomach rather than have it laid to their charge that they had neglected their duty by not satisfying the wants of the stranger, the sick, or the needy . . . because they have a common right to be helped out of the common stock; for if the meat they have been served with was taken from the wood, it was common to all before the hunter took it; if corn and vegetables, it had grown out of the common ground, yet not by the power of man, but by that of the Great Spirit.'[1]

Caesar, who had observed an analogous communism among the Germans who had invaded Belgium and Gaul, states that one of the objects of their customs was 'to uphold in the people the sense of equality, since every man sees his resources equal to those of the most powerful'. And, in effect, this communism in production and consumption presupposes a perfect equality among all the members of the clan and tribe who consider

---

[1] Hobbes, one of the great thinkers of modern times, thought not otherwise. 'Nature hath given to each of us an equal right to all things,' says Hobbes in *DE Cive*. 'In a *state of nature* every man has a right to do and to take whatsoever he pleases: whence the common saying that Nature *has given all things to all men*, whence it follows that in a state of nature utility is the rule of right.'

themselves as derived from a common stock. But not only did this rudimentary communism maintain equality; it developed, also, sentiments of fraternity and liberality which put to shame the much vaunted brotherliness and charity of the Christian, and which have elicited the admiration of the observers of savage tribes before they had been deteriorated by the Bible and brandy, the brutal mercantilism, and pestilential diseases of civilization.

At no subsequent period of human development has hospitality been practised in so simple and perfect a way. 'If a man entered an Iroquois house,' says Morgan, 'whether a villager, a tribesman, or a stranger, and at whatever hour of the day, it was the duty of the women of the house to set food before him. An omission to do this would have been a discourtesy amounting to an affront. If hungry, he eats, if not hungry, courtesy required he should taste the food and thank the giver.'

'To be narrow-hearted, especially to those in want, or to any of their own family, is accounted a great crime, and to reflect scandal on the rest of the tribe,' says another student of the primitive manners of the American Indians. [1] A guest was held sacred, even though an enemy. Tacitus describes the same usages among the barbarian Germans who invaded the Roman Empire. 'No people,' he says, 'are more addicted to social entertainments, or more liberal in the exercise of hospitality. To refuse any person whatever admittance under their roof is accounted flagitious. Everyone according to his ability feasts his guest; when his provisions are exhausted, he who was late the host is now the guide and companion to another hospitable board. They enter the next house, and are received with equal cordiality. No one makes a distinction with respect to the rights of hospitality between a stranger and an acquaintance.'

Tacitus held up the barbarian Germans as an example to his civilized compatriots. Catlin, who, during a period of eight years, from 1832 to 1839, sojourned amongst the wildest Indian tribes of North America, writes: 'Morality and virtue, I venture to say, the civilized world need not undertake to teach them.'

' Travellers, who were not ferocious and rapacious commercial

---

[1] James Adair. *History of the American Indians.* London, 1775.

travellers like Mr Stanley, have not hesitated to bear testimony, with Caesar, to the virtues of the savages, and to attribute those virtues to the communism in which they lived. 'The brotherly sentiments of the Redskins,' says the Jesuit Charlevoix, 'are doubtless in part ascribable to the fact that the words *mine* and *thine*, "those cold words", as St John Chrysostomos calls them, are all unknown as yet to the savages. The protection they extend to the orphans, the widows and the infirm, the hospitality which they exercise in so admirable a manner, are, in their eyes, but a consequence of the conviction which they hold that all things should be common to all men.'[1] So writes the Jesuit Charlevoix. Let us hear what his contemporary and critic, the free-thinker Lahontan, says: 'Savages do not distinguish between *mine* and *thine*, for it may be affirmed that what belongs to the one belongs to the other. It is only among the Christian savages who dwell at the gates of our cities that money is in use. The others will neither handle it nor even look upon it. They call it: *the serpent of the white men*. They think it strange that some should possess more than others, and that those who have most should be more highly esteemed than those who have least. They neither quarrel nor fight among themselves; they neither rob nor speak ill of one another.'[2]

So long as the savage hordes, composed of 30 or 40 members, are nomadic, they wander on the face of the earth, and fix wherever they find the means of sustenance. It is, probably, in following the sea-shores and the course of the rivers which supplied them with food that the savages peopled the continents. Such was the opinion of Morgan. The Bushmen and the Veddahs of Ceylon, who live in this state of savagery, do not dream of vindicating the right of property even in the territories of the chase—the most archaic form of landed property.

Primitive man, who does not till the soil, and who supports himself by hunting and fishing, and lives on a diet of wild fruits, eked out by milk, must have access to vast territories for his own

1 Charlevoix. *Histoire de la Nouvelle France.*
2 *Voyage de Lahontan.* II.

sustenance and that of his herds: it has been computed, I know
not with what accuracy, that each savage, for his subsistence,
requires three square miles of land. Hence, when a country
begins to be populous, it becomes necessary to divide the land
among the tribes.

The earliest distribution of the land was into pasture and
territories of chase common to the tribe, for the idea of individual
ownership of the land is of ulterior and tardier growth. 'The earth
is like fire and water, that cannot be sold, say the Omahas. The
Maoris are so far from conceiving that the land is vendible, that,
'although the whole tribe might have consented to a sale, they
would still claim with every new-born child among them an
additional payment, on the ground that they had only parted with
their own rights, and could not sell those of the unborn. The
government of New Zealand could settle the difficulty only by
buying land for a tribal annuity, in which every child that is born
acquired a share'. Among the Jews and Semitic peoples there was
no private property in land. 'The land shall not be sold for ever,
for the land is mine; for ye are strangers and sojourners with me.'
(Leviticus xxv., 23.) Christians set the commandment of their
God at defiance. Full of reverence as they are for Jehovah and
His laws, still greater is their veneration for almighty Capital.

Mankind underwent a long and painful process of development
before arriving at private property in land.

Among the Fuegians vast tracts of unoccupied land
circumscribe the territories of chase belonging to the tribe.
Caesar relates that the Suevi and Germans founded their pride
upon having vast solitudes round their frontiers. *(De Bello Gallico*
iv., 3.) Savage and barbarian peoples limit their territories by
neutral zones, because an alien found upon the lands of any tribe
is hunted like a wild beast, and mutilated or put to death if taken.
Heckewelder reports that the Redskins cut off the noses and ears
of every individual found on their territory, and sent him back to
inform his chief that on the next occasion they would scalp him.
The feudal saying, *Qui terre a, guerra a*, held good in primitive
times; the violations of the territories of chase are among the chief
causes of dispute and warfare between neighbouring tribes. The
unoccupied areas, established to prevent incursions, came, at a
later period, to serve as market places where the tribes met to
exchange their belongings. Harold, in 1063, defeated the

Cambrians, who made perpetual inroads on the territories of the Saxons; he made a covenant with them that every man of their nation found in arms east of the entrenchment of Offa should have his right hand cut off. The Saxons, on their side, raised parallel trenches, and the space enclosed by the two walls became neutral ground for the merchants of both nations.

Anthropologists have noted with a feeling of surprise that the sexes among savage peoples are isolated and live apart; there is reason for supposing that this separation of the sexes was introduced when it was sought to put a stop to the primitive promiscuity and prevent the sexual intercourse that was the rule between brother and sister. This separation of the sexes within the limits of the tribe, necessary in the interests of morality, was upheld and promoted by a differentiation of pursuits and by property. The man is habitually charged with the defence and the procuring of food, while on the woman devolves the culinary preparation of the food, the fabrication of the clothes or household utensils, and the management of the house once it has sprung into existence.[1] It is, as Marx observes, the division of labour which begins and which is based on sex: property, in its origin, was confined to a single sex.

The man is a hunter and a warrior; he possesses the horses and arms; to the woman belongs the household utensils and other objects appropriate to her pursuits; these belongings she is obliged to transport on her head or back, in the same way that she carries her child, which belongs to her and not to the father, generally unknown.

The introduction of agriculture enhanced the separation of the sexes, while it was the determinant cause of the parcelling of the lands, the common property of the tribe. The man continues a warrior and a hunter; he resigns to his wife the labour of the fields consenting, on occasion, to assist at harvest time; among pastoral peoples he reserves to himself the care of the flocks and herds, which comes to be looked on as a nobler pursuit than agriculture; it is, in truth, the less arduous of the two. The Kaffirs consider the tending of the herds to be an aristocratic occupation; they call the cow the *black pearl*. The earliest laws of the Aryans forbade agriculture, thought degrading, to the two highest classes, the

---

1. 'A man,' said a Kurnai to Fison, 'hunts, fishes, fights, and sits down,' meaning that all besides is the business of the woman.

Brahmins and the Kshattryas, or warriors. 'For a Brahmin and a Kshattryas agriculture is blamed by the virtuous, as the plough with the iron point injures the earth and the beings in it.'[1]

As the use of a thing constitutes the sole condition of its ownership, landed property, on its first establishment among primitive nations, was allotted to the women. In all societies in which the matriarchal form of the family has maintained itself, we find landed property held by the woman; such was the case among the Egyptians, the Nairs, the Touaregs of the African desert, and the Basques of the Pyrenees; in the time of Aristotle two-thirds of the territory of Sparta belonged to the women.

Landed property, which was ultimately to constitute for its owner a means of emancipation and of social supremacy, was, at its origin, a cause of subjection; the women were condemned to the rude labour of the fields, from which they were emancipated only by the introduction of servile labour.

Agriculture, which led to private property in land, introduced the servile labour, which in the course of centuries has borne the names of slave-labour, bond-labour, and wage-labour.

III

So long as primitive communism subsists, the tribal lands are cultivated in common. 'In certain parts of India', says Nearchus, one of Alexander's generals, and eye-witness of events that took place in the 4th century, BC, 'the lands were cultivated in common by tribes or groups of relatives, who at the end of the year shared among themselves the fruits and crops.'[2]

Stephen cites a settlement of Maya Indians composed of 100 labourers, 'in which the lands are held and wrought in common and products shared by all'.[3]

From Tao, an Indian village of New Mexico, Mr Miller, in Dec. 1877, wrote to Morgan: 'There is a cornfield at each pueblo, cultivated by all in common, and when the grain is scarce the poor take from this store after it is housed, and it is in the charge and at the disposal of the Cacique, called the Governor.' In Peru, prior

---

1 Laws of Man. Cap. x.
2 Nearchus apud Strabo, lib xv.
3 Stephen. *Incidents of a travel in Yucatan, II.*

to the Spanish Conquest, agricultural labour possessed the
attraction of a feast. At break of day, from an eminence, or a
tower, the whole of the population was convoked — men, women,
and children, who all assembled in holiday attire and adorned
with their most precious ornaments. The crowd set to work, and
sang in chorus hymns celebrating the prowess of the Incas. The
work was accomplished with the utmost spirit and enthusiasm.[1]
Caesar relates that the Suevi, the most warlike and most powerful
of the Germanic tribes, annually sent forth to combat a hundred
men from a hundred cantons. The men that stayed at home were
bound to maintain the men engaged in the expedition; the
following year it was the combatants who remained at home and
the others who took up arms; in this way, he adds, the fields were
always cultivated and the men practised in war. (De Bello
Gallico, IV. 1.)

The Scandinavians who ravaged Europe had similar
communistic practices, combined with warlike expeditions; the
latter over, they returned home to assist their wives in gathering
in the harvest. This cultivation in common long survived the
stage of primitive communism. In the Russian villages which are
under the régime of collective or consanguine property, a certain
tract of land is often cultivated in common and is called mirskia
zapaschki (fields tilled by the mir); the produce of the harvest is
distributed among the families of the village. In other places the
arable lands are tilled jointly, and are afterwards allotted to the
families. In several communities of the Don the meadows
elsewhere proportioned out remain undivided, the mowing is
performed in common, and it is only after the hay is made that the
partition takes place. Forests, also, are cleared in common. The
co-operative ploughing and digging practised in the village
communities ought probably to be referred to the period of
communist agriculture. In Fiji, when preparing a piece of ground,
a number of men are employed, divided into groups of three or
four. Each man being furnished with a digging stick, they drive
them into the ground so as to enclose a circle of about two feet in
diameter. When by repeated strokes the sticks reach the depth of
18 inches, they are used as levers, and the mass of soil between
them is then loosened and raised. Mr Gomme cites, after Ure, an
analogous practice of the Scotch highlanders.

[1] W. Prescott. Conquest of Peru.

Caesar shows us how the Germans set out annually on predatory expeditions; the booty was, probably, divided among all the warriors, including those who had remained at home to perform the agricultural labour of the community. The Greeks of prehistoric times, also, were audacious pirates, who scoured the Mediterranean and fled with their booty to their citadels, perched on the tops of promontories like eagles' nests, and as inexpugnable as the round towers of the Scandinavians, built in the midst of the waters. A precious fragment of a Greek song, the Skolion of Hybrias, presents us with a picture of the heroic lives of the Greeks. The hero says:—'I have for riches a great lance, and my sword, and my buckler, the rampart of my body; with these I till the ground and reap the harvest and vintage the sweet juice of the grape; thanks to these I am styled the master of the *mnoia* (the slaves of the community). Let those who dare not bear the lance and the buckler kneel to me as to a master and call me the great king.' Piracy is the favourite pursuit of prehistoric times. Nestor inquires of Telemachus, his guest, if he is a pirate (Odyssey III). Solon maintained a college of pirates at Athens (Institutes of Gaius), the Thucydides states that in ancient times piracy was honourable (I, sec. 5).

Wherever the heroes landed, they carried off men, women, cattle, crops, and movables; the men became slaves and common property; they were placed under the supervision of the women, and cultivated the lands for the warriors of the clan. All of the cities of Crete, one of the first islands colonized by these bold pirates, possessed, down to the time of Aristotle, troops of slaves, called *mnotie,* who cultivated the public domains. The Greek cities maintained, besides a public domain, public slaves, and upheld common repasts similar to those described by Heraclides.[1]

Mr Hodgson, in 1830, described a village, thirty miles north-west of Madras, the inhabitants of which were assisted in their agricultural operations by slaves who were common property; for they were transferred with the other privileges of

---

[1] The Greek slaves were divided into two classes, the public slaves *(Koine douleia)* belonging to the state, and the slaves belonging to private individuals, called *Klerotes,* i.e., adjudged by lot. Athens possessed a number of public slaves, who did not cultivate the soil, but discharged the functions of executioner, police agents, and inferior employees of the administration.

the village occupants when those privileges were sold or mortgaged. The mediaeval towns and even villages had serfs in common.[1]

Thus we see that everywhere property in land and its produce, in domestic animals, serfs and slaves, was primarily property common to all the members of the clan. Communism was the cradle of humanity; the work of civilization has been to destroy this primitive communism, of which the last vestiges that remain, in defiance of the rapacity of the aristocrat and the bourgeois, are the communal lands. But the work of civilization is twofold: while on the one hand it destroys, on the other hand it reconstructs; while it broke into pieces the communist mould of primitive humanity, it was building up the elements of a higher and more complex form of communism. I am here concerned to trace out civilization on its double movement of destruction and reconstruction.

---

[1] Transactions of the Royal Asiatic Society, 1830, vol. ii.

3

Family or Consanguine Collectivism

I

THE common tribal property began to break up as the family was being constituted. A few remarks respecting the family will render an exposition of the evolution of property more intelligible to the reader.

We are at present aware that the human species, before arriving at the patriarchal form of the family, in which the father is the head, possesses the estates and transmits his name to all his children, passed through the matriarchal form, in which the mother occupied that high position. We have seen, above, the whole clan living in great joint tenement-houses, containing a certain number of rooms for the married women. The private family is then nascent, when we find it constituted in the matriarchal or patriarchal form, a segmentation has ensued of the communal house into as many private houses as there are households. In the matriarchal family the mother lives with her children and her younger brothers and sisters; receiving her husbands, who belong to a different clan, each in her turn; it is then that family property makes its appearance.

Its beginnings were modest, for, at the outset, it consisted but of the cabin and the small garden surrounding it. Among certain people the patriarchal family may have been constituted and have superseded the matriarchal family prior to the constitution of family property, but the case is not universal; on the contrary it would seem that the revolution in the family was posterior to the formation of family property. Such was the case with the Egyptians, Greeks, and many other peoples the course of whose development was a normal one, undisturbed by the invasion of nations on a higher plane of civilization.

So long as the matriarchal form subsists, the movables and immovables are transmitted by the women; a person inherits from his mother and not from his father, or the relations of his father. In Java, where this form of the family reached a high pitch of development, a man's property reverts to his mother's family; he is not at liberty to make a donation to his children, who belong to the clan of his wife, without the consent and concurrence of his brothers and sisters. If we judge from what we know of the Egyptians and other peoples, the male occupied a very subordinate position in the matriarchate. Among the Basques, who have preserved their primitive customs, notwithstanding Christianity and civilization, when the eldest daughter, on her mother's death, becomes an heiress, she becomes at the same time the mistress of her younger brothers and sisters. The male is under the tutelage of his own family, and when he 'goes out' to get married, with his sister's approbation, he falls under the dominion of his wife; he is subjected throughout life to female authority, as son, brother and husband; he possesses nothing save the small peculium which his sister gives him on his marriage. 'The husband,' says a Basque proverb, 'is his wife's head servant.'

This elevated position of the woman affords a proof, let me observe in passing, that the physical and intellectual superiority of the male, far from being a primordial physiological necessity, is but the consequence of an economical situation, perpetuated during centuries, which allowed the male a freer and fuller development than it permitted to the female, held in bondage by the family. Broca, in the course of his discussion with Gratiolet on the relation of the brain weight and cranial capacity to the intelligence, conceded that the inferiority of the female might be due merely to inferior education. M. Manouvrier, a disciple of Broca, and Professor at the Paris School of Anthropology, has demonstrated that the cranial capacities of the males of the Stone Age, which he had measured, were nearly as great as the average cranial capacities of the modern Parisians, whereas the cranial capacities of the females of the Stone Age were considerably greater than those of the modern female Parisians.[1]

Most disastrous has been the effect on the human species of this female inferiority; it has been one of the most active causes of the degeneration of civilized nations.

Without going to the length of pretending that in all countries the ascendancy of the female assumed the proportions which it attained in Egypt, it is an indubitable fact that wheresoever we meet with the matriarchal family we can note a dependency of the men upon the women, coinciding, frequently, with a degree of animosity between the sexes, divided into two classes. Among the Natchez and among all the nations of the valley of the Mississippi, the term *woman,* applied to a man, was an affront. Herodotus relates that Sesostris, in order to perpetuate the memory of his glorious achievements, erected obelisks among the conquered nations, and that to mark his contempt for those who had offered him no resistance he caused the female sexual organ to be engraved thereon, as emblematic of their cowardice. To apply to a Homeric Greek the epithet *woman* was a grave insult. On the other hand, the warlike women of the tribes of Dahomey employ the word man by way of an injurious epithet. Unquestionably it was the desire to shake off this feminine ascendancy and to satisfy this feeling of animosity which led man to wrest from woman the control of the family.

Presumptively this family revolution was accomplished when the movable goods of individual property had multiplied; and when the family estate was constituted and had been consecrated by time and custom; it was worth the men's while, for the nonce,

---

[1.] The following are M. Manouvrier's figures:—

Average cranial capacity of modern Parisians.

Number of skulls measured	Capacity in cubic centimetres
77 male	1560
41 female	1338

Average cranial capacity of men and women of the Stone Age.

Number of skulls measured	Capacity
58 male	1544
30 female	1422

Thus the average cranial capacity of the male savage is inferior by 26 cubic centimetres, whereas the average cranial capacity of the female savage is superior by 84 cc—L. Manouvrier. 'De la quantité de l'encephale.'—Memoire de la Société d'Anthropoligie de Paris, III. 2nd fascicule, 1885.

to dethrone the women. There took place a positive dispossession
of the women by the men, accomplished with more or less
brutality, according to the nations; while in Lacedaemonia the
women conserved a measure of their former independence (a fact
which caused Aristotle to say that it was among the most warlike
peoples that the women exercised their greatest authority); at
Athens, and in the maritime cities engaged in commerce, they
were forcibly expropriated and despoiled. This dispossession
gave rise to heroic combats; the women took up arms in defence
of their privileges, and fought with such desperate energy that the
whole of Greek mythology and even recorded history have
preserved the memory of their struggles.

So long as property was a cause of subjection, it was
abandoned to the women; but no sooner had it become a means of
emancipation and supremacy in the family and society than man
tore it from her.

Without entering more specially into the history of its
evolution, I would lay stress upon this point, to wit, that the
family, wherever or however constituted, whether affecting the
matriarchal or patriarchal form, invariably breaks up the
communism of the clan or tribe. At first the clan was the common
family of all its members; afterwards there came to exist private
families, having interests distinct from those of the clan
considered as an aggregate of a number of families; the communal
territory of the tribe was then parcelled out so as to form the
collective property of each family.

The existent European family must not be considered as the
type of family founded on collective property. The family was
not reduced to its last and simplest expression, as it is in our day,
when it is composed of the three indispensable elements: the
father, the mother, and the children; it consisted of the father, the
recognised head of the family collectivity; of his legitimate wife
and his concubines, living under the same roof; of his children,
his younger brothers, with their wives and children, and his
unmarried sisters: such a family comprised many members.

---

1 This form of property, under another name than that of *collective property*,
which term I employ in contradistinction to the primitive communist form, has of
recent years been the subject of extensive research. It has been investigated in
Germany by Haxthausen, Maurer, Engels, etc.; in England by Maine, Seebohm,
Gomme, etc.; in Belgium by Laveleye; in Russia by Schepotief, Kovalesky, etc.

II

The arable lands, hitherto cultivated in common by the entire clan, are divided into parcels of different categories, according to the quality of the soil; the parcels are formed into lots, in such wise that each lot contains an equal proportion of the different descriptions of soil; the number of lots corresponds to that of the families. A portion of the land is reserved in view of a possible increase of the population; it is let on lease or cultivated in common. To preclude injustice or grounds for complaint the shares were drawn by lot;[1] hence, in Greek and Latin, the words which designate lot (sors, cleros) signify also goods and patrimony.

If, when a family had complained of unfairness, they proved, on inquiry, that their complaint was justified, satisfaction was granted them by an additional allotment out of the reserve lands. The inquirers who have had opportunities of observing the way in which these partitions of the land are practised, have been struck by the spirit of equality which presides over them, and by the ability of the peasant land surveyors. Haxthausen relates how 'Count de Kinsleff, the minister of the imperial domains, had in several localities of the government of Woronieje caused the land to be valued and surveyed by land taxers and land surveyors. The results went to show that the measurements of the peasants were in all respects, save for a few minor discrepancies, in perfect consonance with the truth. Besides, who knows which of the two was the more accurate?'[2]

The pasture lands, forests, lakes, and ponds, the right of hunting and fishing, and other rights, such as the imposts raised on the caravans, etc., are the joint property of all the members of the clan.

The allotments are cultivated by each family under the direction of its chief and the supervision of the village council; the crops are the property of the family collectively, instead of belonging, as at an earlier period, to the tribe or clan. A family is not allowed to cultivate their lot at pleasure, says Marshall. 'They

---

[1] Dividing the land by lot has been everywhere the primitive mode of distribution. 'The Lord commanded the children of Israel, entering the Land of Canaan, to divide the land by lot.' (Numbers xxxiii., 54; xxxvi., 2.)

[2] Etudes sur la situation intérieure, la vie nationale et les institutions de la Russie, par le Baron A. de Haxthausen. French edition of 1847.

must sow their fields with the same grain as that of the other families of the community.'[1]

The system of cultivation is a triennial rotation (1) corn or rye, (2) spring crops (barley, oats, beans, peas, etc.), (3) fallow. Not only the kind of seed to sow, but also the seed and harvest times, are prescribed by the communal council. Sir G. Campbell informs us that every Indian village possesses its calendar-Brahmin, or astrologist, whose business it is to indicate the propitious seasons for seed time and harvest. Haxthausen, an intelligent and impartial observer of the manners of the collectivist communes of Russia, remarks that 'the most perfect order, resembling a military discipline, presides over the labours of the fields. On the same day, at the same hour, the peasants repair to the fields, some to plough, others to harrow, the ground, etc, and they all return in company. This orderliness is not commanded by the *Starosta,* the village ancient; it is simply the result of that gregarious disposition which distinguishes the Russian people, and that love of union and order which animates the commune.' These characteristics, which Haxthausen considers as peculiar to the Russian people, are but an outgrowth of the collective form of property, and have been observed in all parts of the world. We have seen that, to determine the seed time, the Indians did not obey human orders, but celestial considerations suggested by the astrologer. Maine, who, in his capacity as jurisconsult of the Anglo-Indian government, was in a position to study closely the village communities, writes:—

'The council of the village elders does not command anything, it merely declares what has always been. Nor does it generally declare that which it believes some higher power to have commanded; those most entitled to speak on the subject deny that the natives of India necessarily require Divine or political authority as the basis of their usages; their antiquity is by itself assumed to be a sufficient reason for obeying them. Nor, in the sense of the analytical jurists, is there *right* or *duty* in an Indian village community; a person aggrieved complains not of an individual wrong but of the disturbance of the order of the entire little society.'[2]

---

[1] Marshall. *Elementary and Practical Treatise on Landed Property.* London, 1804.

[2] H. S. Maine. *Village Communities in the East and West,* p. 68.

The discipline referred to by Haxthausen is a natural and spontaneous product, unlike the movements of an army or the manoeuvres of the labourers on the *bonanza* farms of North America, which are produced to order. A Swiss clergyman, who wrote in the last century, teaches us that in the canton of Berne there existed the same orderliness and ardour in work observed in Russia. 'On an appointed evening,' he says, 'the entire commune repairs to the communal meadows, every commoner choosing his own ground, and when the signal is given at midnight, from the top of the hill downwards, every man mows down the grass which stands before him in a straight line, and all that which he has cut till noon of the next day belongs to him. The grass which remains standing after the operation is trodden down and browsed by the cattle which are turned on to it.'[1]

The crops once got in, the lands allotted to the different families become common property again, and the villagers are free to send their cattle to de-pasture them.

Originally, the fathers of the families belonging to the clan, were alone entitled to a share in these allotments. It is only at a later period that the stranger settlers, having obtained the freedom of the city after a term of residence, were admitted to the partition of the land. Landed property belonged to the fathers, whence *patria,* fatherland; in the Scandinavian laws, *house* and *fatherland* were synonyms. At that time a man possessed a *patria* and political rights only if he had a right to a share in the land. As a consequence, the fathers and males of the family alone were charged with the country's defence; they alone were privileged to bear arms. The progress of capitalism consists in confiding the defence of the country to those who do not possess an inch of land — who have no stake in the country — and to accord political rights to men who have no property.

Private property in land does not as yet obtain, because the land belongs to the entire village, and only the temporary usage of it is granted, on condition that it shall be cultivated according to the established customs, and under the supervision of the village elders charged with watching over the maintenance of those

---

[1] *Essai sur l'abolition du parcours et sur le partage des biens communaux,* by Sprungli de Neuenegg; published by Societé D'Economie rurale de Berne (1763), cited by Neufchateau, in his *Voyage agronomique dans la Senatorerie de Dijon, 1806.*

customs. The house alone, with its small enclosure, is the private property of the family; among some peoples, *e.g.* the Neo-Caledonians, the tenement was burnt on the death of the chief of the family, as well as his arms, his favourite animals, and, occasionally, his slaves. According to all appearance, the house for a long time was distinguished from the land, as a movable; it is so qualified in many customaries of France; in that of Lille, among others.

The house is inviolable; nobody has a right to enter it without the master's consent. The justice of the country was suspended at the threshold; if a criminal had penetrated into the house, nay, if he had but touched the door-latch, he was secure from public prosecution and amenable only to the authority of the father of the family, who exercised the legislative and executive power within the precincts of the house. In 186 B.C., the Roman Senate, having condemned to death some Roman ladies, whose orgies compromised public morals, was forced to remit the execution of the sentence to the heads of the families; for the women, as constituting a part of the household, were answerable only to the master of it. To such extremes was this inviolability pushed in Rome that a father could not invoke the assistance of the magistrates or public force in case of his son's resistance. In the Middle Ages this sanctity of the domicile still existed; at Mulhouse, for example, a burgher shut up in his house ceased to be amenable to the justice of the town; the court was bound to transport itself to his house door in order to judge him, and it was open to him to reply to the questions put to him from the window. The right of asylum possessed by the Church was merely a transformation of this sanctity of the house; as we shall see hereafter, the Church was but a sort of communal house.

The habitations are not contiguous, but surrounded by a strip of territory. Tacitus, and numerous writers after him, have assumed that this insulation of the houses was prescribed as a measure of precaution against fire, so dangerous in villages in which the houses are built of wood and thatched with straw. I am of belief that the reason for this very prevalent custom should be looked for elsewhere. It has been shown that the tribal territories were surrounded by a strip of uncultivated land, which served to mark the boundaries of other neighbouring tribes; in like manner the family dwelling is surrounded by a piece of unoccupied land in order to render it independent of the adjacent dwelling-houses; this was the sole land which, subsequently, it was permitted to enclose with palisades, walls, or hedges. In the barbarian codes it is known by the name of legal, legitimate court *(curtis legalis, hoba legitima);* in this spot was placed the family tomb. So indispensable was this insulation held to be that the Roman law of the Twelve Tables fixed the space to intervene the town houses at two-and-a-half feet.[1]

It was not the houses only, but also the family allotments of land which were isolated, so that the fear of fire could not have suggested the measure. A law of the Twelve Tables regulates that a strip of land, five feet in width, be left uncultivated. (Table VII, sec. 4.)

The breaking up of the common property of the clan into the collective property of the families of the clan was a more radical innovation than, in our day, would be a restitution of the landed estates to the community. Collective property was introduced with infinite difficulty, and only maintained itself by placing itself under Divine protection and the aegis of the law. I may add that the law was only invented for the purpose of protecting it. The justice which is other than the satisfaction of revenge, an eye for an eye, a tooth for a tooth — the lex talionis, — made its appearance in human society only after the establishment of property, for, as Locke says, '*Where there is no property there is no injustice,* is a proposition as certain as any demonstrated in Euclid. For the idea of property being a right to anything, and the idea to which the name injustice is given being the invasion or violation of that right.'[2] As the witty Linguet said to Montesquieu, 'L'esprit des lois, c'est l'esprit de la propriété.'

Religious rites and ceremonies were instituted to impress upon the superstitious minds of primitive peoples the respect due to this private property of the family collectivit, so greatly opposed to their communistic usages. In Greece and Italy, on appointed days of the month and year, the chief of the family walked round his fields, along the uncultivated boundary, pushing the victims before him, singing hymns, and offering up sacrifices to the posts or stones, the metes and bounds of the fields, which were converted into divinities — they were the Termini of the Romans,

---

1 Table VII, sec. 1. Restored text after Festus.
2 Locke's *Essay on the Human Understanding.* Book IV, chap. iii, sec. 18.

the 'divine bournes' of the Greeks. The cultivator was not to
approach the landmark, 'lest the divinity, on feeling himself
struck by the ploughshare, should cry out to him,"Stop, this is my
field, yonder is thine." ' The Bible abounds in recommendations
to respect the fields of one's neighbour: 'Thou shalt not remove
thy neighbour's landmark.' (Deut. xix, 14.) 'Cursed be he that
removeth his neighbour's landmark.' Job, who has the soul of a
landlord, numbers among the wickedest the man 'who removes
the landmarks.' (Job xxiv.) The Cossacks, with a view to
inculcating on their children a respect for other people's property,
took them out for walks along the boundaries of the fields,
whipping them all the way with rods. Plato, who drops his
idealism when he deals with property, says, 'Our first law must be
that no man shall lay a hand on the boundary-mark which divides
a field from his neighbour's field, for it must remain unmoved.
Let no man remove the stone which he has sworn to leave in its
place.' (Laws, VIII.) The Etruscans called down maledictions on
the heads of the guilty: 'He who has touched or removed the
landmark shall be condemned by the gods; his house shall
disappear; his race become extinct; his lands shall cease to bear
fruit; hail, rust, and canicular heat shall destroy his harvests; the
limbs of the culprit shall ulcerate and rot.' [1]

The spiritual chastisements, which make so deep an impression
on the wild and fiery imaginations of primitive peoples, having
proved inadequate, it becomes necessary to resort to corporal
punishments of unexampled severity — punishments repugnant
to the feelings of barbarian peoples. Savages inflict the most cruel
tortures on themselves by way of preparing for a life of perpetual
struggle, but such tortures are never punitive; it is the civilised
proprietor who has hit upon the *bene amat, bene castigat* of the
Bible. Catlin, who knew the savages of America well, states that a
Sioux chief had expressed his surprise to him at having seen
'along the frontier white men whip their children; a thing that is
very cruel.'

The worst crime that a barbarian can commit is to shed the
blood of his clan; if he kills one of its members the entire clan
must rise up to take vengeance on him. When a member of a clan
was found guilty of murder or any other crime he was expelled,
and devoted to the infernal gods, lest any should have to reproach

---

[1] Sacred formula cited by Fustel de Coulanges. *Cité Antique.*

himself with having spilt the blood of his clan by killing the murderer. Property marks its appearance by teaching the barbarian to trample under foot such pious sentiments; laws are enacted condemning to death all those who attack property. 'Whosoever,' decrees the law of the Twelve Tables, 'shall in the night furtively have cut, or caused to graze on, the crops yielded by the plough, shall, if he has reached puberty, be devoted to Ceres and put to death; if he has not arrived at puberty he shall be beaten with rods at the will of the magistrate and condemned to repair the damage doubly. The manifest thief (*i.e.,* taken in the act), if a freeman, shall be scourged with rods and delivered up to slavery. The incendiary of a corn-stack shall be whipped and put to death by fire.' (Table VIII, secs. 9, 10, 14.) The Saxons punished theft with death. The Burgundian law surpassed the Roman law in cruelty; it condemned to slavery the wives and children under 14 years of age who had not denounced their husbands and fathers guilty of stealing a horse or an ox. (XLVII, secs. 1, 2.) Property introduced the common informer into the family.

These moral and material punishments, which are met with in all countries and which are everywhere alike ferocious,[1] abundantly prove the difficulty experienced by the collective form of property in introducing itself into the communist tribes.

Prior to the institution of collective property, the barbarian looked upon all the property belonging to the tribe as his own, and disposed of it accordingly; the Lacedaemonian, we have seen, had the right to enter private dwellings without any formalities and to take the food he required. The Lacedaemonians were, it is true, a comparatively civilized people, but their essentially warlike existence had enabled them to preserve their ancient usages. The travellers who have fallen victims to this propensity of the barbarian to appropriate everything within his reach, have described him as a thief; as if theft were compatible with a state of society in which private property is not as yet constituted. But as soon as collective property was established, the natural habit of appropriating what a man sees and covets, became a crime when practised at the expense of the private property of the family,

---

[1] Property is invariably ferocious; until quite recently thieves were hanged after having suffered torture; the forgers of banknotes in civilised Europe were formerly sentenced to death, and are still condemned to hard labour for life.

and, in order to set a restraint upon this inveterate habit, it was found necessary to have recourse to moral and physical punishment; justice and our odious criminal codes followed in the wake of collective property and are an outgrowth of it.

Collective property, if not the sole cause, was, at all events, the pre-eminent cause of the overthrow of the matriarchate by the patriarchate. The fate of the patriarchal family is intimately bound up with the collective form of property: the latter becomes the essential condition of its maintenance, and, so soon as it begins to break up, the patriarchal family is likewise disintegrated and superseded by the modern family; a sorry remnant, destined, ere long, to disappear.

Ancient society recognized the necessity of the integrity of collective property for the maintenance of the family. At Athens the State watched over its proper administration; anybody being entitled to demand the indictment of the head of a family who maladministered his goods. The collective property did not belong to the father, nor even to the individual members of the family, but to the family considered as a collective entity which is perpetual, and endures from generation to generation.[1] The property belonged to the family in the past, present, and future; to the ancestors who had their altars and their tombs in it; to the living members who were only usufructuaries, charged with continuing the family traditions, and with nursing the property in order to hand it down to their descendants. The chief of the family, who might be the father, the eldest brother, the younger brother, or, on occasions, the mother, was the administrator of the estate; it was his duty to attend to the wants of the individuals who composed the collectivity; to see that the lands were properly cultivated and the house kept in order, so that he might transmit the patrimony to his successor in the same state of prosperity in which he had received it at the death of his predecessor. To enable him to fulfil this mission the head of the family was armed with despotic power; he was judge and executioner; he judged, condemned, and inflicted bodily punishment on the members of the family under his control; his

---

[1] Among the Germans and the Bavarians they were known by the name of estates belonging to the genealogies (*genealogiae*); among the Ripuarian Franks under that of *terrae aviaticae;* among the Anglo-Saxons under that of *ethel* or *alod parentum.*

authority stretched so far as to empower him to sell his children into slavery, and to inflict the pain of death on all his subordinates, including his wife, although she enjoyed the protection, precarious enough, it is true, of her own family The quantity of land distributed was generally proportionate to the number of males in the family; the father, with a view to the procuring of servants to cultivate it, married his sons while still in infancy to adult women, who became his concubines. Haxthausen relates that in Russia one could see tall and robust young women carrying their little husbands in their arms.

The worn-out phrase 'The family is the pillar of the state,' which modern moralists and politicians reiterate *ad nauseam* since it has ceased to be exact, was at one time an adequate expression of the truth. Where collective property exists, every village is a petty state, the government whereof is constituted by the council elected in the assembly of the family-chiefs, co-equals in rights and privileges. In India, where the collective form of property was highly developed, the village had its public officers, who were artisans (wheelwrights, tailors, weavers, etc.), schoolmasters, priests, and dancing women for public ceremonies; they were paid by the village community, and owed their services to the members having ancestral shares in the land, but not to stranger settlers. In the Greek republics the state maintained public prostitutes for the use of the males of the patrician families. Sir G. Campbell states, among other curious facts, that the smiths, and the artisans generally, were more highly remunerated in the Indian villages than the priest.

The head man of the village, elected for his ability, his learning, and powers as a sorcerer, is the administrator of the property of the community; he alone is privileged to carry on commerce with the exterior, that is, to sell the surplus of the crops and cattle, and to buy such objects as are not manufactured in the village. As Haxthausen observes: 'Commerce is only carried on wholesale, which is of great advantage to the peasant, who, left to himself, is often under the necessity of selling his products below their real value, and at unfavourable moments. As commerce is in the hands of the chief, the latter is able from his connections with the chiefs of the neighbouring villages to wait for a rise in prices, and take advantage of all favourable circumstances before concluding a sale.' All those who are familiar with the deceptions practised upon peasants by merchants will appreciate the justness of the observation of Haxthausen. The French bourgeois, who pounced upon Algiers and Tunis as on a prey, expressed great moral indignation at being prevented from entering into communication with the Arabs individually, and obliged to treat with the chiefs of the community; they loudly and pathetically bewailed the unhappy lot of the wretched Arabs bereft of the liberty of allowing themselves to be fleeced by the European merchants!

Petty societies, organized on the basis of collective property, are endowed with a vitality and power of resistance possessed by no other social form in an equal degree.

'The village communities are little republics, having nearly everything that they want within themselves and almost independent of any foreign relations,' says Lord Metcalfe. 'They seem to last where nothing else lasts. Dynasty after dynasty tumbles down, revolution succeeds to revolution; Hindu, Pagan, Mogul, Mahratta, Sikh, English are all masters in turn; but the village communities remain the same. In time of trouble they arm and fortify themselves; a hostile army passes through the country, the village communities collect their cattle within their walls and let the enemy pass unmolested. If plunder and devastation be directed against themselves, and the force employed be irresistible, they flee to friendly villages at a distance; but when the storm has passed over they return and resume their occupations. If a country remains for a series of years the scene of continued pillage and massacre, so that the village cannot be inhabited, the scattered villagers nevertheless return whenever the power of peaceable possession revives. A generation may pass away, but the succeeding generation will return. The sons will take the places of their fathers, the same site for the village, the same positions for their houses; the same lands will be re-occupied by the descendants . . . It is not a trifling matter that will turn them out, for they will often maintain their posts throughout times of disturbance and convulsions, and acquire a strength sufficient to resist pillage and oppression with success. Further on he adds: 'The village constitution which can survive all outward shock is, I suspect, easily subverted with the aid of our regulations and Courts of Justice by any internal

disturbance; litigation, above all things, I should think would tend
to destroy it.' [1]

Bourgeois exploitation cannot tolerate, alongside of it, the
collective form of property, which it destroys and replaces by
private property, the adequate form of bourgeois property. What
has taken place in India and Algeria has occurred in France. The
village collectivities that had lasted throughout the entire feudal
period, and survived till 1789, were disorganized by the dissolvent
action of the laws during and after the bourgeois revolution. The
great revolutionary jurist, Merlin *suspect* (so called because he
had been the proposer of the sanguinary *loi des suspects*), did
more towards bringing about the destruction and confiscation of
the communal lands of the village collectivities than the feudal
lords had done in the course of centuries.

Over and above the reasons of a political character which
prompt monarchical governments to patronize the family

---

[1] *Report of Select Committee of the House of Commons*, 1832. The remarkable
deposition of Lord Metcalfe is published *in extenso* in the appendix to Vol. XI.

Jurists, politicians, religious and socialist reformers have repeatedly discussed
the rights of property, and these discussions, how interminable soever, have
always come back to the initial point, to wit, that property had been established by
violence, but that time, which disfigures all things, had added grace and sanctity to
property. Unti' recent years the writers of philosophies of human society ignored
the existence of collective property. Baron Haxthausen, who travelled in Russia in
1840, made the discovery, and published an account of it in his *Etudes sur la
situation intérieure, la vie nationale et les institutions rurales de la Russie*. He
remarked that the *mir* was the realization of the Utopianism of St. Simon, then in
vogue. Bakunin and the liberal Russians, who had never so much as suspected the
existence of collective property in Russia, now re-discovered Haxthausen's
discovery; and as, in spite of their amorphous anarchism, they are above all
things Russian Jingos, who imagine that the Slav race is the chosen race,
privileged to guide mankind, they declared the *mir*, that primitive and exhausted
form of property, to be the form of the future; it only remained for the western
nations to obliterate their civilization and to ape that of the Russian peasants.

In virtue of the principle that it is hardest to see what lies under our eyes,
Haxthausen, who had discovered the *mir* in Russia, was unable to perceive the
remains of the *Mark*, so numerous in Germany; he affirmed that collective
property was a specialty of the Slavs. Maurer has the merit of having
demonstrated that the Germans have passed through the stage of collective
property; and, since Maurer, traces of it have been found in all countries and
among all races. Before Haxthausen, the English officials in India had, indeed,
called attention to this particular form of property in the provinces which they
administered, but their discovery, buried in official reports, had obtained no
publicity; but since the question has come under scientific observation it has been
found that this same form had already been signalized by writers in the last, and in
the first years of the present, centuries, notably by Le Grand d'Aussy, François de
Neufchateau, in France, and the agronomist Marshall, in England.

organization based on collective property, there exist yet others, equally important, of an administrative character. As the collectivist village forms a number of administrative units represented by the chief who directs it and trafficks in its name, the Government makes the latter responsible for the levying of the taxes and the recruiting of the militia, and charges him with additional functions which are not remunerated. In Russia the Imperial Government lends its weight to the decisions of the communal council, incorporating into the army, and even despatching to Siberia, all those whose conduct is not approved of by the elders. In France, the monarchy anterior to 1789 exerted itself to uphold these peasant collectivist organizations, assailed on the one hand by the feudal lords, who brutally despoiled them of their communal possessions and privileges, and on the other by the bourgeoisie, who seized upon their lands by every means.[1]

The feudal lords encouraged the organization of the peasants into family collectivities. Dalloz mentions a contract of the 17th century in which a lord causes his lands to be cultivated by *metayers,* on condition that the peasants shall have 'in common, fire and food and live in perpetual community.' A legist of the 18th century, Dunod, furnishes us with the reason which led to the community of the cultivators: It is that 'the seignorial domains are better cultivated, and the subjects better able to pay the tributes due to the lord when living in common than when forming separate households.'

Collective property, which destroyed the primitive tribal

---

[1] Russian revolutionary socialists believe in the *mir,* and are in favour of its maintenance. They opine that the existence of a class of peasants living in collectivity must facilitate the establishment of agrarian communism. A socialist government, turning to account the communistic sentiments developed by collective property, might conceivably adopt measures favourable to the nationalization of the soil and its social cultivation; but the establishment of a revolutionary socialist power in Russia is highly improbable during the maintenance, as a general fact, of this form of property. All village collectivities, organized on the basis of the *mir,* are independent; they are self-sufficing, and keep up very imperfect relations among one another, and it is an easy matter for any government to stifle whatever disposition they might manifest for federation. This is what has come to pass in India. The English Government, with an army of 50,000 European soldiers, holds in subjection an empire as thickly peopled as Russia. The village collectivities united by no federative bonds are powerless to offer any considerable force of resistance. It may be asseverated that the surest basis of governmental despotism is precisely collective property, with the family and communal organization which corresponds thereto.

communism, established the family communism which secured all its members against want. 'The proletariat is not known in Russia,' wrote Haxthausen, 'and so long as this institution (the *mir*) survives, it can never be found here. A man may become impoverished here and squander his substance, but the faults or misfortunes of the father can never affect his children, for these holding their rights of the commune, and not of the family, do not inherit their father's poverty.'

It is precisely this security against want afforded by collective property which is offensive to the capitalist, whose whole fortune reposes on the misery of the working class.

Collective property is remarkable not only for the tenacity and indestructibility of the small peasant collectivities which it maintained, and the well-being which it afforded to the cultivators of the soil, but also for the grandeur of its achievements. In illustration whereof let me cite the marvellous works of irrigation in India and the terrace-culture of the mountain slopes of Java, covering, Wallace informs us, hundreds of square miles; 'These terraces are increased year by year, as the population increases, by the inhabitants of each village working in concert under the direction of their chiefs, and it is, perhaps, by this system of village culture alone that such extensive terracing and irrigation has been rendered possible.'[1]

The collective form of property, traces of which have been met with wherever researches have been instituted, has survived for shorter or longer periods, according to the industrial and commercial development of the country in which it obtained. This form, created by the splitting up of the common property of the tribe, was bound to disappear in its turn, with the disintegration of the patriarchal family, in order to constitute the individual property of the several members of the dissolved family.

Private property, which was to succeed collective property, grew out of it. The house and garden enclosed by walls and palisades were the private property, absolute and inalienable, of the family; no public authority had the right to trench on it. In the interior of the house the different members, not omitting the slaves, possessed a *peculium*, some private property independent of that of the family; this individual property, acquired by the

---

[1] A. R. Wallace. *The Malay Archipelago*, 1869. Vol. I.

personal toil of its owner, was often considerable; it consisted of slaves, cattle and movables of various kinds. The right to a *peculium* was acquired slowly; in the beginning no one member of the family could possess aught in severalty; all that he acquired reverted of right to the community.

The arable and pasture lands of which the family had but the usufruct became ultimately their private property, and when the family was broken up, *i.e.,* when every male upon marrying quitted the collective dwelling for a house of his own, landed property shared the fate of personal property — it was divided amongst the children and was held in severalty.

The evolution of property, passing from the collective to the private form, has been extremely slow, so slow, indeed, that in many a country collective property, but for an external impulse, might possibly have endured for centuries without suffering a change. Villages founded on collective property form economic units; that is to say that they contain all they require for the intellectual and material wants of their inhabitants, and that contrariwise, they comprise few elements capable of determining change; here all things are accomplished in accordance with traditions prescribed by the elders, and handed down like precious heirlooms. In effect, once a village has arrived at such a degree of industrial and agricultural development as to be capable of satisfying the natural and simple wants of the villagers, it would seem that it no longer finds within itself any cause for change; an impulse from without is required to set it in motion.

Agriculture, which was the determinant cause of the parcelling out of the common tribal property, was, moreover, one of the causes of the splitting up of collectivist property. In proportion as improved methods of culture were introduced, the peasants recognized that one year's possession was insufficient to reap the benefits of the manures and labour incorporated with the lands that had been allotted them. They demanded that the partitions, hitherto annual, should in future take place every two, three, seven, and even twenty years: in Russia the government was constrained to impose the partitions on the taking of the census; the peasants call them *black, i.e., bad* partitions, which shows how uncongenial they were to the families who considered that they had proprietary rights in the lands which had been given them at the last distribution. Hence, it was the arable lands to which improved methods were first applied, which, in the first place, became liable to be divided only after a certain number of years, and which finally became inalienable; whereas the pasture continued to be apportioned annually. So long as the arable lands are not private property, the trees planted in the communal lands belong to those who have planted them, even though they grow in territory which is subject to periodical partition.

In the villages in which collective property obtains all the chiefs of families are co-equals; they all possess an equal right to share in the allotment of the lands, because all originally belonged to the same clan; the strangers who have come to reside there as artificers, fugitives, or prisoners of war, are entitled, after having obtained the freedom of the city, which corresponds to the ancient adoption by the clan, to share in the territorial partition equally with the original inhabitants. This admission of strangers was feasible only so long as the villages grew slowly and as the land to be disposed of remained abundant: the populous villages were forced to disseminate, to send forth colonies and to clear the neighbouring forests. Every family was free, indeed, to make clearances outside a given limit and during a stated period, and was held to have a possessory right in the lands which it had brought under culture. But this abundance of uncultivated land began to fail in the villages situated near the sea shore or by the riverside, which, owing to their more favoured position, attracted a larger number of strangers. Into these villages, which grew into small towns, it became difficult to gain admission, and for a right of sojourn certain fees were levied. [1]

The newcomers were excluded from the territorial partitions, from the right of common pasture, and from the administration of the towns; these rights were strictly limited to the original families, who constituted a privileged body, a sort of communal aristocracy, to wit, the municipal aristocracy, opposed alike to the feudal or warlike aristocracy and to the alien artificers. The latter, in order to resist the continual aggressions of the

---

[1] In his *Histoire des biens Communaux jusqu'au XIII. siècle*, 1856, M. Rivière cites an ordinance of 1223, which states that every stranger for the right of sojourn at Rheims must pay a bushel of oats and a hen to the archbishop, eight crowns to the mayor, and four to the aldermen. The archbishop is the feudal lord: the contributions due to him are comparatively insignificant, whereas those exacted by the mayor and aldermen, who belong to the communal or municipal aristocracy, are very onerous for the period.

communal aristocracy, formed trade corporations. This division of the members of the city was throughout the Middle Ages a constant source of intestine warfare.

A degree of inequality crept into the primitive families: it would happen that to one family fell an undue share of allotments; that others, in order to discharge their debts, were compelled to relinquish the enjoyment of their lots, and so forth. This engrossing of the land profoundly wounded the sentiments of equality which had not ceased to animate the members of the collectivist villages. Everywhere the monopolizers of land have been loaded with maledictions; in Russia they are called the community-eaters; in Java it is forbidden to claim more than one inheritance. Isaiah exclaims: 'Woe unto them that join house to house, that lay field to field, till there be no place, that they may be placed alone in the midst of the earth.' (v. 8.)

But among the causes that operated most powerfully in bringing misery and disorganization into the village collectivities were the fiscal charges, as witness Anglo-India.

At the outset the taxes were paid in kind and proportionally to the nature of the harvest; but this mode of payment no longer answers the claims of a government which becomes centralized; it exacts money payment of the taxes in advance, taking no account of the state of the crops. The villagers, as a consequence, are constrained to apply to the usurers, those pests of the village; this vile brood, who are countenanced by the government, rob the peasant shamelessly; they transform him into a nominal proprietor, who tills his fields with no other object than to pay off his debts, which increase in proportion as he discharges them. The contempt and hatred inspired by the usurers is widespread and intense; if the anti-Semitic campaign in Russia has given rise to such sanguinary scenes in the villages, it is because the peasant made no distinction between the Jew and the usurer; many an orthodox Christian who needed not to be circumcised in order to strip the cultivators as clean as ever the purest descendant of Abraham could have done, was robbed and massacred during the height of the fever of the anti-Semitic movement. These various causes co-operated with the development of industry and commerce to accelerate the monopolizing of the land, vested more and more in private families, and to precipitate the dissolution of the patriarchal family.

4

Feudal Property

I

FEUDAL property presents itself under two forms: immovable property, called *corporeal* by the French feudists, consisting of a castle or manor with its appurtenances and surrounding lands, 'as far as a capon can fly;' and movable or *incorporeal* property, consisting of military service, aids, reliefs, fines, tithes, etc.

Feudal property, of which ecclesiastical property is but a variety, springs up in the midst of village communities based on collective property, and evolves at their expense; after a long series of transformations it is resolved into bourgeois or capitalist property, the adequate form of private property.

Feudal property, and the social organization which corresponds thereto, serve as a bridge from family, or, more correctly, consanguine collectivism to bourgeois individualism.

Under the feudal system the landlord has obligations and is far from enjoying the liberty of the capitalist — the right to use and abuse. The land is not marketable; it is burdened with conditions, and is transmitted according to traditionary customs which the proprietor dares not infringe; he is bound to discharge certain defined duties towards his hierarchical superiors and inferiors.

The system, in its essence, is a compact of reciprocal services; the feudal lord only holds his land and possesses a claim on the labour and harvests of his tenants and vassals on condition of doing suit and service to his superiors and lending aid to his dependants. On accepting the oath of fealty and homage the lord engaged to protect his vassal against all and sundry by all the means at his command; in return for which support the vassal was bound to render military and personal service and make certain payments to his lord. The latter, in his turn, for the sake of protection, commended himself to a more puissant feudal lord, who himself stood in the relation of vassalage to a suzerain, to the king or emperor.

All the members of the feudal hierarchy, from the serf upwards to the king or emperor, were bound by the ties of reciprocal duties. A sense of duty was the spirit of feudal society, just as the lust of lucre is the soul of our own. All things were made to contribute to the impressing of it upon the minds of great and small alike. Popular poetry, that primeval and all-powerful instrument of education, exalted duty into a religion. Roland, the epic hero of feudalism, assailed and overwhelmed by the Saracens at Roncevalles, upbraids his companion-in-arms, Oliver, who complains of Charlemagne's desertion of them, in this wise:

'Ne dites tel ultrage.
Mal seit de l'coer ki el piz se cuardet!
Nus remeindruin en estal en la place;
Par nus i iert e li colps e li caples.

'Pur sun seignur deit hum suffrir granzmals;
E endurer e forz freiz e granz calz
Si'n deit hum perdre del sanc e de la carn
Fier de ta lance e jo de Durendal,
Ma bone espée que li Reis me dunat
Se jo i moerc, dire poet ki l'avrat,
Que ele fut a nobilie vassal!'[1]

---

[1] 'Speak not such outrage.
Curse on the heart that cravens in the breast!
Fast in the place will we maintain our stand.
And blows and sword-thrusts shall be dealt by us.'

'Much evil must one suffer for his lord;
Endure alike the hard cold and high heat;
And for him must one lose his blood and bone!
Fight with thy lance, as I with Durendal,
My good sword that my king did give to me;
And if I die, who gets it well may say,
Right noble was the vassal owned the sword!'
          Chanson de Roland, secs. xciii and xciv

Consanguine collectivism had but created the communal unit; feudalism called forth a provincial and national life by knitting together the independent and insulated groups of a province or a nation by a reciprocity of duties and services. Viewed in this light feudalism is a federation of baronies.

The duties which the lord owed his serfs, tenants, and vassals were manifold and onerous, but with the decay of feudalism he shook off these duties, while, at the same time, he continued to exact and even aggravated, the dues and obligations which, originally, had been but the recompense of services he had rendered. Not content with neglecting his feudal duties, he raised a claim to the lands of his vassals, as also to the communal domains and forests. The feudists, justly stigmatized as 'feudal pens', maintained that the woodlands, forests, and meadows had immemorially belonged to the lord, who had merely resigned the usufruct thereof to his serfs and vassals. The English feudists made shorter work of it. They fabricated history and declared that at some period — 'sometimes vaguely associated with the feudalization of Europe, sometimes more precisely with the Norman Conquest — the entire soil of England

---

The song of Roland was frequently sung at the beginning of a battle. At Hastings, when the two hostile armies were face to face, 'the Earl', (William, Earl of Normandy), says William of Malmesbury, commenced the song of Roland, 'that the warlike example of that man might stimulate the soldiers'. According to Wace, the Trouvère, the song was sung by the Norman, Taillefer:

> 'Taillefer ki moult bien cantout
> Sur un cheval gi tost alout,
> Devant le Duc allout cantant
> De Karlemaigne e de Rollant,
> Ed d'Oliver e des vassals
> Qui moururent en Roncevals.'

Thus Englished by Sir Walter Scott:—

> 'Taillefer, who sang both well and loud,
> Came mounted on a courser proud;
> Before the Duke the minstrel sprung
> And loud of Charles and Roland sung
> Of Oliver and champions mo
> Who died at fatal Roncevaux.'

As Taillefer sang he played with his sword, and, casting it high in the air, caught it again with his right hand, while all in chorus shouted the cry of 'God aid us!'

was confiscated; that the whole of each manor became the lord's demesne; that the lord divided certain parts of it among his free retainers, but kept a part in his own hands to be tilled by his villeins; that all which was not required for this distribution was left as the lord's waste; and that all customs which cannot be traced to feudal principles grew up insensibly through the subsequent tolerance of the feudal chief.' [1]

The bourgeois historians and Merlin, the terrible jurist of the convention and destroyer of the communal lands, solicitous to trace the private form of property to the feudal period, adopted the interested thesis of the aristocrats. The history of the genesis and evolution of feudal property will prove the unsoundness of the feudists' theory and show that seignorial property was built up by fraud and violence.

II.

The feudal system appears as the hierarchical organization of authority, notwithstanding that it was the outgrowth of a society of equals; but equality could never have brought forth despotism but for the co-operation, during centuries, of events which, for the understanding of that genesis, must be kept in mind.

The Teutonic tribes who had invaded Western Europe were a nomad population, in a state of barbarism nearly akin to that of the Iroquois tribes at the time of the discovery of America. Strabo tells us that the barbarians established in Belgium and in the North-East of France were ignorant of agriculture, and lived exclusively on milk and flesh; principally on pork, fresh or salt; that they possessed herds of swine — savage and dangerous as wolves — roaming at large in the immense forests which covered the country, and so abundant as to supply them with food and the means of buying the few articles they stood in need of. Strabo adds that the Gauls had similar manners, and that to know them it required but to contemplate the Germans of his time. When Caesar landed in England he found that the Britons inhabiting

---

[1] H. S. Maine. *Village Communities,* p. 84. This opinion was formulated. in his evidence before the Select Committee of the House of Commons which sat to consider the subject of enclosures. by a lawyer. Mr Blamire. who according to Mr Maine. was 'an official unusually familiar with English landed property in its less usual shapes.'

Kent possessed much the same manners and customs as the Gauls; they did not till the land; they subsisted on a milk diet and on flesh, and were clad in skins. They painted their bodies blue in order to strike terror into their enemies, and had their wives in common by groups of ten or twelve, including brothers, fathers and sons.[1] In Europe and elsewhere the point of departure is the same.

The widest equality reigned among these barbarians, who were all warriors and hunters, and whose manners and usages tended to preserve this heroic equality. When they settled and began to practise a rude kind of agriculture, they undertook warlike expeditions for the purpose of keeping up the exercise of fighting. A war chief of renown needed but to announce that he was starting on a campaign to see warriors flock to him, eager for spoils and glory. During the expedition they owed him obedience, as did the Greek warriors to Agamemnon, but they ate at the same table and banqueted with him without distinction of persons, and the booty was divided equally and by lot. Back again in their villages, they recovered their independence and equality, and the war chief lost his authority.

It is in this free and equal fashion that the Scandinavians, and in fact all barbarians, organized their expeditions. These piratical manners prevailed during the whole of the middle ages; when William the Conqueror and Pope Innocent III wanted to levy an army against the English and the Albigenses, it was only necessary for them to promise a division of the spoils taken from the vanquished. Before the battle of Hastings, just as the troops were about to engage in fight, William, with a loud voice called out to his soldiers: 'Fight bravely and put all to death; if we win, we shall all be rich; what I get, you shall get; if I conquer, you will conquer; if I obtain the land, you will obtain it.' His Holiness the Pope used similar language on the 10th of March, in the year 1208, on stirring up the faithful to fight the heretic Albigenses: 'Up now, soldiers of Christ; root out impiety by every means that God may have revealed to you [the means that the Lord had revealed were fire, rapine, and murder], drive out of their castles the Earl of Toulouse and his vassals, and seize upon their lands, that the orthodox Catholics may be established in the dominions of the

[1] *De Bello Gallico*, V., sec. 14.

heretics.' The Crusades which launched the warriors of Europe
on the East were similarly organized, having the delivery of the
Holy Sepulchre for pretence and plunder for object.[1]

When the barbarians, in quest of territory, had conquered a
country, they either put the inhabitants to death (as the Hebrews
did, by Divine order), or contented themselves with ransacking
the towns; they settled in the country, which they set about
cultivating in their own way, and allowed the vanquished to live
alongside of them according to their own customs and usages. But
when they became sedentary and cultivators of the land, they
little by little lost their warlike habits, although some of them
remained invincibly attached to the primitive manners. The
Germans observed by Tacitus had already lost some of their
savage fierceness; they had established themselves and become
addicted to agriculture; the tribe of the Catti, however, were
dedicated to war. Always in the forefront of battle, they occupied
the most dangerous posts; they possessed neither houses nor
lands, nor had they cares of any sort. Wherever they presented
themselves they were entertained. These warriors formed a kind
of standing army, charged with defending those of their
countrymen who were engaged in agricultural pursuits.

But no sooner had the invading barbarians established
themselves and lost their native vigour than other barbarians
pounced upon them as on an easy prey, and treated them like a
conquered people. During many centuries compact masses of
barbarians overran Europe: in the east, the Goths, Germans, and
Huns; in the north and west, the Scandinavians; in the south, the
Arabians; desolating the towns and country in their passage. And
when from east and north and south this human flood had ceased
to pour down into Europe, and when the barbarians had lost their
nomadic habits and resumed the work of civilization which they
had arrested and frustrated, there was unloosed another scourge;
bands of armed men overspread the country, plundering and
ransacking and levying contributions on every side; the 'battle

---

[1] A celebrated bourgeois economist, M. de Molinari, has innocently compared
the financial enterprises of our times with the predatory expeditions of the Middle
Ages. Both, indeed, aim at plunder, but with this difference, that whereas the
feudal warrior staked his life, the capitalists who gnaw, rat-like, at the 10 and 20
per cent interest, risk their capital alone, which they have taken good care not to
create.

over, the soldiers of the hostile armies fraternized and started on an expedition on their own account.[1]

During many centuries people lived in continual fear of robbery, kidnapping and murder. The invasions of the barbarians that ruined and disorganized the country did not prevent the tribes already settled from quarrelling among themselves. These constant internecine quarrels render barbarian nations powerless in the face of strangers; they are unable to stifle their clan hatreds and their village feuds in front of a common enemy. Tacitus, intent solely on the supremacy of the Romans, adjured the gods to foment this disastrous discord; for, said he, 'fortune can bestow no higher benefit on Rome than the dissensions of her enemies.[2]

The inhabitants of the towns and provinces were constrained, for safety's sake, to live in fortified places. The charters of Auvergne of the 11th and 12th centuries designate such villages by the term of *castra* (camp). In the towns and boroughs houses were constructed in view of the necessity of sustaining a siege.

The village collectivities which, at the outset, were composed almost exclusively of individuals belonging to the same clan, and consequently equals, elected chieftains charged with their defence, who eventually came to gather into their hands the several rights of jurisdiction, of settling differences, of interpreting the customs, and maintaining order. The Franks in their barbarous Latin called such a chieftain *graffio*, from *graf*, the German for count. The elected chiefs of the village collectivities are the feudal barons in embryo.

In the beginning they were simply public officers subject to the authority of the council of the elders and the popular assemblies, and with the execution of whose decisions they were

---

[1] After the battle of Poitiers (1356) the soldiers, being out of employment, associated and made war on their own behalf. In 1360, after the Treaty of Bretigny, which restored King John of France — a prisoner in England — to liberty, the soldiers of the two armies were dismissed. They formed themselves into bands and took the field. One band operated in the north, another, and more considerable one, commanded by Talleyrand Perigord, descended into the valley of the Rhone, and after having ravaged Provence passed through Avignon—where the Pope regaled the chiefs and gave absolution and a present of 500,000 ducats to the soldiers — ransacking the towns and laying waste the country.

[2] *Germania* l, sec. xxviii.

charged; they were severely punished for every neglect of duty.[1]
The graffio of the Frankish tribes who omitted to expel a stranger
whose expulsion had been voted by the assembly was amerced in
a fine of 200 gold solidi. *(Lex Salica.)* This was exactly the sum
assessed as composition for murder. *(Weregild.)*

The powers which were at a later date to become the appanage
of the feudal lords, belonged to the community met in full
assembly. *(Folkmoote.)* All of the inhabitants were bound to
attend in arms, under penalty of a fine; certain village
collectivities possessed serfs, as, later on, did the lords.

The laws of Wales, collected in 940, by order of King Hoel-Du,
and published in 1841 by A. Owen, indicate the mode of election
and the qualities and the functions of these village chiefs which do
not substantially differ from those of the barbarian war-chief. The
chief of the clan was chosen by all the heads of families having
wives and legitimate offspring, and he held his office for life;
among certain peoples his functions were temporary and
revocable. It was imperative 'that he should speak on behalf of
his kin and be listened to; that he should fight on behalf of his kin
and be feared; that he should be security on behalf of his kin and
be accepted.' When he administered justice he was assisted by
the seven oldest villagers; under his orders stood an *avenger*,
charged with executing vengeance; for justice at that epoch was
but revenge — the lex talionis — blow for blow, wound for
wound. On the first alarm, after the clamour, called *haro* by the
Normans and *biafor* by the Basques, the inhabitants were bound
to issue forth from their houses, in arms, and place themselves
under their chieftain's command; he was the military chief, to
whom all owed fidelity and obedience. Whoever failed to respond
to his appeal was fined. In certain boroughs we find a military
organization, *e.g.*, at Tarbes the inhabitants were formed into
tithings having at their head a tithing-man, whose office it was to
see that all the men were armed and that their arms were in good
condition.[2]

---

[1] The customary of Béarn began with a haughty declaration of independence.
'These are the customs of Béarn, which show that of old there existed no lords in
Béarn. But the inhabitants, hearing praise of a knight of Bigorre, set forth in quest
of him and made him a lord for the space of one year. But he being unwilling to
conform to the customs: the popular assembly of Pay summoned him to respect
the customs . . . he, refusing to obey, was killed in the assembly.'

[2] L. Deville, *Etudes historiques sur Tarbes.* Bulletin de la Sociéte Académique
des Hautes Pyrénées, sixième année, deux livraison. 1861.

All functions amongst barbarian tribes tend to become vested certain families; the weaver's, smith's, priest's, and magician's callings are handed down from father to son; it is in this way that castes arise. The chief, charged with the maintenance of order at home and the duty of defence abroad, was chosen out of the body of the inhabitants; but little by little it became the habit to choose him out of the same family, which, ultimately, itself designated the chief of the community and omitted the formality of an election. It would be erroneous to suppose that in the beginning the chieftainship carried with it any special privilege; so far, indeed, was chieftainship from being coveted, that the man elected by the community was made liable to a fine if he refused to accept the charge. At Folkestone, if either the mayor or any of the jurats refused to assume their respective offices upon being elected, 'the commoners were to go and beat down their principal messuage.' At Hastings it was a law that 'if the bailiff will not accept the charge all the commoners will go and beat down his 'tenement'.[1]

Greatness was dangerous: the Scandinavians, in great calamities — in a pressing famine, for example — sacrificed their king, as the highest price with which they could purchase the Divine favour. In this manner the first king of Vermaland, a province of Sweden, was burnt in honour of Odin, to put an end to a great dearth. Earl Hakon, of Norway, offered his son in sacrifice to obtain of Odin the victory over the Jomsburg pirates, and Gideon immolated his daughter to Jehovah for a similar reason.

The Indian village communities observed in our day have, for public officers, weavers, smiths, schoolmasters, brahmins, dancers, etc., who are in the service of the community which rewards them by a lodging, an allowance of grain, and the allotment of a plot of land cultivated by the villagers.[2]

'In early Greece the *demiurgoi* seem to be the analogues of these Hindu officials. Homer mentions the herald, the prophet,

---

[1] Gomme, *Village Communities*, p.254.

[2] These pieces of land frequently bear the name of the trade of the exercise of which they were the reward. 'There are,' says Maine, 'several English parishes in which certain pieces of land in the common field have from time immemorial been known by the name of a particular trade; and there is often a popular belief that nobody not following the trade can legally be the owner of the lot associated with it.'

the bard, all of whom, although we cannot trace their exact
position, appear to have exercised some kind of public function.
Among the Celtic clans similar classes are known to have
existed.'¹

The chiefs elected by the village collectivities were treated in
the same way as the officers of the Hindu villages: their
companions, in reward of their services, allotted them a larger
share of land than to the rest of the inhabitants. Thus, in the
borough of Malmesbury, the alderman, who was the chief man,
was annually granted a piece of land, known as the 'Alderman's
kitchen,' in order that he might devote himself exclusively to the
discharge of his office; his fields were cultivated by the
commoners, who allowed him a share in their harvest and live-
stock.²

At the outset no special distinction marks out the elected chief;
but the practice of continuously choosing him in the same family
ended by creating a privilege that was changed into a hereditary
right; the head of the privileged family became, by right of
succession, and without requiring to submit to an election, the
natural chief of the village. The royal authority had no other origin
than this in the Frankish tribes. The *leudes* must be the heads of
the families of the clan which are charged with furnishing the
military chieftains; just as, among the Hebrews, the tribes of
Levy must furnish the priests. They resided with the king and
were partakers of the royal councils; upon occasions they resisted
him and even offered him violence; it was these *leudes* who
elected the king, whose functions became hereditary.

The village collectivities were perpetually at war with one
another; in the partitions of the conquered lands the share of the
chieftain and his family was, doubtless, more considerable than
that of the commoners; to the privilege of birth was gradually
super-added that of property.

On electing the village chief, the choice fell, we may presume,
on the owner of the most spacious dwelling-house, affording the

---

¹ Dr. Hearn. *Aryan Households*, p. 150.

² 'The Basutos assemble every year to dig up and sow the field appropriated for
the personal maintenance of their chief's first wife. Hundreds of men, in a straight
line, raise and lower their mattocks simultaneously and with perfect regularity.
The entire village concurs in the maintenance of the chieftain.' Casalis. *The
Basutos.*

greatest facilities of defence and the best place of refuge for the peasants in an emergency. This strategical advantage, which, originally, may have been a matter of accident, came to be a condition exacted from every chieftain; in the Indian villages beyond the border the *burj,* or watch tower, is always attached to the house of the chief, and in constant use as a place of refuge and observation. During the feudal period every lord was bound to possess a castle or fortified house having a courtyard protected by moats and drawbridges, a large square tower and a grist mill, to enable the peasants to shelter their crops and cattle, grind their corn and organize their defence. The chieftain's dwelling-house was considered as a sort of common house, and actually became such in times of danger. The members of the village collectivities applied themselves to repairing and fortifying it, surrounding it with walls and trenches; it was the custom for the members of a village to aid in the construction and repair of the houses of all the inhabitants without distinction. This custom is the origin of the right possessed by the feudal lord 'to compel his vassals and tenants to contribute towards the construction of the fortifications in time of war.' and the commentary of the feudal writer indicates the origin of the right. 'And as these fortifications serve alike for the security of the country and the towns, the safety of persons, and the conservation of property, non-residents owning lands in the locality are bound to contribute towards the same.'

The barbarians, who were more of warriors than of cultivators, defended their houses and villages themselves; on the first alarm they rushed forth in battle array and placed themselves under the command of the chieftain, to assist him in beating back the aggressors; in the watch tower they mounted guard by day and watched at night; in many places the lord retained the right to exact from his vassals this service of watch and ward. But when agricultural habits began to get the upper hand, the peasants commuted this military service, which interfered with their pursuits, into a tribute to the chief; on condition that he should maintain a body of men-at-arms, charged exclusively with the work of protection and defence. A proportion of every fine imposed on a delinquent was reserved for the chieftain and his men-at-arms. The chief was thus placed in a position to maintain

an armed force which finally enabled him to impose his will and
dominate his ancient companions.

The village built in the best strategical position became a
centre; in the event of invasion the inhabitants of the adjacent
villages flocked to it for refuge, and in return for the protection
afforded them in the hour of danger they were called on to
contribute towards the costs of repairing the fortifications and
maintaining the men at arms. The authority of these village chiefs
extended to the surrounding country.

In this natural manner were generated in the collectivist
villages, all of whose members were equal in rights and duties, the
first elements of feudalism; they would have remained stable
during centuries, as in India, but for the impulse of external
events which disturbed them and infused them with new life.
Wars and conquests developed these embryonic germs, and by
agglomerating and combining them, built up the vast feudal
system diffused during the Middle Ages, over Western Europe.

What in modern times has taken place in India helps us to
realize the role of conquest in transforming the village chieftain
into the feudal baron. When the English, established along the sea
coasts, extended their dominion inland, they were brought into
contact with villagers organized in the manner described above;
every agricultural group was commanded by a peasant, the
head-man, who spoke in its name, and negotiated with the
conquerors. The English authorities did not trouble to inquire into
the origin and precise nature of his powers, or of the office held
by him in the community; they preferred to take for granted that
he was the master of the village of which he was but the
representative, and to treat him as such; they enhanced and
solidified his authority by all the weight conferred by the right of
the strongest, and on divers occasions assisted the head-man in
oppressing his quondam companions, and despoiling them of
their rights and possessions.

The mediaeval conquerors acted in an analogous fashion; they
confirmed the local chiefs in their possession of those posts in the
villages which were too unimportant to be bestowed as *benefices*
on their liegemen, and in return, made them responsible for the
levying of the taxes and the conduct of their dependents, thereby
according them an authority they had not previously possessed in
the village collectivities. But in every strategical place they

installed one of their own warriors; it was a military post which
they confided to him; the length of tenure of such posts, called
benefices, was subject to variation; at first, they were revoked at
pleasure, afterwards granted for life, and ultimately became
hereditary. The beneficiary tenants took advantage of
circumstances to turn their hereditary possessions into alodial
property, *i.e.*, into land exempt from all obligations. In France the
early kings were repeatedly obliged to make ordinances against
this kind of usurpation. "Let not him who holds a benefice of the
emperor or the church convert any of it into his patrimony," says
Charlemagne in a capitulary of the year 803. (Cap. viii., s. 3.) But
such ordinances were powerless to prevent the conversion of
military chiefs into feudal barons. It may be said, therefore, that
the feudal system had a dual origin; on the one hand it grew out
of the conditions under which the village collectives evolved, and
on the other it sprang from conquest.

The feudal barons, whether village-chiefs transmogrified by the
natural march of events, or military chieftains installed by the
conquerors, were bound to reside in the country which it was
their duty to administer and defend. The territory they possessed
and the dues they received, in the shape of labour and tithes, were
the recompense of services rendered by them to the cultivators
placed under their jurisdiction. The barons and their men-at-arms
formed a permanent army, nourished and maintained by the
inhabitants whom they directly protected. [1]

The baron owed justice, aid, and protection to his vassals, and
these, in their turn, owed fidelity and homage to their lord. At
every change, consequent on the death of either lords or vassals,
the vassal was bound, within a space of 40 days, to repair to the
principal manor—there and not elsewhere, to indicate that he
only swore fealty prospectively to a refuge in the baron's castle; if
the lord was absent and had left no representative, the vassal
made a vow of fealty in front of the manor-door, and caused the
fact to be entered on the records. He was bound to come with his
head uncovered and his belt ungirt, without sword and spurs, and
to kneel down with his hands joined. The lord, in accepting his
oath, took his vassal's hands into his own, in token of union and

---

[1] In the Romance languages the original name of the feudal lord, the term
baron, signified a *strong* man, a *doughty* warrior, which well indicates the
essentially military character of feudalism. *Vassal* similarly bore the sense of
brave, valiant.

protection. The vassal thereupon enumerated the lands and dependencies which he placed under the safeguard of his lord; in early times he brought with him a clod of turf from his fields. Occasionally, too, the lord was the first to take his engagements towards his vassals. In the Fors de Bigorre (customary of Bigorre), it is said that the Comte de Bigorre, 'before receiving the oath of the inhabitants of the land, delegated to that effect, shall himself take the oath that he will change nothing in the ancient customs, nor in such as he shall find the people in possession of; he must have his oath confirmed by that of four nobles of his domain.'

The vassal owed military service to his lord 'when a foreign army had invaded his territory, when he wanted to deliver his besieged castle, or when he set out on a declared war—a war, that is to say, entered upon in the interests of the inhabitants. But, although closely bound to him, the vassal might abandon his lord in certain cases specified in the capitularies of the years 813 to 816, to wit, if his lord had sought to kill him or reduce him to slavery, beaten him with a stick or sword, dishonoured his wife or daughter, or robbed him of his patrimony.

So soon as the authority of the feudal nobility was constituted, it became, in its turn, a source of trouble to the country whose defence it had been charged with. The barons, in order to enlarge their territories and extend their power, carried on continual warfare, among themselves, only interrupted now and again by a short truce necessitated by the tillage of the fields. The wars of the barons may be compared to the industrial and commercial competition of modern times. The outcome is the same; both alike culminate in the concentration of property, and the social supremacy which it bestows. The vanquished, when not killed outright or utterly despoiled, became the vassals of the conqueror, who seized upon a portion of their lands and vassals. The petty barons disappeared for the benefit of the great ones, who became potent feudatories, and established ducal courts at which the lords in vassalage were bound to attend.

It frequently happened that the barons turned highwaymen, who plundered the fields and robbed the towns and travellers; they deserved the epithets of *gens-pille-hommes*, *gens-tue-hommes* (killers and pickers of men) which were applied to them. [1]

The towns were constrained to put themselves under the safeguard of the king or great feudatories, who concentrated the lands and feudal power, and changed the barons into courtiers. But in proportion as the petty barons disappeared, by so much the warfare slackened between castle and castle; a measure of tranquillity was restored to the country, and the necessity for feudal protection ceased to be paramount. The lords, consequently, were in a position to absent themselves from their domains and to betake themselves to the ducal and royal courts; thither they went to play the courtier, and ceased to act as defenders of their vassals and dependents. From the hour that the cultivator no longer stood in need of military service, the feudal system had no reason to exist. Feudalism, born of warfare, perished by warfare; it perished by the very qualities which had justified its existence.

But so long as the feudal system subsisted, there remained traces of the primitive equality which had been its cradle, even though every vestige had disappeared of the equality which had distinguished the relations of the lord with his tenants and vassals. The feudal lord and the vassal became co-equals once again in the communal assemblies which discussed the agricultural interests alike of the villager and the lord; the assemblies met without his sanction, and despite his unwillingness to convoke them. His communal rights were as limited as those of the rest of the inhabitants; the heads of cattle he was entitled to send to pasture on the commons were strictly prescribed. Delisle, in his interesting study of the agricultural classes of Normandy, cites texts which show the limitation of his rights, *e.g.*, the Seigneur de Bricqueville was entitled to send only two oxen and one horse to graze on the meadows. He was so far

---

[1] Vitry, the legate of Innocent III, who in Germany and Belgium preached the crusade against the Albigenses (in 1208), writes: 'The lords, despite their titles and dignities, continue to sally forth for prey and to play the robber and brigand, desolating entire regions by fire.' The manners of the clergy were neither better nor worse. The Archbishop of Narbonne, at the end of the twelfth century, strolled about the fields with his canons and archdeacons, hunting the wild beasts, plundering the peasants, and violating the women. He had in his pay a band of Aragonese *routiers* whom he employed to ransack the country. The bishops and abbots loved mightily, sings a troubadour, 'fair women and red wine, fine horses and rich array; living in luxury, whereas our Lord was content to live in poverty.'

from being privileged that as La Poix de Frémenville, the great feudal jurist, informs us, 'The lord who possesses no cattle of his own is not allowed to introduce any strange cattle, whether by letting on lease, selling, or even lending *gratis* his rights of common.'

III.

The origin of ecclesiastical property is analogous to that of seignorial property. In those turbulent times men fled for protection to the church no less than to the baron's castle; the priestly power, indeed, far outweighed that of the baron; it was the priest who held the key of paradise. Men willed their goods to the church on their death beds in the hope of securing a seat in paradise; this custom, which was voluntary at the outset, became so general that it ended by being imposed as an obligation. 'Any person dying without leaving a part of his possessions to the Church — which was termed dying *déconfés* — was debarred from communion and sepulture. If a man died intestate his relations had to appeal to the bishops to appoint arbiters, who conjointly with themselves fixed the amount which the defunct ought to have bequeathed if he had made a testament.'[1]

The fear of the end of the world in the millennium contributed to multiply the donations to the priests and monasteries, for where was the use of keeping one's lands and chattels, when men and beast were about to perish, and the hour of judgment was at hand? But when the year 1000 had passed away without any sort of cataclysm, people recovered from their fright, and bitterly regretted having parted with their belongings during their lifetime. With a view to intimidating the good people who demanded the restitution of their goods, the Church had recourse to anathemas and malisons. The cartularies of the period abound with formulas of maledictions calculated to strike terror into the hearts of the donator and his relations; here is a sample of the imprecations which frequently recur in the records of Auvergne. 'If a stranger, if any of your relations, if your son or your daughter should be insensate enough to contest this donation, to lay hands upon the goods dedicated to God and consecrated to His saints, may they be struck, like Herod, with an awful wound, may they, like

---

[1] Montesquieu, *L'Esprit des lois*.

Dathan, Abiram, and Judas, who sold the Lord, be tortured in the depths of hell.'[1]

But the property of the Church was derived, also, from other less turbid sources: men gave away their possessions and even their persons in exchange for her temporal protection. 'The major part of the acts of voluntary slavery (*obnoxatio*), says Guérard, were prompted by the spirit of devotion, and by the indulgence practised by the bishops and abbots towards their serfs, and by the benefits which the law accorded them.'[2] The serfs and vassals of the Church and monasteries enjoyed equal privileges with those belonging to the king; they were entitled to a threefold compensation in case of injury, damage, or death. The king and the Church undertook to prosecute the culprit, whereas, ordinarily, that was the business of the family of the injured person.

The convents were fortified places able to sustain regular sieges, and the monks were experts in the use of arms. At Hastings, churchmen fought on both sides; the Abbey of Hida, a convent situated in Winchester, had brought Harold a contingent of twelve monks, who all fell fighting. The high dignitaries of the church were military chieftains, who laid down their cross and chasuble to grasp a sword and don a cuirass. Many, like the Bishop of Cahors, when they officiated, solemnly deposited on the altar their casque, cuirass, sword, and iron gauntlet. Roland at Roncevalles says to Oliver, in praise of Archbishop Turpin:—

> "Li arceves ques est mult bons chevaliers:
> Nen ad meilleur en terre, desuz ciel,
> Bien set ferir e de lance e d'espiet."

In their enthusiasm for his prowess,

> "Dient Francais: 'Ci ad grant vasselage,
> En l'arceves que est bien la croce salve,
> Kar placet Dieu qu 'assez de tels ait Carles.' "[3]

---

[1] Cited by H. F. Rivière in his *Historie des Institutions de l'Auvergne*, 1874.

[2] B. Guérard, *Polyptique de L'Abbe Irminon*, section 145.

[3] "A right good cavalier, the Archbishop,
None better on the earth, under the sky;
Expert in fight alike with lance and spear."

During the feudal period the clergy alone possessed education this, like their weapons, they placed at the service of the parishioners who maintained them. Many a time they interposed between the rural populations and the lords who oppressed them; just as in Ireland, nowadays, the inferior clergy make common cause against the landlords with the farmers and peasants who provide for their subsistence. But if between the rural and urban populations and the priests there subsisted a close union, the clergy were often at war with the feudal nobility. If in their fits of superstitious terror and feverish piety the barons were capable of stripping themselves of a portion of their lands and riches in favour of the churches and monasteries, in their calmer moments they hankered after the possessions of the monks and priests, and seized the first opportunity of securing them.

The early kings and military chieftains bestowed churches and monasteries on their liege men and soldiers as rewards; from the 8th to the 11th centuries a considerable number of churches were in the hands of laymen. The kings of France down to the 18th century had conserved the *droit de régale*, which entitled them to all the fruits of the vacant bishoprics. When Henry VIII, the Bluebeard of English story and Supreme Pontiff of England, in order to reform the Church, suppressed not fewer than 645 monasteries, 90 colleges, 2,347 chantries and free chapels, 100 hospitals, with revenue amounting to two millions per annum, and shared the plunder with his courtiers and concubines, he practised on a larger scale what all his predecessors had done.

The nobility and clergy, the two classes who during the Middle Ages struggled for supremacy, discharged important and necessary functions; the tithes and socage-duty they received were the price of the services they rendered.

IV

THE feudal burdens outlasted the feudal barons, who vanished when they had grown useless; these dues became the appanage of nobles, often of middle-class origin, who did not render the services of which these dues had been the meed. Violently

---

'The French cry out: "Here be great bravery;
The Cross is in safe keep with the Archbishop;
Would God that Charles had more knights like to him!"'

attacked by the bourgeois writers, and energetically defended by the feudists, they were definitely suppressed in France by the revolution of 1789. The earlier English revolution which established bourgeois authority, the House of Commons by the side of the House of Lords, has allowed a number of feudal privileges to subsist which are anachronisms at a time when the aristocratic or landed classes are simply a wing of the 'great middle class' in every sense of the word.

The political economists and liberal bourgeois of this century, instead of investigating the origin of feudal obligations, exposing the transformations they have undergone, and explaining the necessity thereof, have fancied that they were giving proofs of learning and liberality of spirit by a sweeping condemnation of everything in any way connected with the feudal system. Howbeit, it is imperative for the understanding of the social organization of the Middle Ages to ascertain the signification of these obligations, which are the movable form of feudal property. It would be wearisome to pass in review all of the feudal obligations. I will confine myself to those which have more especially aroused the ire of the bourgeois writers, and try to show that if they were maintained and aggravated by force, they had been, at the origin, freely consented to.

SOCAGE. — We have seen that the feudal baron, when not a military chieftain installed by a conqueror, was, as a rule, a simple citizen, a member of the community distinguished by no special privileges from the rest of the villagers, his co-equals; like these he received his allotment in the partition of the lands, and if his acres were cultivated for him by the commoners this was done that he might devote himself exclusively to their defence. Haxthausen has observed that the Russian lord continued to receive a quarter or a third of the territory of the *mir* which was cultivated by the villagers. Latruffe-Montmeylian says that in France the proportion of the communal lands allotted to the lord varied according to the nature of the rights of the inhabitants. It amounted to two thirds when the peasants' rights of common extended to the demèsne forests, and to a third only when the rights were confined to the communal forest.[i] With the increase

---

[i] Latruffe-Montmeylian, *Du Droit des Communes sur les biens Communaux* Paris 1825. Montmeylian is one of the rare French writers who had the courage to defend communal property against the rapacity of the capitalists.

of the possessions of the barons and the monks, there followed a lack of serfs to cultivate their lands, wherefore they gave their arable *en bordelage* to peasant collectivities, 'eating from the same pan and off the same loaf,' to use the language of the period.[1] But, whether Freemen or serfs, the tenants owed a certain number of days of work to the feudal lord, to till his field or house his corn.

As, at this period, production of commodities and commerce did not as yet exist, the baron, no less than the peasant, was obliged to produce all that was requisite to supply his wants. In the feudal habitation there existed workshops of every description for the manufacture of arms, farming implements, stuffs, clothing, etc., in which the peasants and their wives were bound to work for a certain number of days in the year. The female labourer was under the direction of the lady of the manor herself, and the workshops for the same were termed *geniciae*. The monasteries likewise possessed workshops for females.[2] These workshops were rapidly turned into harems for the lords and their retainers, and even into dens of debauchery, in which the barons and the priests debauched their female serfs and vassals. The word *geniciaria* (woman working in the genicia) became synonymous with prostitute. Our modern brothels, as we see, have a religious and aristocratic origin.

In the beginning the number of days of work due to the baron by his vassal was insignificant; in some places it amounted to three days in the year.[3] In France, the royal ordinances, in default of a contract or custom, prescribed the number of twelve days. Villein socage was harder; but the service was not to exceed three days a week, and the serfs had, further, the enjoyment of a small field which the lord had ceded to him and from which he could not be expelled; he had also a share in the baron's harvest and a right of pasture in the forest and arable

---

1 *Bordelage* is a feudal system of tenure resembling *metayage*, inasmuch as the rent for the land is paid not in money, but in a portion of the produce. This tenure has been general in all feudal Europe; in France it lasted till the Revolution of 1789. Guérard found it flourishing in the 9th century, on the lands of the Abbey of St. Germain des Près. Mr L. Gomme, in his *Village Communities* describes similar peasant associations in England, Scotland, and Ireland.

2 In the donation made in 728 by Count Eberhard to the monastery of Merbach, mention is made of 40 workwomen employed in the Geniciae.

3 "Let the freeman enjoy liberty and go three times a year into the count's service," ordains the Customary of Bigorre.

lands. Count Gasparin, who was Minister of Agriculture under Louis XVIII., in his treaty on *Fermage*, published in 1821, states his belief in the superiority, as regards the landed proprietor, of the system of *metayage* to that of *socage*. But in the decline of the feudal system the lords abused their power to aggravate socage. 'They had usurped such authority,' says Jean Chenu, a writer of the beginning of the seventeenth century, 'that they exacted the labour of tillage, the gathering their grapes and a thousand other services, with no better title than the peasants' fear of being beaten or eaten up by their men at arms.' When, in the fourteenth century, peace was gradually established in the interior of Europe, every useful function had been taken away from the feudal baron; and the nobles who succeeded the barons became parasites and tyrants.

BANS DE MOISSON.—It has been supposed that the lord's right of prescribing the days on which to mow the fields, gather the grapes, reap the corn, etc., was a purely feudal one, whereas its origin is traceable to the period in which collective property obtained. We have seen above that in order to allow the arable lands to remain open to the cattle of the village, the elders fixed the days for the various harvests. This usage, established in the interests of the villagers, could only be diverted from its true ends when the lord began to traffic with his crops. He substituted his own authority for that of the council of the elders, or influenced their decisions so as to retard the proclamation of the *ban des moissons* and be beforehand with his own crops, and able, consequently, to sell them earlier and on better terms than the produce of the communal fields.

BANALITE [1]— The term is feudal; but the custom which it designates is a communistic one. In the village collectivities, certain offices, as aforeshown, were filled by individuals maintained at the expense of the commune; there was the village herdsman, who drove the cattle to pasture; there were common forges, mills, slaughter-houses, and animals to breed from, at the disposal of the community. Private families, instead of baking their own bread, sent it to be baked in the communal oven; a custom introduced from the economical consideration of reducing the consumption of fuel. The charge of watching over and attending

---

[1] The term signifies the compulsory usage of a thing belonging to the lord on condition of a due.

to these ovens was entrusted to the council of elders; thereafter to the lord, who, whenever it was in his interest to do so, substituted his own authority for that of the men commissioned by the commune. A small tax was levied for this right of usage of the common objects; in an ordinance of 1223, of Guillaume Blanchemain, Archbishop of Reims, it is said that 'the prelate shall be the proprietor of the common oven and be entitled to the tribute of a loaf for every batch of thirty-two loaves.' Boucher d'Argis cites decrees of 1563 and 1673 fixing the right of grinding in the common mills at a 16th and a 13th; it is computed that, at present, the miller deducts more than a tenth.*

These sort of institutions could exist only in the absence of the production of commodities; they hampered commerce and stood in the way of private enterprise; the revolutionary bourgeois of France pronounced them tainted with feudalism, and abolished them in 1790.

The CHURCH, which eventually became the exclusive property of the clergy, and is now closed to the public out of the hours of worship, was previously the joint property of the curate, the baron, and the peasants. The chancel and altar belonged to the lord and curate; they were bound to repair the woodwork, flooring, seats, etc, but the nave belonged to the peasants, who used it for their markets, communal assemblies, and dancing parties, or as a storehouse for their crops in case of need.[2] Mr Thorold Rogers says that in all cases the Church was the common hall of the parish, and a fortress in time of danger, occupying the site of the stockade which had been built when the first settlers occupied the ground.[3] The church bells, likewise, belonged to the peasants, who set them pealing to announce their assemblies, or to apprise the villagers of fires or hostile attacks. In the judicial archives of the French provinces of the 17th and 18th centuries, we find frequent mention of judgments rendered against the bells for having warned the peasants of the arrival of the collectors of

---

1 Boucher d' Argis. Code rural Ch. xv. Des banalités.

2. A synodical statute of 1529 prohibits — "To hold or suffer in the church or cemeteries here any festivals, dances, games, merrymakings, representations, markets, and other illicit assemblies; for the church is ordained solely to serve the Lord, and not for suchlike follies." The naïve believers of the Middle Ages saw no harm in dancing, and representing their mysteries, in the house of the Lord.

3 Thorold Rogers, *Economical Interpretation of History.*

the salt-tax; they were sentenced to be taken down and whipped by the hands of the executioner, 'notwithstanding that they had been consecrated and blessed by a most solemn ceremony, in which the oil of St Chrism and myrrh and incense had been used and many prayers recited.' The Church was the house of God, elevated in the face of the feudal manor, and the feudal peasants gathered together under the shadow of it as around a strong and tender mother.

The TITHE raised on the harvests of the peasants and the nobles in favour of the Church, was, in the beginning, optional; just as it is in Ireland at the present hour; it was paid alike to the priest and sorcerer. Agobard, an archbishop of the 9th century, complains that the ecclesiastical tithe is paid with far less regularity than that accorded to the *tempestarii,* men endowed with the power to lay storms and conjure up foul weather. But from being optional the tithes became compulsory in virtue of the feudal adage 'no land without its tithes and burdens'; they were converted into a seignorial right, and accorded to lay lords and abbots, who re-sold them to other laymen. Discretionary at the outset, the tithes became obligatory; and, in the sequel, constituted an oppressive impost that no performance of services any longer authorized: even so is refined gold transmuted into vile copper!

V.

Just as the seignorial obligations, which became onerous and iniquitous when the feudal barons had ceased to afford protection to their vassals, tenants, and serfs, had at one time been voluntarily acquiesced in; in like manner, the landed property of the nobles, — at first a military post, entrusted temporarily to a warrior, or, simply a right to a share in the agrarian divisions, — grew and expanded by dint of fraud and violence, and generally at the expense of the communal lands.

Marx, in his admirable 27th chapter of *Capital,* 'on the expropriation of the agricultural population from the land,' to which I refer the reader, has described the prompt and brutal fashion in which the Scotch and English lords stole the posses-sions of the yeomen, 'The great encroachers,' as Harrison, the editor of *Holinshed's Chronicle,* calls them, went to work expeditiously. In the 15th century the immense majority of the population consisted of peasant proprietors, whatever was the feudal title under which their right of property was hidden. Macaulay calculates that 'the number of proprietors was not less than 160,000, who with their families must have made up more than one-seventh of the whole nation. The average income of these small landlords was estimated at between £60 and £70 a year.'

The chief period of eviction began with the 16th century. The great feudal lords drove the peasantry by force from the land, to which they had the same feudal right as the lord himself, and seized upon the common lands. The rapid rise of the Flemish wool manufacture, and the corresponding rise in the price of wool in England, gave a direct impulse to these evictions. The sheep drove out the men. 'The shepe that were wont to be so meke and tame,' says Thomas More, 'and so small eaters, now, as I heare say, be become so great devourers and so wylde, that they eate up and swallow downe the very men themselves.'[1]

In the last decade of the 17th century, the yeomanry, the class of independent peasants, were more numerous than the class of farmers. They had formed the backbone of Cromwell's strength, and, even according to the confession of Macaulay, stood in favourable contrast to the drunken squires and to their servants, the country clergy, who had to marry their masters' cast-off mistresses. About 1750 the yeomanry had disappeared, and so had in the last decade of the 18th century the last trace of the common land of the agricultural labourer. In the 19th century the very memory of the connection between the agricultural labourer and the communal property has, of course, vanished in England. The agricultural population has received not a farthing of compensation for the 3,511,770 acres of common land which between 1800 and 1831 were stolen from them by parliamentary devices presented to the landlords by the landlords.

The last process of wholesale expropriation of the agricultural population from the soil is, finally, the so-called clearing of estates, i.e., the sweeping men off them. But what 'clearing of estates' really and properly signifies we learn only in the promised land of modern romance, the Highlands of Scotland. There the process is distinguished by its systematic character, by the magnitude of the scale on which it is carried out at one blow

---

[1] *Utopia*, translated by Robinson. Ed. Arber, London, 1869.

(in Ireland, landlords have gone to the length of sweeping away several villages at once; in Scotland areas as large as German principalities are dealt with), finally by the peculiar form of property under which the embezzled lands were held.

The Highland Celts were organized in clans, each of which was the owner of the land on which it was settled. The representative of the clan, its chief or 'great man', was only the titular owner of this property, just as the Queen of England is the titular owner of all the national soil. When the English Government succeeded in suppressing the intestine wars of these 'great men', and their constant incursions into the lowland plains, the chiefs of the clans by no means gave up their time-honoured trade as robbers; they only changed its form. On their own authority they transformed their nominal right into a right of private property, and as this brought them into collision with their clansmen, they resolved to drive them out by open force. 'A king of England might as well claim to drive his subjects into the sea,' says Professor Newman. This revolution, which began in Scotland after the last rising of the followers of the Pretender, can be followed through its first phases in the writings of Sir James Steuart and James Anderson. As an example of the method obtaining in the 19th century, the 'clearing' made by the Duchess of Sunderland will suffice here. This person, well instructed in economy, resolved, on entering upon her government, to effect a radical cure, and to turn the whole country, whose population had already been, by earlier processes of a like kind, reduced to 15,000, into a sheep walk. From 1814 to 1820 these 15,000 inhabitants, about 3,000 families, were systematically hunted and rooted out. All their villages were destroyed and burnt, all their fields turned into pasturage. British soldiers enforced the eviction, and came to blows with the inhabitants. One old woman was burnt to death in the flames of the hut which she refused to leave. Thus this fine lady appropriated 794,000 acres of land that had from time immemorial belonged to the clan. She assigned to the expelled inhabitants about 6,000 acres on the sea shore — two acres per family. The 6,000 acres had until this time lain waste, and brought in no income to their owners. The duchess, in the nobility of her heart, actually went so far as to let these at an average rent of 2s. 6d. per acre to the clansmen who for centuries had shed their blood for her family. The whole of the stolen clan-land she divided into 29 great sheep farms, each inhabited by a single family, for the most part imported English farm servants. In the year 1835 the 15,000 Gaels were already replaced by 121,000 sheep. The remnant of the aborigines flung on the sea shore tried to live by catching fish. They became amphibious and lived, as an English author says, half on land and half on water, and withal only half on both.

The plunder of the State lands on a large scale began with William of Orange. 'These estates were given away, sold at a ridiculous figure, or even annexed to private estates by direct seizure. All this happened without the slightest observation of legal etiquette. The crown lands thus fraudulently appropriated, together with the robbery of the Church estates, as far as these had not been lost again during the Republican Revolution, form the basis of the today princely domains of the English oligarchy. The bourgeois capitalists favoured the operation with the view, among others, to promoting free trade in land, extending the domain of modern agriculture on the large farm system, and to increasing their supply of the free agricultural proletarians ready to hand.'

After the restoration of the Stuarts the landed proprietors had carried by legal means an act of usurpation, effected everywhere on the Continent without any legal formality. In 1660 a House of Commons in which the landlords were supreme relieved their estates of all feudal dues, then amounting to about one-half of the entire revenues of the State. Military service, purveyance, aids, reliefs, premier seisin, wardship, alienation, escheat, all disappeared in a day. In their place were substituted excise duties. By 12 Charles II., c. 23 the great bulk of taxation was for the first time transferred from the land to the people, who have borne it ever since.

Landed property monopolized by the lords was exempted from all dues towards the State, as the lord had been discharged from all obligations towards his vassals and tenants: feudal property had been changed into capitalist property.

This transformation was accomplished in Great Britain in the midst of the most awful misery of the peasant class; the cultivators were expelled from the land wholesale and made beggars. Their numbers became a social danger against which the most barbarous measures were taken. Legislation treated them as 'voluntary' criminals, and assumed that it depended on their own will to go on working under the old conditions that no longer existed. In England this legislation began under Henry VII.

Henry VIII., 1530:— 'Beggars old and unable to work receive a beggar's license. On the other hand, whipping and imprisonment for sturdy vagabonds. They are to be tied to a cart tail and whipped until the blood streams from their bodies, then to swear an oath to go back to their birth place, or to where they have lived the last three years, and to put themselves to labour.' What grim irony! In 27 Henry VIII. the former statute is repeated, but strengthened with new clauses. 'For the second arrest for vagabondage the whipping is to be repeated and half the ear sliced off, but for the third relapse the offender is to be executed as a hardened criminal and enemy of the commonweal.'

Elizabeth, 1572:— 'Unlicensed beggars above 14 years of age are to be severely flogged and branded on the left ear unless someone will take them into service for two years; in case of a repetition of the offence, if they are over 18 they are to be executed, unless someone will take them into service for two years; but for the third offence they are to be executed without mercy as felons.' Similar statues, 18 Elizabeth, c. 13, and another of 1597, James I:— 'Anyone wandering about and begging is declared a rogue and a vagabond. Justices of the Peace in petty sessions are authorized to have them publicly whipped, and for the first offence to imprison them for six months, for the second two years. Whilst in prison they are to be whipped as much and as often as the Justices of the Peace think fit. Incorrigible and dangerous rogues are to be branded with an 'R' on the left shoulder and set to hard labour, and, if they are caught begging again, to be executed without mercy.' —These statutes, legally binding until the beginning of the 18th century, were only repealed by 12 Ann, c. 23.

Albeit not a single nation in Europe can boast of having raised an aristocracy that accomplished its work of monopolizing the land with anything like the rapacity and ferociousness of the Scotch and English landlords, nevertheless in all countries the peasant class has been in great part despoiled of its territorial possessions; and no means have been left untried to bring about that most laudable and lucrative consummation. Let me enumerate a few of the devices that were resorted to in France.

The feudal obligations, aids, and fines became so excessive that the peasants commuted for them by ceding to the lords a portion of the common lands. These cessions of territory, greedily hungered after by the feudal lords, would appear, well-nigh all of them, to have been obtained by the aid of artifice; the nobles corrupted a certain number of villagers who managed to constitute in their own persons the general assembly of the commune that voted the cessions; hence we come across royal ordinances in France which specify that for a cession of territory to be valid it must be voted in an assembly of all the inhabitants of the Commune.

The robbers of the communal lands did not invariably employ Jesuitical means; they often plundered with open brutality. In the 16th century, a period when the industrial and commercial bourgeoisie were rapidly developing, the communal lands were coveted at one and the same time by the nobles and by the bourgeois speculators. The towns were enlarged to meet the new requirements, and agriculture increased its yield. The development of agriculture was the great object of the speculators; under the pretext of giving increased extension to the arable lands, they induced the King to grant them, by royal edict, the right of bringing under culture the waste lands; they hastened to include in the category of waste lands the communal territories, and proceeded to wrest them from the peasants, who took up arms in their defence; and to vanquish whose resistance the speculators were compelled to appeal for aid to the armed force of the State.

The nobles had recourse to chicanery in order to win possession of the village territories; they pretended that the lands owned by the peasants did not correspond with their title deeds, which was perfectly true; they insisted on the verification of their claims, and confiscated what was held by imperfect titles for their own benefit. Upon occasion they proceeded after a revolutionary fashion; they destroyed the title-deeds which they had got hold of, and so disabled the peasants from establishing their rights to the fields now left without an owner; whereupon in virtue of the feudal adage *pas de terre sans seigneur*, the nobles seized upon the peasants' territory. The *autos da fé* of proprietary titles, held by the peasants during the revolution of 1789, were in retaliation of the suppression of the peasant titles perpetrated by the nobility of the 16th century.

The forests were grabbed up more brutally: eschewing all legal formalities, the lords adjudged to themselves the ownership of the woods and underwood; they enclosed the forests and forbade hunting, and abolished the right of estovers; the right of taking wood for fuel and for the repairs of houses, fences, implements, etc. These encroachments of the nobles on the forest-lands, which were the common property of the village, gave rise to terrible revolts of the peasants. The *jacqueries* [1] which broke out in the middle of the 14th century in the provinces of the North and the centre of France, were, in fact, occasioned by the pretensions of the nobles to forbid hunting and to interfere with the rights of common in the forests, and the enjoyment of the rivers. Similar conflicts arose in Germany, such as the famous revolt of the Saxons against the Emperor Henry II., and that of the Swabian peasants, who, in the time of Luther, took up arms against the lords who debarred them from the enjoyment of the forests. These peasant insurrections compelled the lords on several occasions to respect the ancient rights of common which consisted in the right — limited only by the peasant's wants — to take wood and brushwood for hedging, firing, and repairing his implements (hedge-bote, fire-bote, and plough-bote); and in the right of common pasture, or the right to send his cows, horses, swine, and in some cases his goats, to graze on the commons throughout the year, the month of May alone excepted. So firmly rooted were these rights that Lapoix de Fréminville declared, in 1760, that even in the event of their abuse by the peasants they could not be taken away from them: 'for the right of usage is perpetual, and being so, it is accorded alike to the actual inhabitants and to those who may come after them; one cannot strip of an acquired right even those who are as yet unborn.' But the revolutionary bourgeoisie of 1789 felt none of the feudal legist's respect for the peasants' rights, and abolished them for the benefit of the landed proprietor.

If the lords did, as a matter of fact, occasionally bow to the peasants' rights of common, they nevertheless constantly declared that these were enjoyed on sufferance only; for they looked upon themselves as the proprietors of the forests; just as in later times they came to pretend to the ownership of the

---

[1] *Jacqueries* were insurrections of the peasants; a term derived from the insulting epithet of *Jacques Bonhomme* applied to the peasants by the nobles.

vassals' lands. In the Middle Ages, when a free man, an alodial proprietor, *commended* himself to a lord, sought the protection, that is to say, of a powerful person, he presented him with a clod of turf, and vowed fealty and homage to him; yet he remained the master of his field. But in a number of provinces, *e.g.*, in Brittany, the lord considered himself as the owner of the subsoil, while he recognized the peasants' rights to the *superficies*, i.e., the crops, trees, buildings, etc. It is in virtue of such legal fictions; that during the bourgeois period the nobles expropriated the peasants, descendants from the vassals, their ancestors. In Scotland, the robbery of the peasant property was perpetrated with such undisguised brutality as to arouse the public indignation. Karl Marx, in *Capital*, has related how the pious Duchess of Sutherland dispossessed the peasants whose fathers had built up the glory and the grandeur of her house.

Until the bourgeois revolution of 1789 had established private property in land, the landed estates in France, including those of the nobility, were subjected to rights of common, which periodically took from them the character of private property. Once the harvest was secured, the forests and arable land appropriated by the nobility became common property again, and the peasants were free to turn their cattle on them. The vines were liable to a similar usage. Francois de Neufchateau, in his *Agronomical Voyage*, 1806, cites a Memoire, published in 1763, by the *Société d'Economie Rurale en Berne*, in which it is complained that 'after the vintage the vineyards are laid open to the sheep, who grass there as on common land.' But not only were the landlords bound to permit the pasturing on their lands of the village cattle; they were moreover forbidden to cultivate the soil according to their own methods; they were constrained to conform to the council of the elders, and required permission for the planting of their vines. A permission of this kind was refused a few years before the French Revolution to Montesquieu, greatly to the scandal of the political economists. The proprietor was not allowed to leave his lands uncultivated; for a royal ordinance of Louis XIV, enacted in 1693, and which but consecrated an ancient usage, authorizes—in the event of the owner not cultivating his land himself—'any person to sow the same and to gather the fruits.'

Landed property, under the feudal system, was anything but

free; not only was it burdened with obligations, but it belonged to the family collectively; the owner could not dispose of it at pleasure; he was only the usufructuary possessor whose mission it was to transmit his estates to his descendants. The Church estates, likewise, bore this character; they were the property of the Church, the great Catholic family; the abbots, monks, and priests who occupied the lands were merely the administrators—the very faithless administrators—of them. In order to claim immunity from impositions, the French clergy down to the time of the revolution, pretended that ecclesiastical possessions ought not to be considered as ordinary property; that it was nobody's property *(res nullius)*, because it was sacred, religious property *(res sacrae, res religiosae)*. The revolutionary bourgeois took them at their word; they declared that the clergy were not the proprietors of the ecclesiastical estates, which belonged to the Church. Now, the Greek word *ecclesia*, whence is derived *eglise* (church). signifies the assembly, the reunion of all the faithful, which is the nation at large; wherefore the estates of the Church are national property. By the help of such subterfuge did the revolutionary bourgeois, like Henry VIII of England, lay hands upon the Church property and distribute amongst themselves the estates which belonged to the poor.

It is these obligations of feudal property which the political economists and Liberal historians attack with special virulence; obligations which were vestiges of the primitive communism that secured a measure of well-being to the peasants, and which they forfeited as soon as private property had superseded feudal property.

The bourgeois historians have invented the legend of the Revolution of 1789 bestowing the land upon the peasant, and freedom and happiness therewithal; whereas the plain truth is that the great Revolution stripped him of his rights of common and other secular rights of equal importance, delivering him up, defenceless, into the clutches of the usurers and middle-men; loading him with taxes and forcing him to enter into competition with the great landed proprietor, equipped with capital and machinery. The great bourgeois revolution was fraught with misery and ruin for the peasant. According to the official census, there were, in 1857, 7,846,000 landed proprietors in France; out of these 3,600,000 were so poor that they paid no direct contributions; the number of proprietors, great or small, was consequently reduced to 4,246,000. In 1879 the various questions were ventilated of an agricultural credit, of the application to the landlords of the law of bankruptcy, of the simplification of the law of procedure in expropriations; and an inquiry was instituted to determine the number of landed proprietors entitled to a share in the famous credit. *La Republique Française,* conducted by Gambetta, much interested in the question, stated in its issue of 25th August 1879, that there existed in France only 2,826,000 landed proprietors, offering the necessary guarantees entitling them to a share in the credit. Thus from 1851 to 1879 the number of landed proprietors deserving of the name had dwindled to 1,420,000.

To dissipate the errors and falsehoods which the bourgeois writers have propagated respecting the status of the cultivator during the feudal period, and the benefits accruing to him from the Revolution, it suffices to compare the conditions of labour of the mediaeval cultivator with those of the modern agricultural labourer. The researches made by men of learning during the last 50 years, and the numerous documents discovered in different towns and convents, enable us to institute such a comparison.

L. Delisle, in his afore-cited study of the condition of the labouring classes in Normandy, points out how the lord shared the fortune of the labourer; for the rent was based upon the harvest. For instance, the tenants of the monks of St Julien de Tours contributed the sixth sheaf; in other parts the tenant contributed the tenth sheaf; in still others the twelfth. Now, we may rummage the bourgeois world and shall not find a landlord contenting himself with a twelfth or even a sixth of the crops gathered on his estate. These conditions were not confined to a single province, for in the south of France, at Moissac, we meet with identical ones. Enactments of 1212 and 1214 show us the monks of the Abbey of Moissac receiving only a third, a fourth or even as little as a tenth of the crops harvested by the peasants who tilled their lands. Lagrèze-Fossat, who has studied these enactments, remarks that 'a mutual agreement was come to between the peasants and the monks, and the contribution of the produce demanded by the latter does not bear the character of an impost; it was debated beforehand, and freely consented to.'*

In the 11th and 12th centuries, when the vine was cultivated in Normandy, the landlords claimed only one half of the crops; the other half. belonged to the cultivators. Nowadays, in the vine-growing countries, the peasant rarely tastes the wine he produces.

Guérard has discovered and published the account-book of the Abbey of St. Germain des Près; this precious document, which dates from the time of Charlemagne, enables us to study the lives of the serfs and peasants of the 9th century. The abbey lands were cultivated, not by individuals, but by collectivities of peasants, composed of from 20 to 30 adult persons living together, and the dues paid by them would appear ridiculously small to a modern farmer.

The abbey lands were divided into three categories, the *manses ingenuiles,* the *manses lidiles,* the *manses serviles.* At that period certain qualities were inherent in the land; it was seignorial, free, or servile: Guérard calculates that the peasants paid in labour and in kind 5s 6d. per acre for the free lands, 8s 1d for the tributary lands, and 10s for the servile lands. The cultivators employed on the abbatial lands, and who, to judge from their names, were mostly Germans, attained, with their families, to the respectable figure of 10,026. The condition of these peasants, considering their great numbers, must have been the normal condition of the cultivators; and what labourer of our day, I ask, would not gladly consent to barter his bourgeois landlord of the 19th for the monk of the 9th century, and hold servile lands at the rate of 10s per acre?*

The condition of the English labourer was no worse. 'There is one very unpleasing remark,' says Hallam in his *View of the State of Europe during the Middle Ages,* 'which everyone who attends to the subject of prices will be induced to make, that the labouring classes, especially those engaged in agriculture, were better provided with the means of subsistence in the reign of Edward III

---

* A. Lagrèze-Fossat, *Etudes Historiques sur Moissac,* 1872. Moissac is a small town in the Department of Tarn et Garonne, of considerable importance in the Middle Ages.

* *Polyptique de l'Abbé Irminon on dénombrement des manses' serfs et revenus de l'Abbaye de St Germain des Près sous le règne de Charlemagne.* Publié par Guérard, 1844.

or of Henry VI than they are at present. In the fourteenth
century, Sir John Cullum observes, a harvest man had fourpence
a day which enabled him in a week to buy a comb of wheat; but to
buy a comb of wheat a man must now (1784) work ten or twelve
days. So under Henry VI, if meat was at a farthing-and-a-half the
pound, which, I suppose, was about the truth, a labourer earning
threepence a day, or eighteenpence in the week, could buy a
bushel of wheat at six shillings the quarter, and twenty-four
pounds of meat for his family. Several Acts of Parliament regulate
the wages that might be paid to labourers of different kinds. Thus
the Statute of Labourers in 1830 fixed the wages of reapers during
harvest at threepence a day, without diet, equal to five shillings at
present; that of 23 H. VI, c. 12, in 1444, fixed the reapers' wages
at fivepence, and those of common workmen in building at
threepence-halfpenny, equal to 6s 8d and 4s 8d; that of 11 H. VII,
c. 22, in 1496, leaves the wages of labourers in harvest as before,
but rather increases those of ordinary workmen. The yearly
wages of a chief hind or shepherd by the Act of 1444, were £1 4s,
equivalent to about £20; those of a common servant in
husbandry, 18s 4d, with meat and drink; they were somewhat
augmented by the Statute of 1496. Yet, although these wages are
regulated as a maximum by Acts of Parliament, which may
naturally be supposed to have had a view rather towards
diminishing than enhancing the current rate, I am not fully
convinced that they were not rather beyond it; private accounts at
least do not always correspond with these statutable prices. And
it is necessary to remember that the uncertainty of employment,
natural to so imperfect a state of husbandry, must have
diminished the labourers' means of subsistence. Extreme dearth,
not more owing to adverse seasons than to improvident
consumption, was frequently endured. But after every allowance
of this kind, I should find it difficult to resist the conclusion that,
however the labourer has derived benefit from the cheapness of
manufactured commodities and from many inventions of common
utility, he is much inferior in ability to support a family to his
ancestors three or four centuries ago.'[1]

When the French Revolution broke out in 1789 feudal property
had not as yet succeeded in enfranchising itself from the manifold

---

[1]. *The Student's History of the Middle Ages.* Henry Hallam. Adapted by
William Smith. Part II, chap. ix, pp. 566-7.

obligations which recalled its collectivist origin, and which prevented it from being converted into private property having the right to use and to abuse.

5

Bourgeois Property

I.

WE have seen that landed property was originally common to the entire tribe in the shape of woodland, pasture, and even arable land; that it was converted into collective property when the clan broke up into the matriarchal or patriarchal families, and, lastly, into private property, on the disintegration of the patriarchal family and the constitution of the modern family, including the parents with their children, and a few supernumeraries, say the grandparents or an odd uncle or aunt who has failed in securing an establishment of his or her own, and whose inheritance is greedily coveted after.

The march of movable property has been a different one; though, starting from the communist form, it far more rapidly arrived at the private form; even among savages, living in community, the arms and ornaments are considered as attached to the individual, and are frequently interred with the corpses.1

The instruments of labour have at all times been considered as the personal property of him who wielded them; during the periods of slavery and serfdom, the tools and the soil were surrendered to the slave or serf who used them and for whom they constituted a sort of property. Individual appropriation of the instrument of labour results from its personal character, and it

---

1 Immortality, that dreary idea, says Frederick Engels, so long the torment of humanity, is an invention of the savages; just as they bestow a soul upon their bodies, or rather a double, who leaves them during sleep and at death, so they attribute to animals, vegetables, and even to inanimate objects, a soul capable of living outside of them; thus, on the burial of a warrior, they destroyed his arms, and killed the animals that were to follow him into the other world.

owes this character to the fact that it is small, of little value, and capable of being manipulated by a single individual — from this point of view the implement of the artificer may be assimilated to the field of the peasant cultivator, which is small, of little value, and usable by a single individual, that is to say, cultivable by himself and the members of his family.

Landed property, as it evolved, prior to the bourgeois property, on the one hand ran into small peasant property and on the other into feudal property. Agriculture was the prime motor of this evolution. Commerce was the motor of the evolution of the property of the instruments of labour and industrial products, which, once it has attained a certain degree of development reacts, as Marx has demonstrated, on landed property, and accelerates its transformation into bourgeois property.

II.

In the collectivist village the peasants produce all that they consume (bread, meat, flax, wool, etc.), and the artificers (smiths, weavers, tailors, etc.) are only admitted into it when their services are required. They reside, as a rule, on the outskirts of the village, and, after a certain term of sojourn there, generally that of a year and a day, they obtain the right of city; are authorized to send their cattle to graze on the common pasture, and are entitled to a share in the land. At the outset there takes place no exchange of products in these villages; the handicraftsmen are public functionaries in the service of the community, and are paid by an annual tribute of provisions. They only work to order; the raw materials are supplied them, and, wherever feasible, they work in the houses of their customers. When they ceased to be public officials, their work was paid in kind or by service, in the same way as the man-at-arms was paid for his work of defence. This primitive form of industrial labour persisted as long as the villages continued to be small and retained the collectivist form of landed property. The villages situated at the intersection of the roads, frequented by the caravans of travelling merchants, or near the mouths of rivers, or the seaside, were the first to undergo a change; a temporary market was established there for which the handicraftsmen wrought. Wherever the artificers found means to sell their products they multiplied; instead of finding themselves repulsed or received indifferently, they were sought and welcomed. The population of the villages — transformed into towns and boroughs — composed of specialized handicraftsmen practising different crafts and standing in need of one another's services, came to establish a permanent market where the inhabitants exchanged their products or sold them, during the fairs, to itinerant traders.

The character of industry then experiences a change; the artificer becomes independent of his customer. He no longer waits for the latter to supply him with the material he must work up; he buys it, and keeps a stock of it on hand; he ceases to work to order, and works only with a view to sell. To his quality of producer is superadded that of trader; he buys the raw material, and sells his finished work; he enlarges his shop, and seeks the help of apprentices and journeymen, who work under his direction and side by side with him, lodging in his house and eating at his table. The fund he requires is of so modest a description as hardly to deserve the name of capital, in the sense in which Marx employs the word, even although this fund be capital in embryo.

The increase of the population in the mediaeval villages forbids the access of new-comers to the communal lands, and precludes their sharing in the agrarian divisions. The village lands remained the exclusive property of the original inhabitants and their descendants, who constituted a sort of municipal aristocracy, while, in the country, the exigencies of defence called into life the feudal aristocracy. The urban aristocracy has survived in certain towns of democratic Switzerland. In the Alsatia of our day these urban aristocrats have become great manufacturers.

By way of resisting the despotism of the aristocrats of the towns, who monopolized the land and power, the handicraftsmen organized guilds, which, in the beginning, were open to all the artificers of the locality without distinction. These guilds not only defended the craftsmen against the municipal aristocrats, but protected them against their mutual competition. The market in which they sold their wares acquired a capital importance; as it was restricted to the inhabitants of the town and the itinerant hawkers of the fairs, the corporations were bound to see that the market was not overstocked with goods. The corporations now became close, and the number of persons admitted into them, and at liberty, consequently, to open a shop in the town, was limited, as was also the number of journeymen the masters might employ and wares they might turn out. In order to facilitate the quantity of and to render effective the supervision of the syndics of the corporations, the craftsmasters were obliged to work with open doors and windows, and sometimes in the streets. Each guild possessed its speciality, to which its members were strictly bound to adhere — *e.g.*, the bootmakers were restricted to the making of new boots; the repairing and soling of old boots was prohibited, as belonging of right to the corporation of cobblers.

The right of sale was no less jealously protected than that of production; at the fairs the seller was only allowed to accost the buyer as he passed in front of the stall; once he had stepped beyond it, the seller had forfeited the right to call him back, or to offer him goods for sale, for he now pertained to the owner of the neighbouring stall. These multiplex and minute regulations attest the importance already acquired by the market, the expansion of which was, at a later date, to transform the mode of production and the correlative social relations.

In handicraft production lay this inherent contradiction: if the handicraftsman was a synthetic labourer, combining in his person the intellectual and manual functions of his handicraft, production and the instruments of production were, on the contrary, scattered over the land. Every province, every borough and town, every seignorial domain and peasant farmstead produced the food and other necessaries of life required by its inhabitants, selling only what was superfluous, and buying only a few articles of luxury. As they imported none of the articles of consumption, the mediaeval towns and provinces were economically independent, and, as a consequence, able to live in a state of isolation; they formed so many distinct petty States, habitually at war with one another.

The economic theory which corresponded to this dispersion of production tended to promote their independence. The agriculturists, who were the economic theoreticians of the feudal epoch, advised the landed proprietor to produce all on his own domain, so as to have nothing to purchase outside its limits, and we have seen that in the manors of the feudal lords there existed workshops for manufacturing all and everything, not excepting arms.

That theory remained valid long after the phenomena which had given rise to it had disappeared. When, in the 16th century, the silk industry was imported into France from Italy, the royal policy, instead of concentrating it in the locality in which it had a chance of success, disseminated it over the provinces. Attempts were made to rear the silk-worm in countries in which it was difficult if not impossible to cultivate the mulberry-tree, on the leaves of which it feeds. During the Revolution of 1789 it was sought to acclimatize the cotton-plant, to avoid having to buy it abroad; and it was the desire to shake off the tribute paid to the colonies by the purchase of the sugar-cane which led to the discovery of the saccharine properties of the beetroot.

When the warfare between castle and castle abated, owing to the disappearance of the vanquished, whose lands were engrossed by the victor, and there ensued a greater security of the highways, commercial intercourse between the different provinces became possible and great centres of handicraft production sprang up. The city of Ghent, which manufactured cloths from wool imported chiefly from England, possessed in the 14th century a population of upwards of half-a-million inhabitants. The development of commerce shook the social organization of the feudal city.

In the towns which prospered industrially, the guildmasters of handicrafts developed into closed corporations the freedom of which was obtainable only by the privilege of birth, money or royal favour, or else — unless one chanced to be a son or relation of a guildmaster — by serving a long term of apprenticeship; it was necessary to pay for learning the handicraft, for the right of exercising it, and again on being made free of the trade. The guildmasters excluded a number of artificers who no longer worked on their own account, but in the workshops of their masters. Heretofore the handicraftsman could hope to become a master and a shopkeeper in his turn; but in proportion as commerce and industry were developed the men lost all prospect of this; shut out from the incorporated trades, and at enmity with the masters who employed them, they formed vast associations of journeymen which were at once national and international, whereas the guilds of the masters were essentially local. The masters, enriched by the development of production, allied themselves with the municipal aristocrats in order to cope with the apprentices and journeymen, who on several occasions were set on and supported by the feudal nobility, jealous of the growing municipal aristocracy. All the industrial towns of the Middle Ages were stained with blood by the conflicts between journeymen and craftsmasters.

The discovery of the passage of the Indies by rounding the Cape of Good Hope, and that of America, which date from the end of the 15th century, by bringing the gold of America into the European market, and by introducing transoceanic commerce, depreciated the value of landed property, gave a decisive impulse to the rising bourgeois production in the cities of the Mediterranean, the cities of the Low Countries, and the Hanseatic League, and opened the era of modern revolution.[1]

The countries newly discovered in India and America were put to plunder, and turned into markets for the industrial and agricultural products of Europe. England exported corn to America; Auvergne cheese, wine, etc.

The creation of the colonial market and the importation of American gold furthered the development of manufacturing industry. Private individuals were enabled to accumulate the funds required for the establishment of manufactories, which in the beginning were simply workshops of artificers, only distinguished from these by the greater number of workmen employed, and the larger quantity of commodities manufactured. As these workshops infringed all the regulations of the guilds, and encroached on the privileges of the masters, they could not be established in the towns, but had to be set up in the suburbs, the country or the maritime cities which, newly founded, possessed neither municipal aristocracy nor incorporated trades. In London and Paris, it was outside the city walls, in Westminster,

---

[1] It is the habit to describe as revolutionary political events of a tumultuous and explosive character, while vastly less importance is attached to economic events of far greater revolutionary influence upon the march of society and the conditions of human existence. The manners and customs of the peasant have subsisted unmodified throughout many centuries in spite of wars, changes of frontiers, and social and political vicissitudes. An English anthropologist Mr. Farrer, has remarked that the superstitions of the peasant singularly resemble those of the savage. Country people have only of quite recent years been roused by the establishment of railways. In our day economic phenomena exert such preponderating influence that in France changes of government occur, to effect which there is no need to make the cannon speak; it is enough if the Deputies to the Chambers speak.

Southwark, and the Faubourg St. Antoine that the manufactories were created. They were established by merchants enriched by the colonial trade, and not by the guildmasters, bound in the chains of routine, and fettered by corporative bonds. In the present day we see railways constructed and directed, not by the masters of stage-coach companies, but by financial men.

Manufacture, which struck at the corporations, and ruined the guildmasters of handicrafts, were equally prejudicial to the artificer, whom it apparently benefited by affording a greater regularity and a greater quantity of labour and a higher salary. Division of labour was introduced into the manufactories; all the operations of a trade were disjoined and isolated; the manufacture of a pin, for example, was decomposed into some twenty different operations, performed by an equal number of specialized labourers. The artificer who, heretofore, had been familiar with all the processes of his craft, and each of which he accomplished in turn, became now a detail labourer, condemned for life to execute a single operation.

The impulsion given to commerce and to production hastened the expansion of the towns, which were compelled to burst their bounds and spread over the adjoining fields. An economical difficulty then arose: it became necessary to find the means of existence for these newly-created populations.

During the primitive collectivist period, the town had not come to exist, even as the residence of the military chief, exercising royal power. The Merovingian kings, like the Indian princes, travelled with a more or less numerous retinue of men-at-arms and retainers, followed by artificers of divers trades. The spot on which they camped became a temporary city: they subsisted on the fees and donations of the surrounding country. The absence of roads and the difficulty of communication precluded all permanent conglomeration of persons; whom there was no means of supporting. The feudal cities, dependent on the agricultural produce of the neighbouring localities for their means of subsistence, were necessarily bound to restrict themselves to a limited number of inhabitants. So long as the absence of roads, or the insecurity of such as existed, rendered all commercial intercourse between the towns impossible or difficult, there was no question of guarding against the exportation of the means of subsistence. But so soon as the means of communication began to be improved, and as men began to transport grain from one province to the other, all the towns and provinces took measures for prohibiting the exportation of corn from their territories, and preventing it being monopolized. In all the European towns we meet with regulations for the sale of cereals in the markets at stated times; a maximum price was fixed, and the quantity allowed to be purchased was determined; the proprietors, under penalty of confiscation, were prohibited from garnering corn for more than two years; it was, furthermore, forbidden to buy the standing corn or that already housed. The extension of the towns, and the difficulty of procuring provisions outside their own territories, turned every bad harvest year into a year of dearth or famine. The paramount concern of the municipal authorities was to prevent famines; they ordained the storing of provisions capable of supplying the town for at least three months, and saw to it that a sufficient quantity of land was annually sown with corn. An edict of 1577, in France, restricted the planting of vineyards, which became, yearly, more important, and required that for every portion of land planted with vines a double portion be devoted to corn.

In order to meet the new requirements it was necessary that agriculture should be developed; new lands were brought under culture, woodlands were deforested and marshlands reclaimed, while the cornfields were enlarged. In years of good harvests the corn was so abundant that the price of it ceased to be remunerative; it became urgent to create fresh markets. In France the circulation of corn was permitted between the provinces, and also the exportation of it to England and the Colonies. These economic liberties were but short-lived, for no sooner had corn attained a certain price in a locality than its exportation was prohibited. From 1669 to 1683, during a period of fourteen years, the exportation of corn was permitted on nine occasions and prohibited during six years.

These regulations were powerless to prevent local famines; nay, it happened that they intensified the same by prohibiting the exportation of corn from a province in which it was superabundant; the towns confiscated corn in its transit through their territories, whenever fearful of competition or threatened with famine. Colbert was constrained to employ force to get 2,500 sacks of corn, which the Parliament of Bordeaux sought to retain, expedited to Paris. It would happen that a town suffered from famine, whilst at a distance of some fifty miles the wheat supply was abundant. The circulation of wine, wool, etc., was subjected to similar restraint; seaports like Bordeaux and Marseilles, in order to command a better sale for their own wines, prevented the shipment of the wines of the neighbouring provinces. Prior to the Revolution of 1789, the last royal ministers endeavoured to show the danger and uselessness of these regulations; they caused them to be temporarily suspended, but were always in the last instance compelled to re-establish them. It required a revolution to abolish them and to strip the peasants of their privileges, which burdened landed property and hampered the development of modern agriculture, just as the privileges of the corporations had shackled the development of industry.

The incorporated trades that opposed the establishment of manufacturers in their towns stood in fear, above all things, of innovations; in order to maintain the industrial equality of the masters of handicrafts, and to prevent the one from enjoying an advantage not shared by the other, the introduction of new processes and improvements of any kind were prohibited. Argand, the inventor of a lamp with a double air-current, which tripled the lighting capacity of the oil, was, in the 18th century, brought before the Parliament of Paris, by the corporation of tinworkers, who claimed the exclusive right of manufacturing lamps. It was due to the influence of the royal courtesans, Mesdames Pompadour, Du Barry, and Marie Antoinette that printed calicoes were allowed to be sold; for the chambers of commerce of Rouen, Lyons, and Amiens had protested energetically, predicting the ruin of industry and a cataclysm in France if the manufacturing of these cottons was authorized.

The feudal fetters which impeded the development of agriculture and industry once broken, bourgeois property was free to implant itself and begin its evolution.

The landlord obtained the right of enclosing his fields; the people's right of pasture after the harvest was abolished. This right of enclosure was of supreme importance, for, anterior to it, the landlord could apply no other methods of culture than those employed by the commoners in general, on pain of seeing his harvests prowled on by their cattle. This right of enclosure was, too, the right most loudly clamoured for in France in the 18th century. The common lands, wherever it was possible, were divided; were given away, that is, to the bourgeois; for the inhabitants of the community to whom they were apportioned sold them at a nominal price; this partition of the land, for which a multiplicity of philanthropical and moral reasons has been adduced, was but a means of preventing the small peasant from possessing cattle, and of depriving him of his resources in order to turn him into a wage-labourer. The church property, which ought to have been restituted to the poor, to whom it belonged, was plundered with the utmost brutality and cynicism in England as well as in France; for everywhere the bourgeois is animated by the same thievish instincts.

Leopold Delisle, in the preface of his history of the agricultural classes of the Middle Ages, observes: 'A significant fact is the stationary condition of our agriculture for the last five centuries, from the 10th to the 15th. Almost all of the practices described in our old records hold good to this day among our labourers; to such an extent that a 13th century peasant who should visit one of our small farms, would experience but little surprise.' But this same 13th century peasant would feel lost in one of the great modern farms on which the methods of mechanical agriculture are applied.

The most improved methods of culture have transformed agricultural products and increased the produce. Modern agriculture is ruinous; it exhausts the soil, alike by the abundance of the crops and their exportation abroad. Their consumption in the towns interferes with the circulation of matter which formerly went on between the soil and animals and man, in the form of meat, grain, and fruit, etc., consumed by him and back from man and beast to the soil, in the shape of excrements. So long as the consumption of the harvest took place upon the spot the circulation was complete; to remedy the present defective circulation it has become necessary to restore the fertility of the soil by artificial means — by gorging it with manures brought from afar, from South America and the Napoleonic battlefields, and with artificial and chemical manures.

Modern agriculture demands a vast expenditure of labour; but in proportion as more labour was required, in the same proportion the industrial towns drew off the labourers and depopulated the country. 'There is a lack of agricultural hands', has been the

general cry for the last eighty years; and it is this dearth of
agricultural labourers which furnished the necessary incitement
for the procurement of the means of labour in abundance. The
application of machinery to agricultural labour became an
imperative necessity; but machinery can only be applied on great
farms; wherefore the concentration of land was a pre-requisite for
the application of machinery and the introduction of scientific
agriculture.

In 1857 M. Léonce de Lavergne cited, by way of example, a
farm of the Department of l'Oise on which 1,250 acres of beetroot
were cultivated, and 8,250 bushels of wheat were gathered.
'There is nothing more colossal to be met with in England', he
exclaimed exultingly.[1]

But how insignificant do these colossal farms appear when
compared with the Bonanza farms of the New World.

Since 1874 an American cultivator, Mr Dalrymple, whose name
has obtained a world-wide celebrity, has directed the operations
of six farms, of an area of 75,000 acres, belonging to a financial
company. He divided these farms into sections of 2,000 acres,
sub-divided into three lots of 650 acres. These 75,000 acres are
cultivated by a regiment of 600 labourers, under a military
discipline. At harvest time the central administration engages
from 500 to 600 supplementary labourers, and distributes them
among the different sections. As soon as the autumn operations
are ended the men are discharged, with the exception of the
foreman and 110 men per section. In certain farms of Dakota and
Minnesota the mules and horses do not winter on the field of
operation; once the ground is broken they are sent southward
and return only in the following spring. Mounted mechanics
accompany the ploughs, sowing machines, etc., ready at a
moments notice to repair the machinery out of order. The grain is
conveyed to the threshing machines, which are in operation night
and day; it is threshed and winnowed and sacked automatically,
and despatched to the railroads which adjoin the farms, and from
thence to Duluth or Buffalo. Every year Mr Dalrymple increases
the acreage under culture by 5,000 acres; in 1880 it amounted to
25,000 acres.

At the same time that the bourgeoisie of Europe stripped the
peasants of the communal lands and feudal privileges, it imposed

1 Léonce de Lavergne, *'L'Agriculture et la Population'*. Paris, 1857.

upon them tributes of blood and money; it left them at the mercy of the usurers, who converted them into nominal proprietors, exposed to the competition of the great land owners and farmers of America and India. These and other causes combined to accelerate the expropriation of the peasant and his conversion into a proletarian. In America, where financial agriculture is carried to the highest pitch of perfection, we meet also with the most highly developed agricultural proletariat.

The cultivators of the corn-growing States of the Union may be classed under four great categories: 1, the day labourers or agricultural proletarians; 2, the small farmers (peasant proprietors and *métayers*); 3, proprietors who direct the cultivation of their land; 4, great financial farmers of whom, in Europe, the only counterparts are to be found in different parts of Roumania and in the south of Russia.

The great majority of the cultivators is composed of proletarians, who do not possess an inch of land or a hut of mud; they do not own the bed on which they lie or the spoon they eat with; they realize the ideal of men stripped of all private property save that which they directly appropriate in the shape of food or clothing. They have no fixed abode in the fields they cultivate, and which they abandon as soon as the work is done. The managers of the financial farms recruit the labourers everywhere; in the villages and large towns the latter are hired by the day, week or month. The men are engaged for the agricultural campaign, placed under the direction of overlookers and foremen and conveyed to the farms; they are lodged and fed and supplied with medicine and paid a wage. They are drilled and formed into regular agricultural regiments, and subjected to a military discipline. They rise, feed, and go to bed at prescribed hours; throughout the week spirits are prohibited; on Sundays the men are free to go and drink at the neighbouring ale-houses. When the work is performed in autumn they are discharged; during the winter months only a small number of men is kept on at the farms to tend the cattle and to take care of the farm implements. The rest return to the towns and villages to practise whatever trade they can put themselves to.

The transformation of landed property and of its mode of culture was necessitated by the transformation undergone by industrial and financial property. The country, in order to supply the men and money required by industry for its workshops and colossal enterprises (railways, tunnels, etc.), unparalleled since the giant achievements of the period of primitive communism, was drained of its population, and the hiding-places in which the peasants had deposited their savings were cleared out.

At previous epochs the citizens, with the exception of an infinitesimal minority of noblemen, priests, and artificers, satisfied all their wants by cultivating the land; in the bourgeois world an ever-increasing mass of citizens is divorced from agricultural labour, and engaged in industrial and commercial pursuits, and dependent for their means of subsistence on the population employed in tilling the soil.

III

A mediaeval village was an economic unit, because within its limits all the handicrafts were practised which the villagers required. Capitalist production begins by destroying this economic unit; it dissociates the handicrafts and isolates them, assigning to special centres the exercise of distinct crafts. A town or province no longer produces all the articles required by its inhabitants; it relies upon other towns or provinces for the manufacture of special goods. The silk manufactures that it had been sought to disperse over France were, by the end of the last century, almost wholly concentrated in Lyons and its environs. The textile manufactures of wool, flax, and cotton are centralized in certain districts, whilst the production of iron, beetroot-sugar, etc., is confined to others.

The ancient communal and provincial units have been destroyed, and in their place units of a different sort have been constituted. The ancient units were complex; they were formed by the conglomeration, in a township or province, of all the industries required by it; whereas the modern economic units are simple. They are constituted each by a single industry — iron or sugar here, cotton or leather yonder. A capitalistic nation, like France, is not subdivided into provinces or departments in harmony with its geographical configuration and historical traditions, but is divided into simple economic units: into cotton districts or wine districts, corn-growing or sugar-growing regions, carboniferous or silk producing centres. All of these industrial units are interdependent from their reciprocal wants, no one industrial centre being capable, like the mediaeval cities, of subsisting a month or even a week without the support of other centres. If, for example, the town of Rouen supplies the whole of France with cotton goods, she imports her corn from La Beauce, her cattle from the north, her coals from the Loire, her oil from Marseilles, and so forth. A capitalistic nation is a gigantic workshop, and every speciality of social production is executed in special centres, situated at great distances from one another but narrowly knit together by reciprocal wants. The political autonomy of the mediaeval townships has become an impossibility; the correlation of economic wants serves as a basis for the political unity of the nation. Capitalist production, which has destroyed the local and provincial unity of handicraft production, is about to destroy the national unity of its own creation and to replace it by a vaster, an international unity.

England, that was the first nation to apply machinery, had manifested the pretension of constraining the rest of the nations to become exclusively agricultural countries, reserving for herself the industrial *role*. Lancashire was to weave all the cotton produced by the Indies and the United States. This premature attempt at an international industrial monopolization has miscarried. America, at the present day, manufactures cotton goods in excess of her requirements, and India, whose cotton industry had been ruined by England, has taken to weaving by machinery. Sixteen years ago the consumption of cotton by the manufactories of India amounted to 87,000 bales; in 1885 the consumption of cotton amounted to 585,000 bales.[1]

India was the cradle of the cotton industry; calicoes first came from Calcutta, and muslin from Mosul; ere long the Indian cottons, manufactured in the proximity of the cottonfields, will once again invade the European markets and, in their turn, ruin the industry of Manchester and the cotton centres of the Continent. The cotton goods of India and the United States will supplant those of Rouen and Manchester. A Yankee merchant, impressed by the impending fate of the Lancashire manufacturers, charitably advised them to transport their machinery to Louisiana, where they would have the raw material close at hand, and so save the expense of its conveyance. The

[1] Thomas Ellison. *The Cotton Trade of Great Britain*. 1886.

international displacement of an industry goes on under our eyes; the manufactories are drawn into the sphere of the agricultural centres which produce the raw material. But before they had become industrial centres India and the United States had held Europe in subjection, thanks to their agricultural production. The War of Secession of the United States, from 1861 to 1865, threw out of work the weavers of France and England; and exaggerated the cultivation of cotton, 'the golden plant,' in Egypt, whilst it ruined the fellahs and delivered up Egyptian finance into the hands of Rothschild and other cosmopolitan bankers.

Wheat production is in the act of being centralized in certain parts of the world. England, that in the 17th century produced corn sufficient for her home consumption, with a surplus for exportation, at the present moment imports from America, Australia, and India more than one-half of the wheat she consumes. The nations of Europe to-day are in a state of economic dependence on one another, and on the half-civilized countries. This international economic interdependence is on the increase, and will, in times to come, form the basis of the political unity of human kind, a unity which will be founded on the ruins of the existing national unities.

IV.

Capitalist production has advanced from the local and provincial political units to the national political units by creating industrial organisms which could not have been constituted but for the local concentration of production and the decomposition of the process of production. Thus, while manufacturing production agglomerated the labourers and the means of production in its workshops, it introduced the division of labour which decomposed the instrument of labour and condemned the labourer to the lifelong execution of a single operation. The implements of the artificer were few and simple, whereas those of the industrial manufacturer are complex and multifarious. In proportion as the fractional labourer became unfit for all save a single operation, the instrument of labour — developing on the same lines — was differentiated and became specialized. In certain manufactories from four to five hundred hammers of different shapes and weights were employed, each hammer serving exclusively to execute a special operation. Great mechanical industry has undone the work of manufacture; it has torn the instruments of labour out of the hands of the detail labourer, and has annexed them to a framework of steel and iron, which is, so to say, the skeleton of the machine tool, while the instruments annexed to it are its organs. The machine tool is a mechanical synthesis.

But capitalist production has produced yet another synthesis.

In domestic industry there is an economic unit; the same family transforms the raw material (wool, flax, etc.) which it has produced; this unit has been decomposed. Already in the most primitive communities we see certain industries fall to the lot of certain individuals, who are professional wheelwrights, smiths, weavers, or tailors, etc.; later on, in order to obtain an economic unit, we have no longer to consider an isolated family but the entire village or burgh. With the development of commerce and the progress of industry, these distinctive industries were multiplied and became specialities devolving upon certain artificers, grouped in corporations.

It is on the basis of the specialisation of industries in the cities that capitalist production was built up. It commenced by establishing weavers', dyers', wheelwrights', and cabinet makers' workshops, in the interior of which the division of labour and the machine accomplished their revolutions. But these manufactures, which subsequently were converted into colossal factories, remained, like the small artificer's workshop, restricted to a special industrial process, or to the production of a commodity and its varieties; weavers did nothing but weave and spinners did nothing but spin. But these specialized manufactories cease to be isolated; a number of them come to be agglomerated and are attached to a factory. Dyeworks, printworks, etc., establish themselves in the neighbourhood of mechanical weaving and spinning industries, so that under one and the same capitalistic administration the raw material goes through the entire series of its industrial transformations. And this conglomeration has not been confined to complementary industries, but has taken place in quite independent industries. This centralization does not necessarily occur in one and the same spot; frequently the different factories are set up in different localities, situated at a considerable distance from one another, but under the control of the same administration.

The National Banks, such as the Banks of England and France, are types of these complex industrial organizations which spread all over the land. A national bank possesses paper mills for the manufacture of the paper for its bank-notes; printing presses and engravers' workshops for printing and engraving the same; and photographic apparatus for the detecting of forgeries; it founds hundreds of branch offices in commercial and industrial centres; enters into connection with town and country bankers at home, as well as the national bankers of foreign countries. The central bank becomes, so to say, the heart of the financial system of the country; and so ingeniously organized is the system that the pulsations of the national bank — the rise or fall of its rate of discount — find an echo in the remotest villages of the country, and even react on the money markets of foreign nations.

Another striking type is *The Times* newspaper. This industrial organism employs a legion of correspondents, scattered over the four quarters of the globe; telegraph wires connect it with the great capitals of Europe; it manufactures its own paper, founds its own type, and employs a set of mechanics to superintend and repair its machinery; it composes, stereotypes, and publishes its sixteen large pages of printed matter, and possesses horses and carts for distributing the papers to other retail vendors. All that it still wants are alfa-fields in Africa to supply the raw material for the paper, and these it will, in good time, no doubt, contrive to acquire. There will come a day when American and Indian manufacturers will adjoin to their factories fields for the cultivation of the cotton plant and workshops for the working up of their calicoes into articles of clothing. Scotch woollen manufacturers have already opened establishments in London in which they sell in the shape of ready-made garments the woollen goods they have manufactured. Capitalistic industry is in the act of reconstituting the economic unit of domestic production; heretofore the same peasant family produced the raw material which it wrought up into industrial products; one and the same capitalistic administration will by-and-by undertake to produce the raw material, transform it into industrial products, and sell these to the customer.

By means of the division of labour, capitalist production began by destroying the unit of labour represented by the handicraftsman; thereupon it proceeded to reconstitute that unit of labour, no longer represented by the labourer, but by 'the iron man,' the machine. At present it tends to constitute giant organisms of production, composed of industries the most diverse and opposite; the special industries which are, so to say, the organs of these monsters, may exist apart, at enormous distances from one another, and be divided by political frontiers and geographical obstacles (mountains, rivers, or seas). These international ogres of labour consume heat, light, electricity, and other natural forces, as well as the brain power and muscular power of man.

Such is the economic mould in which the human material of the nineteenth century is run.

V.

Simultaneously with the extension of the manufacturing system and the factories, property, under the form of gold and silver, underwent a change. At the outset, these two metals, even when stamped and converted into money, were property of an essentially private character; their owner hoarded them or used them for personal ornament. In India and the countries of the East the latter is still one of the uses they are chiefly put to. They but rarely served as a means of exchange, the products themselves being ordinarily bartered. The feudal kings could utter false coin, or debase the coin, without very materially injuring the commercial transactions of their subjects. But when, with the advent of the commercial period, gold and silver became the representative signs of value, the standard measure of all commodities, these metals acquired the right to breed legitimately, to bear legal interest; till then lending on interest had been considered dishonourable; a practice defensible only towards the stranger—'who is the enemy,' says the unlovely God of the Jews. Lending money for profit was condemned by the Pope and Councils. Such as were addicted to the practice were hated and condemned. Exposed to danger of every sort, they jeopardized their lives and fortunes. The Jews of the Middle Ages, those accumulators of gold and silver, alive to the risks incurred by their beloved gold, put their faith in the promises neither of king nor nobles, and only advanced moneys on the deposits of precious stones, or on equally good security.

The bourgeois rehabilitated usury, and exalted the business of the money-lender into one of the most lucrative and honourable of civilized functions; to live on one's income as a fund-holder is the bourgeois' ideal life. In the 16th century, while Calvin, the authorized representative of the religious manifestation of the bourgeois economic revolution, was legitimating lending on, interest in the name of all the theological virtues, the Chancellor Duprat laid the foundations, in France, of the public debt by creating in 1522 perpetual annuities at a rate of interest of 8 per cent., called *rentes de l'hôtel de ville*. The public debt became the savings-bank of the bourgeoisie, where they deposited the money they could find no employment for in business. In earlier ages, the temple of Jerusalem, the house of Jehovah, filled that office; it served as a bank for deposits, and the Jews from every part of the world stored their precious metals there; but those deposits bore no interest.

The public debt is a bourgeois improvement. The kings of France, prior to 1789, still imbued with feudal ideas on usury, were wont, on an emergency, to lower the rate of interest by a fourth or one-half, and at times even to suspend payment. Other European sovereigns acted quite as unceremoniously by their fund-holders. This aristocratic fashion of treating their creditors has been made a constant reproach to the feudal government by the bourgeoisie: one of the first acts of the Bourgeois Revolution of 1789 was to proclaim the inviolability of the public debt and to place it above all political revolutions and all contingent changes of government. The public debt was thenceforward solidly constituted. 'The public debt,' says Marx, 'becomes one of the most powerful levers of primitive accumulation. As with the stroke of an enchanter's wand, it endows barren money with the power of breeding, and thus turns it into capital without the necessity of exposing itself to the troubles and risks inseparable from the employment in industry or even in usury. The State creditors actually give away nothing, for the sum lent is transformed into public bonds, easily negotiable, which go on functioning in their hands just as so much hard cash would,'[1] It is just as if the bank-notes bore interest.

The establishment of the public credit, while it afforded a hitherto unparalleled security to the individual capitalist, enhanced the influence of the financiers to whom the Government

1 KARL MARX, *Capital*, chap. xxxi.

were obliged to apply for money, a fact, however, which in no wise prevented the kings of the old *régime* from treating them like the Jews of the Middle Ages; dragging them before the courts of justice, despoiling and hanging them. Howbeit, a century before the Revolution of 1789 their influence in society had become so considerable that the highest nobility solicited the favour of giving their daughters in marriage to the upstarts of finance, in order to acquire the right of sharing their millions.

The social ascendancy gained by finance, which keeps on growing, is an economical necessity at a time when great commercial, industrial, and agricultural enterprises, banks, railways, canals, high furnaces, etc, have outgrown the means of private capitalists to carry them out, and require associated capital for their execution; the function of the financier is first to accumulate capital and afterwards to distribute it according to the requirements of industry and commerce. In a society based on mechanical industry, the importance of the capital sunk in the instruments of labour (the *constant capital* of Marx); the quantity of circulating capital *(variable capital);* the rapidity and abundance of production; the distance from the markets, the time required for the sale of the goods and realization of the payments, all make of finance the pivot of the economic system.

But finance, mechanical industry, and modern methods of cultivation could not develop without essentially modifying the character of property, by converting it from a personal thing into an impersonal thing; biding the time when it shall resume its primitive form and once again become common.

In the system of small landed property and petty industry, property was an appendage of the proprietor, as his implement was an appendage of the artificer. An industrial enterprise depended upon the personal character of the proprietor: his thrift, activity, and intelligence, just as the perfection of his work depended upon the skill of the artificer who handled the implement. It was impossible for the proprietor to sicken, age, or retire without endangering the success of the industrial undertaking of which he was the soul. He fulfilled a social function that had its pains and penalties, its profits and rewards. Property, at that epoch, was truly personal, whence the popular saying: *'La propriété est le fruit du travail.'* But modern production has reversed the terms; the capitalist is no longer an appendage of his property whose prosperity no longer depends upon his individual worth. The *eye of the master* has lost its occupation. All great financial, agricultural, and industrial undertakings are directed by administrations more or less successfully organized and highly paid. The function of the modern proprietor consists in pocketing his income and squandering it on wine and women; not a social function is, in our day, assigned to the proprietor in the technical organization of producers who are all wage-labourers. After having filled a useful part in production, the proprietor has become useless and even a nuisance, as a bourgeois economist remarks. [1]

Political economists, who are but the overpaid apologists of bourgeois society, have sought to justify the tax levied by capital on the produce of labour in the shape of interest, ground rent, profits, etc, by pretending that the capitalist renders useful service by his *abstinence,* his administrative ability, and so forth. If it was possible for Adam Smith to defend this specious proposition with some show of reason, the Giffens, Roschers, Leroy-Beaulieus, and other such small fry of political economy, ought really, if they would continue to draw their salaries from the middle-class for their interested special pleadings, to set their wits to work to devise something less palpably absurd than the pretended usefulness of the capitalist in the modern system of great mechanical production.

Mechanical production has robbed the artisan of his technical skill and turned the wage labourer into a servant of the machine; the capitalistic organization of industry has made a parasite of the capitalist. The parasitical nature of his *role* is recognized and proclaimed by the creation of anonymous companies whose shares and obligations—the bourgeois' titles of property—pass from hand to hand, without exerting any influence on production, and on the Stock Exchange change hands a dozen times a day.

---

[1] 'In an enterprise carried on by a company the body of directors may possess but a small fraction of capital; they might, conceivably, possess none at all, and, contrary to the generally received opinion, such a state of things would be the most satisfactory one as regards a proper administration of the company; a body of directors who should be shareholders having no right to administer themselves. It is enough if they possess the requisite capacity, competency, and morality for their functions, all of which qualities are to be found more readily, and at less cost, apart from capital than associated with it. (G. DE MOLINARI. *L'évolution économique du xix siecle.* 1880, p. 38.)

The Rothschilds, Grants, Goulds, and other financiers of that stamp, practically demonstrate to the capitalists that they are useless, by cheating them out of their shares and bonds by Stock Exchange swindling, and other financial hanky-panky, and by accumulating in their strong-boxes the profits derived from the great organisms of production.

In the days when the feudal baron dwelt in his fortified castle, in the midst of his vassals, administering justice to them in time of peace, and donning his armour and putting himself at the head of his men to defend them in cases of invasion, the feudal nobility was a class essentially useful and which it was impossible to suppress; but so soon as a relative tranquillity had been established in the country, and as the towns and boroughs, converted into strongholds, became capable of defending themselves, the nobles ceased to be wanted; they abandoned their castles and betook themselves to the ducal, episcopal, royal and imperial courts, in which they ended by becoming a body estranged from the nation, and living on it parasitically: that very moment their doom was sealed. If the nobility have not in all European nations been as brutally mowed down as they were during the French Revolution in 1789, they have yet everywhere forfeited their feudal privileges, and become merged in the ranks of the bourgeois, from whom, at present, they only distinguish themselves by the absurdity of their aristocratic pretensions. In capitalistic nations the nobility have disappeared as a ruling class. The same fate awaits the capitalist class. The day that the capitalist ceased to have a function to perform in social production, the death-warrant of his class was signed; it remains but to execute the sentence pronounced by the economic phenomena, and the capitalists who may survive the ruin of their order will lack even the grotesque privileges of the pedigreed nobility to console them for the lost grandeur of their class. Machinery which has killed the artificer will kill the capitalist.

VI.

Civilization, after having destroyed the rude and simple communism of the beginnings of humanity, elaborates the elements of a complex and scientific communism. Just as in primitive times, labour is to-day performed in common, and the producer owns neither the instruments of labour nor the products of his labour. The produce of labour is not, as yet, shared in common, as was the case with the savage and barbarian tribes; it is monopolized by idle capitalists whose suppression is now but a question of time and opportunity. Let the parasites of property be swept away, and communistic property will affirm itself and implant itself in society. In primitive society property was common only among members of the same tribe, connected by the ties of blood; every human being not included in the narrow circle of kinship was a stranger, an enemy; but in the society of the future, property will be held in common by all the members of the great human family, without distinction of nationality, race, or colour; for the workers, bowed under the same capitalistic yoke, have recognized that brothers in misery, brothers in revolt, they must remain brothers in victory.

This final communist and international revolution of property is inevitable; already, in the midst of bourgeois civilization, do the institutions and communistic customs of primitive times revive.

Universal suffrage, the mode of election employed by savages and barbarians in electing their military chiefs and *sachems,* is re-established, after having been set aside by the bourgeois governments who had proclaimed it the basis of political power.

In primitive ages, habitations were common, repasts were common, and education was common. In our municipal schools children are taught gratuitously and in common; in some cities they are beginning to receive gratuitous repasts. In our restaurants civilized folk are being poisoned and cheated in common, and in the many-storied houses of our large cities they are cooped up in common like rabbits in a hutch.

If universal suffrage is a juggle; if our town houses are unwholesome; if the rest of our institutions, affecting a mock communistic character, are a bane to those whom they profess to benefit, it is because they evolve in a bourgeois society and are established for the sole behoof of the capitalist. None the less are they of capital importance; they destroy individualistic instincts and form and fashion men for the communistic habits of the society to come.

Communism exists in a latent form in bourgeois society; circumstances, not to be foreseen, will cause it to burst forth openly, and will re-instate it as the only possible form of future society.

SOCIAL AND PHILOSOPHICAL STUDIES

The mode of production of the material means of life dominates as a rule the development of the social, political and intellectual life.

KARL MARX

1

Causes of belief in God

I

THE RELIGIOUS BOURGEOISIE AND THE IRRELIGIOUS PROLETARIAT

BOURGEOIS free thought under the auspices of two illustrious scientists. Berthelot and Haeckel, has set up its platform at Rome, opposite the Vatican to hurl its oratorical thunder-bolts against Catholicism, which with its hierarchical clergy and its alleged immutable dogmas stands in the bourgeois mind for religion.

Do the free-thinkers, because they are putting Catholicism on trial, think they are emancipated from belief in God, the foundation of all religion? Do they think that the bourgeoisie, the class to which they belong, can dispense with Christianity, of which Catholicism is a manifestation?

Christianity, though it has succeeded in adapting itself to other social forms, is first and foremost the religion of societies founded on individual property and the exploitation of wage labour, and that is why it has been, is, and shall be, whatever is said, and whatever is done, the religion of the bourgeoisie. For more than ten centuries all its movements, whether for organizing itself, emancipating itself, or spreading into new territory, have been accompanied and complicated by religious crises; it has always put the material interests whose triumph it sought under the cover of Christianity, which it claimed that it wished to reform and bring back to the pure doctrine of the Divine Master.

The bourgeois revolutionists of 1789, imagining that France could be de-christianized, persecuted the clergy with unequalled vigour; the more logical of them, thinking that nothing would be accomplished as long as the belief in God existed, abolished God by decree, like a functionary of the old regime, and replaced him by the Goddess of Reason. But when the revolutionary fever had run its course, Robespierre re-established by a decree the Supreme Being, the name of God being still out of fashion, and a few months later the priests emerged from their cells and opened their churches, where the faithful held love feasts, and Bonaparte to satisfy the bourgeois mob signed the Concordat: then appeared a Christianity of a romantic, sentimental, picturesque and macaronic character, adapted by Chateaubriand to the tastes of the triumphant bourgeoisie.

The powerful intellects of free thought have affirmed and still affirm, in spite of evidence, that science would disencumber the human brain of the idea of God by making it useless for a comprehension of the mechanism of the universe. Nevertheless the men of science with but few exceptions are still under the charm of that belief; if in his own field a scientist, to use Laplace's phrase, has no need of the hypothesis of God to explain the phenomena that he studies, he does not venture to declare that it is useless in accounting for those which are not summed up in the list of his researches; and all scientists recognize that God is more or less necessary for the proper working of the social gearings and for the morals of the masses.* Not only is the idea of God not completely banished from the brains of the scientists, but the

---

* La Revue Scientifique of November 19, 1904, corroborates these assertions. M. H. Pieron, in his discussion of a work on 'Scientific Materialism,' recognizes that 'God is the convenient residual cause of all that can not be explained ... that faith has always been framed to supplement science, ... and that science has nothing to do with beliefs or faith ... but that religion is not absolutely incompatible with science, on condition, however, that it be shut up in a thoroughly tight compartment.' He protests also against 'the succession of present-day scientists who are searching in science for nothing but proofs of the existence of God or the truth of religion, as well as against the sophism of one who should search in science for proofs of the non-existence of God.' Up to the modern epoch, it was considered a denial of the existence of God, if one did not recognize his incessant action for the maintenance of order in the universe. Socrates reproached Anaxagoras for having wished to explain the motions of the heavenly bodies without the intervention of the gods, and Plato relates that the Athenians held as atheists the philosophers who admitted that the revolutions of the stars and the phenomena of nature were regulated by law (Laws, VII: 21). In another passage, he demonstrates the existence of God by the creation, the order that reigns in it, and the consent of all nations, Greeks and barbarians (the same, X., 1). God is 'he who balances the world,' said the Egyptian priests.

grossest superstition flourishes, not in the backwoods and among the ignorant, but in the capitals of civilization and among the educated bourgeois; some enter into sessions with spirits to get news from beyond the tomb, others prostrate themselves before St. Anthony of Padua to find something lost, to guess the lucky number at the lottery, to pass an examination at the Polytechnic; they consult palmists, clairvoyants, card-readers, in order to learn the future, interpret dreams, etc. The scientific knowledge that they possess does not protect them against the most stupid credulity.

But while in all the groups of the bourgeoisie the religious sentiment retains its vitality and shows itself in a thousand fashions, the industrial proletariat is characterized by a religious indifference that is unreasoning, but unshakable.

Mr. Charles Booth, the well-known sociologist, at the close of his vast inquiry into the religious state of London, which his army of assistants 'have visited district by district, street by street, and often house by house,' states that 'the mass of the people make no profession of faith and take no interest in religious observances.... The great section of the population which passes, by the name of the working classes, lying socially between the lower middle class and the "poor", remains, as a whole, outside of all the religious bodies.... The churches have come to be regarded as the resorts of the well-to-do, and of those who are willing to accept the charity and patronage of the people better off than themselves.... The average working man of to-day thinks more of his rights or of his wrongs than of his duties and his failure to perform them. Humility and the consciousness of sin, and the attitude of worship, are perhaps not natural to him.'* These undeniable proofs of the instinctive irreligion of the London workingmen, usually thought so religious, can be matched by the most superficial observation of the industrialized cities of France. If labourers are found there who assume religious sentiments, or who really have them (these latter are rare) it is because religion strikes them as a form of charitable relief; if others are fanatical free-thinkers, it is because they have suffered from the meddling of the priest in their families or in their relations with their employer.

---

* Religious Influences: Series III of the investigation undertaken by Charles Booth into the 'Life and Labour of the People of London.'

indifference in religious matters, the most serious symptom of irreligion, to quote Lamennais, is inborn in the modern working class. While the political movements of the bourgeoisie may have taken on a religious or anti-religious form, no inclination can be seen in the proletariat of the great industries in Europe and America toward elaborating a new religion to replace Christianity, nor any desire to reform it. The economic and political organizations of the working class in both hemispheres are uninterested in any doctrinal discussion on religious dogmas and spiritual ideas; this however does not prevent their making war on priests of all cults, regarding them as the domestics of the capitalist class.

How comes it that the bourgeois, who receive a scientific education of greater or less extent, are still trammelled by religious ideas, from which the workers, without the education, have freed themselves?

II

NATURAL ORIGINS OF THE IDEA OF GOD IN THE SAVAGE

To declaim against Catholicism as the free-thinkers do, or to ignore God as the positivists do does not take account of the persistence of the belief in God in spite of the progress and the popularization of scientific knowledge, nor does it take account of the persistence of Christianity in spite of the railleries of Voltaire, the persecutions of the revolutionists, and the results of exegetic criticism. It is easy to declaim and ignore and it is hard to explain, for to do that one must begin by inquiring how and why belief in God and spiritualistic ideas slipped into the human brain, took root there, and developed; and answers to these questions are found only by going back to the ideology of the savages, where are clearly outlined the spiritualistic ideas which encumber the brains of civilized people.

The idea of the soul and of its survival is an invention of the savages, who allowed themselves an immaterial and immortal spirit to explain the phenomena of dreams.

The savage who has no doubt of the reality of his dreams imagines that if during his sleep he hunts, fights, or takes vengeance, and if on awakening he finds himself in the place where he lay down it is because another self, a double, as he says, impalpable, invisible and light as air has left his sleeping body to go far away to hunt or fight, and if it comes about that he sees in his dreams his ancestors and his dead companions he concludes that he has been visited by their spirits, which survive the destruction of their corpses.

The savage, 'that child of the human species,' as Vico calls him has, like the child, puerile notions about nature. He thinks that he can give orders to the elements as to his limbs, that he can with words and magic rites command the rain to fall, the wind to blow, etc.; if for example he fears that the night may overtake him on his march he knots up in a certain fashion certain herbs to stop the sun, as the Joshua of the Bible did with a prayer. The spirits of the dead having this power over the elements to a higher degree than the living, he calls on them to produce the phenomenon when he fails in bringing it about. Since a brave warrior and a skilful sorcerer have more effect upon nature than simple mortals, their spirits when they are dead must consequently have a greater power over it than the doubles of ordinary men; the savage chooses them out of the crowd of spirits to honour them with offerings and sacrifices and to beg them to make it rain, when drought compromises his harvests, to give him victory when he takes the field, to cure him when he is sick. Primitive man starting out with a mistaken explanation of dreams elaborated the elements which later served for the creation of one sole God, who is when defined nothing more than a spirit, more powerful than the other spirits.

The idea of God is neither an innate idea, nor an *a priori* idea, but an *a posteriori* idea, just as all ideas are, since man can not think until he has come in contact with the phenomena of the real world which he explains as he can. It is impossible to set forth in an article the logically deductive manner in which the idea of God proceeded from the idea of the soul, invented by the savages.

Grant Allen, bringing together and summing up the observations and researches of explorers, folk-lorists, and anthropologists and interpreting them and illuminating them by his ingenious and fertile criticism has followed out in its principal steps the process of formation of the idea of God in his remarkable work entitled, the *Evolution of the Idea of God; an Enquiry into the Origin of Religions*, London, 1903. He also

demonstrated with ample proofs that primitive Christianity with
its Man-God, dead and raised again, its Virgin-Mother, its
Holy-Spirit, its legends, its mysteries, its dogmas, its ethics, its
miracles, and its ceremonies, merely assembled and organized
into a religion, certain ideas and myths, which for centuries were
current in the ancient world

III

ECONOMIC ORIGINS OF THE BELIEF OF GOD IN THE BOURGEOIS

It might reasonably have been hoped that the extraordinary
development and popularization of scientific knowledge and the
demonstration of the necessary linking of natural phenomena
might have established the idea that the universe ruled by the law
of necessity was removed from the caprices of any human or
superhuman will and that consequently God became useless since
he was stripped of the multiple functions which the ignorance of
the savages had laid upon him; nevertheless it cannot but be
recognized that the belief in a God, who can at his will overthrow
the necessary order of things, still persists in men of science, and
that such a God is still in demand by the educated bourgeois, who
asks him as the savages do for rain, victory, cures, etc.

Even if the scientists had succeeded in creating in bourgeois
circles the conviction that the phenomena of the natural world
obey the law of necessity in such sort that, determined by those
which precede them, they determine those which follow them, it
would still have to be proved that the phenomena of the social
world are also subject to the law of necessity. But the economists,
the philosophers, the moralists, the historians, the sociologists,
and the politicians who study human societies, and who even
assume to direct them, have not succeeded, and could not
succeed in creating the conviction that social phenomena depend
upon the law of necessity like natural phenomena; and it is
because they have not been able to establish this conviction that
the belief in God is a necessity for bourgeois brains, even the
most cultivated ones. If philosophical determinism reigns in the
natural sciences it is only because the bourgeoisie has permitted
its scientists to study freely the play of natural forces, which it has

every motive to understand, since it utilizes them in the production of its wealth; but by reason of the situation that it occupies in society it could not grant the same liberty to its economists, philosophers, moralists, historians, sociologists and politicians, and that is why they have not been able to introduce philosophical determinism into the sciences of the social world. The Catholic Church for a like reason formerly forbade the free study of nature, and its social dominance had to be overthrown in order to create the natural sciences.

The problem of the belief in God on the part of the bourgeoisie cannot be approached without an exact notion of the role played by this class in society. The social role of the modern bourgeoisie is not to produce wealth, but it is to have it produced by wage workers, to seize upon it and distribute it among its members after having left to its manual and intellectual producers just enough for their nourishment and reproduction.

The wealth taken away from the labourers forms the booty of the bourgeois class. The barbarian warriors after the taking and sacking of a city put the products of the pillage into a common fund, divided them into parts as equal as possible and distributed them by lot among those who had risked their lives to conquer them.

The organization of society permits the bourgeoisie to seize upon wealth without any one of its members being forced to risk his life. The taking possession of this colossal booty without incurring dangers is one of the greatest marks of progress in our civilization. The wealth despoiled from the producers is not divided into equal parts to be distributed by lot; it is distributed under form of rents, incomes, dividends, interests, and industrial and commercial profits, proportionately to the value of the real or personal property; that is to say, to the extent of the capital possessed by each bourgeois.

The possession of a property, a capital, and not that of physical, intellectual or moral qualities is the indispensable condition for receiving a part in the distribution of the wealth. A child in swaddling clothes, as well as an adult, may have a right to its share of the wealth. A dead man possesses it so long as a living man has not yet perfected his title to his property. The distribution is not made among men, but among properties. Man is a zero, property alone counts.

A false analogy has been drawn between the Darwinian struggle which the animals wage among themselves for the means of subsistence and reproduction and that which is let loose among the bourgeois for the distribution of wealth. The qualities of strength, courage, agility, patience, ingenuity, etc., which assure victory to the animal, constitute integral parts of his organism, while the property which gives the bourgeois part of the wealth which he has not produced is not incorporated in his individuality. This property may increase or decrease and thus procure for him a larger or smaller share without its increase or diminution being occasioned by the exercise of his physical or intellectual qualities. At the very most it might be said that trickery, intrigue, charlatanism, in a word, the lowest mental qualities permit the bourgeois to take a part larger than that which the value of his capital authorizes him to take; in that case he pilfers from his bourgeois brothers. If then the struggle for life can in a number of cases be a cause for progress among animals, the struggle for wealth is a cause of degeneracy for the bourgeois.

The social mission of grasping the wealth produced by the wage-workers makes of the bourgeoisie a parasitic class; its members do not contribute to the creation of wealth, with the exception of a few whose number is constantly diminishing, and the labour which they furnish does not correspond to the portion of wealth which falls to them.

If Christianity, after having been in the first centuries the religion of the mendicant crowds whom the state and the wealthy supported by daily distributions of food, has become that of the bourgeoisie, the parasitic class par-excellence, it is because parasitism is the essence of Christianity.

Jesus in his sermon on the mount explained its character in a masterly fashion; it is there that he formulates the 'Our Father,' the prayer which every believer must address to God to ask him for his 'daily bread' instead of asking him for work; and in order that no Christian worth of the name may be tempted to resort to work for obtaining the necessaries of life, the Christ adds, 'Consider the birds of the air, they sow not neither do they reap, and your Heavenly Father feedeth them ... take no thought therefore and do not say, to-morrow what shall we eat, or what shall we drink, or wherewithal shall we be clothed.... Your Heavenly Father knoweth that you have need of all these things.'

The Heavenly Father of the bourgeoisie is the class of manual and intellectual wage workers; this is the God who provides for all its needs.

But the bourgeoisie cannot recognize its parasitic character without at the same time signing its death warrant; so while it leaves the bridle on the neck of its men of science, that without being troubled with any dogma nor stopped by any consideration they may give themselves up to the freest and most profound study of the forces of nature, which it applies to the production of its wealth, it forbids to its economists, philosophers, moralists, historians, sociologists, and politicians the impartial study of the social world, and condemns them to the search of reasons that may serve as excuses for its phenomenal fortune.* Concerned only with the returns received or to be received, they are trying to find out, if by some lucky chance social wealth might not have other sources than the labour of the wage-worker, and they have discovered that the labour, the economy, the method, the honesty, the knowledge, the intelligence, and many other virtues of the bourgeois manufacturers, merchants, landed proprietors, financiers, shareholders, and income-drawers, contributed to its production in a manner far more efficacious than the labour of the manual and intellectual wage-workers, and therefore they have the right to take the lion's share and to leave the others only the share of the beast of burden.

The bourgeois hears them with a smile, because they sing his praises, he even repeats these impudent assertions, and calls them eternal truths; but, however slender his intelligence, he can not admit these things in his inmost soul, for he has only to look around him to perceive that those who work their life through, if they do not possess capital, are poorer than Job, and that those

---

* The history of political economy is instructive. At a time when capitalist production, in the first stage of its evolution, had not yet transformed the mass of the bourgeois into parasites, the Physiocrats, Adam Smith, Ricardo, etc., could make an impartial study of economic phenomena, and search out the general laws of production. But since the machine-tool and steam require the co-operative efforts of wage-workers alone in the creation of wealth, the economists confine themselves to the collection of facts and statistical figures, valuable for the speculations of commerce and the Stock Exchange, without endeavouring to group and classify them, so as to draw theoretical conclusions, since these could only be dangerous to the dominance of the possessing class. Instead of building up science they are fighting socialism; they have even wished to refute the Ricardian theory of value because socialist criticism had taken possession of it.

who possess nothing but knowledge, intelligence, economy, honesty, and who exercise these qualities, must limit their ambition to their daily pittance, and rarely hope for anything beyond. Then he says to himself: 'If the economists, the philosophers, and the politicians with all their wit and literary training have not been able, in spite of their conscientious search, to find more valid reasons for explaining the wealth of the bourgeoisie, it is because there is something crooked in the business, some unknown cause whose mysteries are beyond us.' An Unknowable of the social order plants itself before the capitalist's eyes.

The capitalist, for the sake of social peace, is interested that the wage-workers should believe his riches to be the fruit of his innumerable virtues, but in reality he cares as little to know that they are the rewards of his good qualities as to know that truffles, which he eats as voraciously as the pig, are vegetables capable of cultivation; only one thing matters to him, namely, to possess them, and what troubles him is to think that he may lose them without any fault of his own. He cannot help having this unpleasant perspective, since even in the narrow circle of his acquaintance, he has seen certain persons lose their possessions, while others became rich after having been in distress. The causes of these reverses and strokes of fortune are beyond him as well as beyond the people who experienced them. In a word, he observes a continual going and coming of wealth, the causes of which are for him within the realm of the Unknowable, and he is reduced to setting down these changes of fortune to chance, to luck.*

* The capitalist mind has in all ages been tormented by the constant uncertainty of fortune, represented in Greek Mythology by a winged woman standing upon a wheel with her eyes bandaged. Theognis, the Megarian poet of the fifth century before the Christian era, whose poetry, according to Isocrates, was a text book in the Greek schools, said: 'No man is the cause of his gains and of his losses, the Gods are the distributors of wealth.... We human beings cherish vain thoughts, but we know nothing. The Gods make all things come about according to their own will.... Jupiter inclines the balance sometimes to one side and sometimes to the other, according to his will, that one may be rich, and then at another time may possess nothing.... No man is rich or poor, noble or commoner, without the intervention of the Gods.' The authors of Ecclesiastes, Psalms, Proverbs and Job make Jehovah play the same part. The Greek poet and the Jewish writers express the capitalists thought. Megara, like Corinth, its rival, was one of the first maritime cities of ancient Greece in which commerce and industry developed. A numerous class of artisans and capitalists took shape there and stirred up civil wars in its struggle for political power. About sixty years before the birth of Theognis, the democrats, after a victorious revolt, abolished the debts due to the aristocrats and

It is too much to hope that the bourgeois should ever arrive at a positive notion of the phenomena of the distribution of wealth, since in proportion as mechanical production develops, property is depersonalized and takes on the collective and impersonal form of corporations with their stocks and bonds, the titles to which are finally dragged into the whirlpool of the stock exchange. There they pass from hand to hand without the buyers and sellers having seen the property which they represent, or even knowing exactly the geographical place where it is situated. They are exchanged, lost by some and won by others, in a manner which comes so near gambling that the distinction is difficult to draw. All modern economic development tends more and more to transform capitalist society into one vast international gambling house where the bourgeois win and lose capital, thanks to unknown events which escape all foresight, all calculation, and which seem to them to depend on nothing but chance. The Unknowable is enthroned in bourgeois society as in a gambling house.

Gambling, which on the stock exchange is seen without disguise, has always been one of the conditions of commerce and industry; their risks are so numerous and so unforeseen, that often the enterprises which are conceived, calculated and carried out most skilfully fail, while others undertaken lightly, in a happy-go-lucky fashion, succeed. These successes and failures, due to unexpected causes generally unknown and apparently arising only from chance, predispose the bourgeois to the mental attitude of the gamester; the game of the stock exchange fortifies and vivifies this mental cast. The capitalist whose fortune is invested in stocks sold on the exchange, who is ignorant of the reason for the variations of their prices and dividends, is a

required the restitution of the interest which had been extorted. Theognis, although a member of the aristocratic class and although he cherished a ferocious hatred against the democrats, whose black blood as he said he would gladly have drunk, because they had robbed and banished him, could not escape the influence of the bourgeois social environment. He is impregnated with its ideas and sentiments, and even with its language; thus on several occasions he draws metaphors from the assaying of gold, to which the merchants were constantly obliged to resort that they might know the value of the coins and ingots given them in exchange. It is precisely because the gnomic poetry of Theognis, like the books of the Old Testament, carried the maxims of bourgeois wisdom, that it was a school book in democratic Athens. It was, said Xenophon, a treatise on man such as a skilful horseman might write on the art of riding.

professional gamester. Now the gamester, who can account for his gains or losses only as a good run or a bad run, is an eminently superstitious individual; the frequenters of gambling houses all have magical charms to compel good fortune; one mumbles a prayer to St. Anthony of Padua, or no matter what spirit from Heaven, another plays only when a certain colour has won, another holds a rabbit's foot in his left hand, etc.

The Unknowable of the social order envelops the bourgeois as the Unknowable of the natural order surrounded the savage; all or nearly all the acts of civilized life tend to develop in him the superstitious and mystical habit of assigning everything to chance, like the professional gamester. Credit, for example, without which commerce and industry are impossible, is an act of faith in chance, in the unknown, performed by him who gives the credit, since he has not positive guarantee that the one who receives the credit will be able to meet his obligations at maturity, his solvency depending upon a thousand and one accidents that can not be foreseen nor understood.

Other economic phenomena instil every day into the bourgeois mind the belief in a mystical force without material support; detached from everything material. The bank note, to cite a single example, holds within itself a social force so far beyond its small material consequence that it prepares the bourgeois mind for the idea of a force which should exist independently of matter. This miserable rag of paper, which no one would stoop to pick up, were it not for its magical power, gives its possessor all material things most to be desired in the civilized world; bread, meats, wine, house, lands, horses, women, health, consideration, honours, etc., the pleasures of the senses and the delights of the soul: God could do no more. Bourgeois life is woven out of mysticism.*

Commercial and industrial crises confront the terrified bourgeois — uncontrollable, unchecked forces of a power so irresistible that they scatter disasters as terrible as the wrath of the Christian God. When they are unchained in the civilized

---

* Renan, whose cultivated mind was clouded with mysticism, had decided sympathy for the impersonal form ot property. He relates in his *Memories of Childhood* (VI), that instead of devoting his gains to the acquirement of real estate he preferred buying 'stocks and bonds, which are lighter, more fragile, more ethereal.' The bank note is a value quite as ethereal as stocks and bonds.

world they ruin capitalists by thousands and destroy products and means of production by hundreds of millions. For a century the economists have recorded their periodical returns without being able to advance any plausible hypothesis of their origin. The impossibility of finding their causes on earth has suggested to certain English economists the idea of looking for them in the sun; its spots, they say, destroying by droughts the harvests of India, might diminish its capacity for purchasing European merchandise and might determine the crises. These grave sages carry us back scientifically to the judicial astrology of the Middle Ages, which subjected the events of human societies to the conjunction of the stars, and to the belief of savages in the action of shooting stars, comets, and eclipses of the moon upon their destinies.

The economic world swarms with fathomless mysteries for the bourgeois, mysteries which the economists resign themselves to leaving unexplored. The capitalist, who, thanks to his scientists has succeeded in domesticating natural forces, is so amazed by the incomprehensible effects of economic forces that he declares them uncontrollable, like God, and he thinks that the wisest course is to endure patiently the ills which they inflict and accept gratefully the favours which they grant. He says with Job: 'The Lord gave and the Lord hath taken away, blessed be the name of the Lord.' Economic forces appear to him in a fantasm as friendly and hostile spirits.*

The terrible and inexplicable phenomena of the social order which surround the capitalist and strike him without his knowing why or how, in his industry, his commerce, his fortune, his well-being, his life, are as disquieting for him as were for the savage the terrible and inexplicable phenomena of nature which excited and over-heated his exuberant imagination. Anthropologists account for the primitive man's belief in witchcraft, in the soul, in spirits and in God, on the ground of his ignorance of the natural world: the same explanation holds for the civilized man; his spiritualist ideas and his belief in God should be attributed to his ignorance of the social world. The uncertain

---

* Crises impress the bourgeois so vividly that they talk of them as if they were corporeal beings. The celebrated American humorist Artemus Ward relates that hearing certain financiers and manufacturers in New York affirm so positively, 'The crisis has come, it is here,' he thought it must be in the room, and to see what kind of a head it had, he began looking for it under the tables and chairs.

duration of his prosperity, and the unknowable causes of his fortunes and misfortunes, predispose the bourgeois to admit, like the savage, the existence of superior beings, which act on social phenomena as their fancies lead them, whether favourably or unfavourably, as described by Theognis and the writers of the Old Testament. To propitiate them he practises the grossest superstition, communicates with spirits from the other world, burns candles before sacred images and prays to the trinitarian God of the Christians or the one God of the philosophers.

The savage, in daily contact with nature, is especially impressed by the unknown things of the natural order, which on the contrary worry the bourgeois but slightly; the only nature he knows about has been agreeably decorated, trimmed, gravelled, raked off and generally domesticated. The numerous services that science has already rendered for his enrichment, and those he still expects from her, have engendered in his mind a blind faith in her power. He does not doubt but that some day she will solve the unknown problems of nature and even prolong indefinitely his own life, as promised by Mechnikov, the microbe-maniac. But it is not so with the unknown things of the social world, the only ones that trouble him; these seem to him impossible of comprehension. It is the unknowable of the social world, not of the natural world, which insinuates into his unimaginative head the idea of God, an idea which he did not have the trouble of inventing, but found ready to be appropriated. The incomprehensible and insoluble social problems make God so necessary that he would have invented Him, had need been.

The bourgeois, vexed by the bewildering come and go of fortunes and misfortunes, and by the puzzling play of economic forces, is furthermore confused by the brutal contradiction of his own conduct and that of his fellows with the current notions of justice, morality, honesty; he repeats these sententiously, but refrains from regulating his acts by them, although he insists that they be observed strictly by the people who come into contact with him. For example, if the merchant hands his customer goods that are damaged or adulterated, he still wishes to be paid in sterling money; if a manufacturer cheats the labourer on the measurement of his work, he will not submit to losing a minute of the day for which he pays him; if the bourgeois patriot (all bourgeois are patriots) seizes the fatherland of a weaker nation, his commercial dogma is still the integrity of his country, which according to Cecil Rhodes is a vast commercial establishment. Justice, morality, and other principles more or less eternal, are valuable for the bourgeois, but only if they serve his interests; they have a double face, an indulgent and smiling one turned toward himself, and a frowning and commanding face turned toward others.

The constant and general contradiction between people's acts and their notions of justice and morality, which might be thought of a nature to disturb the idea of a just God in the bourgeois mind, rather confirms it, and prepares the ground for that of the immortality of the soul, which had disappeared among nations that had reached the patriarchal period. This idea is preserved, strengthened and constantly revivified in the bourgeois by his habit of expecting a reward for everything he does or does not do.* He employs labourers, manufactures goods, buys, sells, lends money, renders any service, whatever it be, only in the hope of being rewarded, of reaping a benefit. The constant expectation of profit results in his performing no act for the pleasure in it, but to pocket a recompense; if he is generous, charitable, honourable, or even if he limits himself to not being dishonest, the satisfaction of his conscience is not enough for him; a reward is essential if he is to be satisfied and not feel that he has been duped by his good and candid feelings; if he does not receive his reward on earth, which is generally the case, he

---

* Theognis, like Job and other Old Testament authors, is embarrassed by the difficulty of reconciling the injustice of men with the justice of God. 'O son of Saturn,' says the Greek poet, 'how canst thou grant the same-lot to the just and to the unjust?... O king of the immortals, is it just that he who has committed no shameful act, who has not transgressed the law, who has sworn no false oaths, but who has always remained honourable, should suffer?... The unjust man, full of himself, who fears the wrath neither of men nor of gods, who commits deeds of injustice, is gorged with riches, while the just man shall be despoiled and shall be consumed by hard poverty.... What mortal is he that, seeing these things, shall fear the gods?' The Psalmist says: 'Behold, these are the ungodly, who prosper in the world; they increase in riches.... When I thought to know this, it was too painful for me.... I was envious of the foolish (those who fear not the Eternal) when I saw the prosperity of the wicked.' (Psalm LXXIII.) Theognis and the Jews of the Old Testament, not believing in the existence of the soul after death, think that it is on earth that the wicked is punished, 'for higher is the wisdom of the gods,' says the Greek moralist. 'But that vexes the spirit of men, since it is not when the act is committed that the immortals wreak vengeance for the fault. One pays his debt in his own person, another condemns his children to misfortune.' Men are punished for Adam's sin, according to Christianity.

counts on getting it in heaven. Not only does he expect a reward
for his good acts, and his abstention from bad acts, but he hopes
to receive compensation for his misfortunes, his failures, his
vexations and even his annoyances. His ego is so aggressive that
to satisfy it he annexes heaven to earth. The wrongs in civilization
are so numerous and so crying, and those of which he is the
victim assume in his eyes such boundless proportions, that his
sense of eternal justice cannot conceive but that some day they
shall be redressed; and it is only in another world that this day can
shine; only in heaven is he assured of receiving the reward for his
misfortunes. Life after death becomes for him a certainty, for his
good God, just and adorned with all bourgeois virtues, cannot but
grant him rewards for what he has done and has not done, and
amends for what he has suffered; in the business tribunal of
heaven, the accounts not adjusted on earth will be audited.

The bourgeois does not give the name of injustice to his
monopolizing of the wealth created by wage-workers; for him this
robbery is justice itself, and he cannot conceive how any
imaginable God could have a different opinion on the subject.
Nevertheless, he regards it as no violation of eternal justice to
allow the labourers to cherish the desire to improve their
conditions of life and of labour; but as he is keenly aware that
these improvements would have to be made at his expense, he
thinks it good policy to promise them a future life, where they
shall feast like bourgeois. The promise of posthumous happiness
is for him the most economical way to satisfy the labourers'
demands. Life beyond the grave, at first a pleasure of hope for the
satisfaction of his ego, becomes an instrument of exploitation.

Once it is settled that in heaven the accounts of earth are to be
definitely settled, God necessarily becomes a judge having at his
disposal an Eldorado for some and a prison for others, as is laid
down by Christianity, following Plato.* The celestial judge
renders his decrees according to the judicial code of civilization,

---

* Socrates, in the tenth and last book of the Republic, cites as worthy of belief
the story of an Armenian who, left for dead ten days on the battle-field, came to
life again, like Jesus, and related that he had seen in the other world 'souls
punished ten times for each unjust act committed on earth.' They were tortured by
'hideous men, who appeared all on fire.... They flayed the criminals, dragged
them over thorns, etc.' The Christians, who drew part of their moral ideas from
the Platonic sophistry, had but to complete and improve Socrates' story to
establish their hell, adorned with such frightful horrors.

enriched by a few moral laws which cannot figure in it, owing to the impossibility of establishing the offence and finding the proof.

The modern bourgeois occupies himself mainly with the rewards and compensations beyond the tomb; he takes but a moderate interest in the punishment of the wicked, that is to say, the people who have injured him personally. The Christian hell disturbs him little; first, because he is convinced that he has done nothing and can do nothing to deserve it, and second, because his resentment against his fellows who have sinned against him is but short-lived. He is always disposed to renew his relations of business or pleasure with them if he sees any advantage in it; he even has a certain esteem for those who have duped him, since after all they have done to him only what he has done or would have liked to do to them. Every day in bourgeois society we see persons whose pilferings had made a scandal, and who might have been thought forever lost, return to the surface and achieve an honourable position; nothing but money was demanded of them as a condition for resuming business and making honourable profits.*

Hell could only have been invented by men and for men tortured by the hate and the passion of vengeance. The God of the first Christians is a pitiless executioner, who takes a savoury pleasure in feasting his eyes on the tortures inflicted for all eternity on the infidels, his enemies. 'The Lord Jesus,' says St. Paul, 'shall ascend into heaven with the angels of his power, with burning flames of fire, working vengeance against those who know not God and who obey not the Gospel; they shall be punished with an everlasting punishment before the face of God and before the glory of his power.' — II. Thess. i, 6-9. The Christian of those days expected with an equally fervent faith for the reward of his piety and the punishment of his enemies, who became the enemies of God. The bourgeois, no longer cherishing these fierce hates (hate brings no profits), no longer needs a hell to assuage his vengeance, nor an executioner-God to chastise his associates who have clashed with him.

---

* Emile Pereire, the day after the scandalous crash of the Credit Mobilier, of which he was the founder and manager, meeting on the boulevards a friend who made as though he would not recognize him, went straight to him and said loudly: 'You can salute me, I have several millions yet.' The challenge, interpreting so well the bourgeois feeling, received due comment and appreciation. Pereire died an hundred times a millionaire, honoured and regretted.

The belief of the bourgeoisie in God and in the immortality of the soul is one of the ideological phenomena of its social environment; it will never lose it till it is dispossessed of its wealth stolen from wage-workers, and transformed from a parasitic class into a productive class.

The bourgeoisie of the eighteenth century, which struggled in France to grasp the social dictatorship, attacked furiously the Catholic clergy and Christianity, because they were props of the aristocracy; if in the ardour of battle some of its chiefs, Diderot, La Mettrie, Helvetius, d'Holbach, pushed their irreligion to the point of atheism, others, quite as representative of its spirit, if not more so, Voltaire, Rousseau, Turgot, never arrived at the negation of God. The materialist and sensualist philosophers, Cabanis, Maine de Biran, de Gerando, who survived the Revolution, publicly retracted their infidel doctrines. We must not waste our time in accusing these remarkable men of having betrayed the philosophical opinions which, at the opening of their career, had assured them fame and livelihood; the bourgeoisie alone is guilty. Victorious, it lost its irreligious combativeness, and like the dog in the Bible, it returned to its vomit. These philosophers underwent the influence of the social environment: being bourgeois, they evolved with their class.

This social environment, from the workings of which not even the most learned nor the most emancipated of the bourgeois can free themselves, is responsible for the deism of men of genius, like Cuvier, Geoffroy Saint-Hilaire, Faraday, Darwin, and for the agnosticism and positivism of contemporary scientists, who, not daring to deny God, abstain from concerning themselves with him. But this very act is an implicit recognition of the existence of God, whom they need in order to understand the social world, which seems to them the plaything of chance, rather than ruled by the law of necessity, like the natural world.

M. Brunetière, thinking to dart an epigram at the free-thought of his class, quotes the phrase of the German Jesuit Gruber, that 'the Unknowable is an idea of God appropriate to Freemasonry.' The Unknowable cannot be any one's idea of God; but it is its generating cause, in savages and barbarians as well as in Christian bourgeois or Freemasons. If the unknown elements of the natural environment made necessary for the savage and barbarian the idea of a God, creator and ruler of the world, the unknown elements of the social environment make necessary for the bourgeois the idea of a God who shall distribute the wealth stolen from the manual and intellectual wage-workers, dispense blessings and curses, reward good deeds, avenge injuries and repair wrongs. The savage and the bourgeois are drawn unsuspectingly into the belief in God, just as they are carried along by the rotation of the earth.

IV

EVOLUTION OF THE IDEA OF GOD

The idea of God, planted and germinated in the human brain by the unknown elements of the natural environment and the social environment, is not something invariable, it varies on the contrary according to time and place; it evolves in proportion as the mode of production develops, transforming the social environment.

God, for the Greeks, the Romans and other ancient peoples, had his dwelling in a given spot, and existed only to be useful to his adorers and hurtful to their enemies; each family had its private gods, the spirits of deified ancestors, and each city had its municipal or state god. The municipal god or goddess dwelt in the temple consecrated to him or her and was incorporated into the image which often was a block of wood or a stone; he or she was interested in the fate of the inhabitants of the city, of these alone. The ancestral gods concerned themselves only with family affairs. The Jehovah of the Bible was a god of this kind; he lodged in a wooden box, called Ark of the Covenant, which was carried along when the tribes changed their location; they put it at the head of the army, that Jehovah might fight for his people; if he chastised them cruelly for their infractions of his law, he also rendered them many services, as the Old Testament reports. When the municipal god was not in the best of circumstances, they associated another divinity with him; the Romans, during the second Punic war, brought over from Pessinonte the statue of Cybele, that the goddess from Asia Minor might aid them in their defence against Hannibal. The Christians had no other idea of divinity when they demolished the temples and broke the statues of the gods in order to oust them and keep them from protecting the pagans.

The savages thought that the soul was the replica of the body, so their defied spirits, though incorporated into stones, blocks of wood or beasts, preserved the human form. Similarly for St. Paul and the apostles, God was anthropomorphic, they made of him a Man-God, like to themselves both in body and mind; while the modern capitalist conceives him as without head or arms, and present in all the nooks and corners of the earth, instead of being quartered in one certain locality.

The Greeks and Romans, like the Jews and the first Christians, had no thought of their god being the only god of creation; the Jews believed in Moloch, Baal and other gods of the nations with which they warred as firmly as in Jehovah, and the Christians of the first centuries and of the Middle Ages, while they called Jupiter and Allah false gods, still took them for gods, who, could work wonders quite as well as Jesus and his Eternal Father.* This belief in a multiplicity of gods made it possible for each city to have a god attached to its service, shut up in a temple and incorporated into a statue or some such object; Jehovah was in a stone. The modern capitalist who thinks that his God is present in all places of the earth cannot but arrive at the notion of one sole God: and the ubiquity which he attributes to his God prevents his representing him with face and buttocks, arms and legs, like Homer's Zeus and St. Paul's Jesus.

The municipal divinities, which belonged to the warlike cities of antiquity, always at strife with neighbouring peoples, could not answer to the religious needs which mercantile production created in the bourgeois democracies of the commercial and industrial cities, obliged on the contrary to maintain pacific relations with surrounding nations. The necessities of commerce and industry forced the new-born bourgeoisie to demunicipalize the city divinities and create cosmopolitan gods. Six or seven centuries before the Christian era we observe in the maritime cities of Ionia, Magna Grecia and Greece attempts to organize religions whose gods should not be exclusively monopolized by one city, but should be recognized and worshipped by different nations, even hostile ones. These new divinities, Isis, Demeter,

---

* Tertullian in his *Apologetics* and St. Augustin in his *City of God* relate as undeniable facts that Esculapius had raised several persons, mentioned by name, from the dead, that a Vestal had carried water from the Tiber in a sieve, that another Vestal had towed a ship with her girdle, etc.

Dionysos, Mithra, Jesus, etc., several of whom belonged to the matriarchal epoch, still took on the human form, though the need was beginning to be felt of a Supreme Being which should not be anthropomorphic; but it is not until the capitalist epoch that the idea of an amorphous god has imposed itself, as a consequence of the impersonal form taken on by the property of corporations.

Impersonal property, which introduced a mode of possession absolutely new and diametrically opposed to that which had previously existed, was necessarily destined to modify the habits and customs of the bourgeois and consequently transform his mentality. Until its appearance, the possibilities of ownership were limited to a vineyard in the Bordelais, a weaving establishment at Rouen, a forge at Marseilles or a grocery in Paris. Each of these properties, distinct in the character of the industry and in its geographical situation, was possessed by one single individual, or by two or three at the most; it was a rare thing for one individual to possess several of them. It is otherwise with impersonal property: a railroad, a mine, a bank, etc., are possessed by hundreds and thousands of capitalists, while one and the same capitalist may have side by side in his portfolio bonds of France, Prussia, Turkey and Japan, with stocks of gold mines in the Transvaal, electric railways in China, a line of transatlantic steamers, a coffee plantation in Brazil, a coal mine in France, etc. No such ties of affection can link the capitalist to the impersonal property he possesses as bind the bourgeois to the property that he administers, or that is operated under his control; his interest in it is proportioned only to the price paid for the stock and the rate of dividend it bears. It is a matter of absolute indifference to him whether the dividend be declared by a scavenger enterprise, a sugar refinery or a cotton-spinning mill, and whether the production be carried on at Paris or at Pekin. Once the dividend becomes all-important, the distinguishing characteristics of the properties producing it disappear, and these properties in different industries, differently situated, are for the capitalist one sole dividend-bearing property, whose certificates, circulating on the stock exchange, continue to keep various names of trades and of countries.

Impersonal property, embracing all trades and extending all over the globe, unrolls its tentacles armed with suckers greedy for dividends, in a Christian nation just as it does in realms of

Mohammedanism, Buddhism or fetishism. The accumulation of wealth is the absorbing and mastering passion of the capitalist, and so this identification of properties of different sorts and countries in one sole and cosmopolitan property was bound to reflect itself in his intelligence and to influence his conception of God.* Impersonal property without any doubt leads him to amalgamate the gods of the earth into one sole and cosmopolitan God, who according to the various countries bears the name of Jesus, Allah or Buddha, and is worshipped according to different rites.

It is a matter of historical fact that the idea of one sole and universal God, which Anaxagoras was one of the first to conceive, and which through the centuries lived only in the brains of a few thinkers, did not become a current idea until capitalist civilization appeared. But as by the side of this impersonal, sole and cosmopolitan property there still exist countless personal and local properties, so certain local and anthropomorphic gods touch elbows in the capitalist's brain with the one and cosmopolitan God. The division into nations, which are commercial and industrial rivals, compels the bourgeoisie to parcel out its one God into as many gods as there are nations; thus every nation of Christendom thinks that the Christian God, who is all the while the God of all the Christians, is its national god, like Jehovah of the Jews and Pallas-Athene of the Athenians. When two Christian nations declare war, each prays its national and Christian God to fight on its side, and if it is victorious, it sings *Te Deums* to thank him for having beaten the rival nation and its national and Christian God. The pagans made different gods fight among themselves, the Christians make their one God fight with himself. The one and cosmopolitan God could not completely dethrone the national gods in the bourgeois brain unless all the bourgeois nations were centralized into one single nation.

Impersonal property possesses other qualities, which it has transmitted to its one and cosmopolitan God. The proprietor of a wheat field, a carpenter's shop or a haberdashery can see, touch, measure, and appraise his property, the clear and precise form of which strikes his senses. But the owner of government bonds and of shares in a railroad, a coal mine, an insurance company or a

---

* 'Wealth engenders not saiety,' says Theognis, 'the man who has the most strives ever to double it.'

bank cannot see, touch, measure, appraise the parcel of property
represented by his bonds and stocks, in whatever forest or
government building, in whatever wagon, ton of coal, insurance
policy or bank safe he might suppose it to be found. His fragment
of property is lost, buried in a vast whole that he cannot even
picture to himself; for if he has seen locomotives and stations, as
well as subterranean galleries, he has never seen a railroad nor a
mine in its entirety; and a national debt, a bank and an insurance
company are not capable of being represented by any image
whatever. The impersonal property of which he is one of the
co-proprietors cannot assume in his imagination other than a
vague, uncertain, indeterminate form; it is for him rather a
rational being, which reveals its existence by dividends, than a
tangible reality. Nevertheless this impersonal property, though
indefinite as a metaphysical conception, provides for all his
needs, like the Heavenly Father of the Christians, without
requiring from him any more labour of body and brain than to
take in his dividends: he receives them in blessed laziness of body
and soul as a Grace of Capital, of which the Grace of God, 'the
truest of Christian doctrines,' as Renan says, is the religious
reflection. He troubles his brain as little to study the nature of the
impersonal property which gives him interest and dividends as he
does to know whether his one and cosmopolitan God is man,
woman or beast, intelligent or idiotic, and whether he possesses
the qualities of strength, ferocity, justice, kindness, etc., with
which the anthropomorphic gods had been endowed. He wastes
no time on prayers, because he is sure that no supplication will
modify the rate of interest or dividend on the impersonal property
of which his one and cosmopolitan God is the intellectual
reflection.

At the very time when impersonal property was transforming
the anthropomorphic God of the Christians into an amorphous
God and a rational being — into a metaphysical conception — it
was taking away from the religious feeling of the bourgeoisie the
virulence which had produced the fanatical fever of martyrs,
crusaders and inquisitors; it was transforming religion into a
matter of personal taste, like cookery, which each suits to his
fancy, with butter or with oil, with garlic or without. But if the
capitalist bourgeoisie needs a religion, and finds liberal
Christianity to its taste, it cannot accept without serious

amendments the Catholic Church, whose inquisitorial despotism descends to the details of private life, and whose organization of bishops, priests, monks and Jesuits, disciplined and obedient to wink and nod, is a menace to its public order. The Catholic Church was endurable for the feudal society, all of whose members, from serf to king, were graded in a hierarchy and bound to each other by the reciprocal rights and duties, but it cannot be tolerated by bourgeois democracy, whose members, equal before the law, but divided by their interests, wage perpetual industrial and commercial war among themselves, and always claim the right to criticize the constituted authorities, and hold them responsible for their economic mischances.

The capitalist, who does not want any obstacle to his getting rich, found it equally impossible to tolerate the guild organization of master-workmen, which supervised the manner of producing and the quality of the product. He crushed it. Freed from all control, he now has but his own interest to consult in making his fortune, each according to the means at his disposal: on his elastic conscience alone depends the quality of the goods that he makes and sells; it is for the customer to see that he is not deceived with regard to the quality, weight and price of what he buys. Every one for himself, and God, in other words money, for all. The freedom of industry and commerce could not but reflect itself in his way of conceiving religion, which each one understands as he likes. Each makes his own arrangements with God, as with his conscience in a business matter; each according to his interests and his light interprets the teachings of the church and the words of the Bible, which is put into the hands of the Protestants, as the Code is put into the hands of all the capitalists.

The capitalist can be neither martyr nor inquisitor, because he has lost the furore of proselytism which inflamed the first Christians. They had a vital interest in increasing the number of believers, in order to swell the army of malcontents, giving battle to pagan society. Yet he has a sort of religious' proselytism, without breath and without conviction, which is conditioned by his exploitation of woman and of the wage-worker.

Woman must be pliable to his wishes. He wishes her faithful and unfaithful according to his desires. If she is the wife of a brother capitalist, and if he is courting her, he demands her infidelity as a duty toward his Ego, and he unfurls his rhetoric to relieve her of her religious scruples; if she is his lawful wife, she becomes his property, and must be inviolate; he requires from her a fidelity equal to every test, and employs religion to force conjugal duty toward him into her head.

The wage-worker ought to be resigned to his lot. The social function of exploiter of labour requires the capitalist to propagate the Christian religion, preaching humility and submission to God, who chooses the masters and sets off the servants, and to complete the teachings of Christianity by the eternal principles of democracy. It is quite to his interest that the wage-workers exhaust their brain power in controversies on the truths of religion and in discussions on Justice, Liberty, Ethics, Patriotism and other such booby-traps, in order that they may not have a minute left to reflect on their wretched condition and the means for improving it. The famous radical and free-trader, John Bright, appreciated this stultifying method so thoroughly, that he devoted his Sundays to reading and commenting on the Bible for his labourers. But the profession of Biblical brain-destroyer, which English capitalists of both sexes may undertake to kill time or as a whim, is of necessity irregular, like any amateur work. The capitalist class needs to have at its disposal professionals in brain destroying to fulfil this task. He finds them in the clergy of all cults. But every medal has its reverse side. The reading of the Bible by wage-workers presents dangers that one day some pious Rockefeller will recognize; and to meet this situation he will organize a company for the publication of popular Bibles expurgated of the plaints against the iniquities of the rich and of the cries of envious wrath against their scandalous good fortune. The Catholic Church, foreseeing these dangers, had provided against them, by forbidding the faithful to read the Bible, and by burning Wycliffe, the first to translate it into a vulgar tongue. The Catholic clergy, with its *novenas,* its pilgrimages, and its other mummeries, is of all clergies that which practices most wisely the art of brain-destruction, it is also the best equipped for furnishing ignorant brothers and sisters to teach in primary schools, and nuns to stand guard over women in factories. The great industrial capitalists, on account of its manifold services, sustain it politically and financially, in spite of their antipathy for its hierarchy, its rapacity, and its intrusion into family affairs.

V

CAUSES OF THE IRRELIGION OF THE PROLETARIAT

The numerous attempts made in Europe and America to Christianize the industrial proletariat have completely miscarried; they have not succeeded in moving it from its religious indifference, which becomes general in proportion as machine production enlists new recruits from the peasants, artisans and petty tradesmen into the army of wage-workers.

Machine production, which makes the capitalist religious, tends on the contrary to make the proletariat irreligious.

If it is logical for the capitalist to believe in a Providence attentive to his needs, and in a God who elects him among thousands of thousands, to load with riches his laziness and social inutility, it is still more logical for the proletarian to ignore the existence of a divine Providence, since he knows that no Heavenly Father would give him daily bread if he prayed from morning to evening, and that the wage which produces for him the bare necessities of life is earned by his own labour; and he knows only too well that if he did not work he would starve, in spite of all the Good Gods of heaven and all the philanthropists of earth. The wage-worker is his own providence. His conditions of life make any other providence inconceivable for him; he has not in his life, as the capitalist in his, those strokes of fortune which might by magic lift him out of his sad situation. Wage-worker he is born, wage-worker he lives, wage-worker he dies. His ambition cannot go beyond a raise in wages and a job that shall last all the days of the year and all the years of his life. The unforeseen hazards and chances of fortune which predispose the capitalist to superstitious ideas do not exist for the proletarian, and the idea of God cannot appear in the human brain unless its coming is prepared for by certain superstitious ideas, no matter what their source.

If the wage-worker were to let himself be drawn into a belief in that God, whom he hears talked of without paying attention, he would begin by questioning his justice, which allotted to him nothing but work and poverty; he would make the God an object of horror and of hate, and would picture him under the form and aspect of a capitalist exploiter, like the black slaves of the colonies, who said that God was white, like their masters.

Of course the wage-worker has no more idea of the course of economic phenomena than the capitalist and his economists, nor does he understand why, as regularly as night succeeds day, the periods of industrial prosperity and work at high pressure are followed by crises and lock-outs. This failure to understand, which predisposes the mind of the capitalist to belief in God, has not the same effect on that of the wage-worker, because they occupy different positions in modern production. The possession of the means of production gives the capitalist the absolute and arbitrary direction of the production and distribution of products, and obliges him, consequently, to concern himself with the causes which govern them: the wage-worker, on the contrary, has no right to trouble himself with them. He has no part in the direction of the productive process, nor in the choice and the procuring of the raw materials, nor in the manner of producing, nor in the sale of the product; he has but to furnish labour like a beast of burden. The passive obedience of the Jesuits, which arouses the wordy indignation of the free-thinkers, is the law in the army and the workshop. The capitalist plants the wage-worker in front of the moving machine, loaded with raw materials, and orders him to work; he becomes a cog of the machine. He has in production but one aim, the wage, the sole interest which capitalism has been forced to leave him; when he has drawn this, he has nothing more to claim. The wage being the sole interest that it has permitted him to keep in production, he therefore has to concern himself simply with having work so as to receive wages; and as the employer or his representatives are the givers of work, it is they, men of flesh and blood like himself, that he blames, if he has or has not work, and not economic phenomena, which he may be entirely ignorant of; it is against these men that he is irritated on account of the reductions of wage and slackness of work, and not against the general perturbations of production. He holds them responsible for all that comes to him, good or evil. The wage-worker personalizes the accidents of production which affect him, while the possession of the means of production is depersonalized in proportion as they take the form of machinery.

The life led by the labourer in the great industries has removed him even more than the capitalist from the influences of the environment of nature which in the peasant keep up the belief in ghosts, in sorceries, in witchcraft and other superstitious ideas.

He sees the sun only through the factory windows; he knows nature only from the country surrounding the city where he works, and that he sees only on rare occasions; he could not distinguish a field of wheat from a field of oats nor a potato plant from hemp; he knows the products of the earth only in the form under which he consumes them. He is completely ignorant of the work of the fields and the causes affecting the yield of the harvests; drought, excessive rains, hail, cyclones, etc., never make him think of their action on nature and her harvests. His urban life shelters him from the anxieties and the troublesome cares which assail the mind of the farmer. Nature has no hold upon his imagination.

The labour of the mechanical factory puts the wage-worker in touch with terrible natural forces unknown to the peasant, but instead of being mastered by them, he controls them. The gigantic mechanism of iron and steel which fills the factory, which makes him move like an automaton, which sometimes clutches him, mutilates him, bruises him, does not engender in him a superstitious terror as the thunder does in the peasant, but leaves him unmoved, for he knows that the limbs of the mechanical monster were fashioned and mounted by his comrades, and that he has but to push a lever to set it in motion or stop it. The machine, in spite of its miraculous power and productiveness, has no mystery for him. The labourer in the electric works, who has but to turn a crank on a dial to send miles of motive power to tramways or light to the lamps of a city, has but to say, like the God of Genesis, 'Let there be light', and there is light. Never sorcery more fantastic was imagined, yet for him this sorcery is a simple and natural thing. He would be greatly surprised if one were to come and tell him that a certain God might if he chose stop the machines and extinguish the lights when the electricity had been turned on; he would reply that this anarchistic God would be simply a misplaced gearing or a broken wire, and that it would be easy for him to seek and to find this disturbing God. The practice of the modern workshop teaches the wage-worker scientific determinism, without his needing to pass through the theoretical study of the sciences.

Since the capitalist and the proletarian no longer live in the fields, natural phenomena can no longer produce in them the superstitious ideas, which were utilized by the savage in elaborating his idea of God; but if the former, since he belongs to the ruling and parasitic class, undergoes the action of the social phenomena which generate superstitious ideas, the other, since he belongs to the exploited and productive class, is removed from their superstition-breeding action. The capitalist class can never be de-christianized and delivered from belief in God until it shall be expropriated from its class dictatorship and from the wealth that it plunders daily from the wage-working labourers.

The free and impartial study of nature has engendered and firmly established in certain scientific circles the conviction that all phenomena are subject to the law of necessity, and that their determining causes must be sought within nature and not without. The study has, moreover, made possible the subjection of natural forces to the use of man.

But the industrial use of natural forces has transformed the means of production into economic organisms so gigantic that they escape the control of the capitalists who monopolize them, as is proved by the periodic crises of industry and commerce. These organisms of production, though of human creation, disturb the social environment, when crises break out, as blindly as the natural forces trouble nature when once unchained. The modern means of production can no longer be controlled except by society, and for that control to be established, they must first become social property; then only will they cease to engender social inequalities, to give wealth to the parasites and inflict miseries on the wage-working producers, and create world-wide perturbations which the capitalist and his economists can attribute only to chance and to unknown causes. When they shall be possessed and controlled by society, there will no longer be an Unknowable in the social order; then and only then, will belief in God be definitely eliminated from the human mind.

The indifference in religious matters of our modern labourers, the determining causes of which I have been tracing, is a new phenomenon, now produced for the first time in history: the popular masses have, till now, always elaborated the spiritual ideas, which the philosophers have merely had to refine and to obscure, as well as the legends and the religious ideas, which the priests and the ruling classes have merely organized into official religions and instruments of intellectual oppression.

2

The origin of abstract ideas

I

CONTRADICTORY OPINIONS REGARDING THE ORIGIN OF ABSTRACT IDEAS

IT often happens in the history of thought that hypotheses and theories, after having been the object of study and discussion, disappear from the field of intellectual activity to reappear only after a season of oblivion more or less prolonged. Then they are examined anew in the light of the knowledge accumulated during the interval, and sometimes they end by being included in the baggage of acquired truths.

The theory of the continuity of species — unconsciously admitted by the savage, who takes for his ancestors plants and animals endowed with human qualities, scientifically foreseen by the thinkers of antiquity and the Renaissance, brilliantly defined by the naturalists at the close of the eighteenth century — had sunk into so deep an oblivion after the memorable debate between Geoffroy Saint-Hilaire and Cuvier that its conception was attributed to Darwin when he revived it in 1859 in his *Origin of Species*. The proofs, which in 1831 had been lacking for Geoffroy Saint-Hilaire to bring victory for his thesis, *Unity of Plan*, had been accumulated in·such abundance that Darwin and his disciples had been able to complete the theory and impose it on the scientific world.

The materialistic theory of the origin of abstract ideas had a similar experience: put forth and discussed by the thinkers of Greece, taken up in England by the philosophers of the seventeenth century, and in France by those of the eighteenth century — it has since the triumph of the bourgeoisie been eliminated from philosophical preoccupations.

Alongside of the ideas which correspond to things and persons, there exist others which have no tangible counterpart in the objective world, such as the ideas of the Just, the True, the Good, the Evil; of Number, Cause and Infinity. If we are ignorant of the cerebral phenomenon which transforms the sensation into an idea — just as we do not know how a dynamo transforms motion into electricity — we have no trouble in taking account of the origin of the ideas which are the conceptions of objects apprehended by the senses; while the origin of the abstract ideas which do not correspond to any objective reality, has been the object of studies which have not yet given definite results.

The Greek philosophers, whom we meet at the entrance of all the avenues of thought, have stated and tried to solve the problem of abstract ideas. Zeno (the founder of the Stoic School) looked upon the senses as the source of knowledge, but the sensation became a conception only after having undergone a series of intellectual transformations.

The savages and barbarians, who were the creators of the Latin and Greek languages, anticipating the philosophers, seemed to have believed that thoughts proceeded from sensations, since in Greek *eidos*, the physical appearance of the object, that which strikes the view, signifies 'idea'; and in Latin *sapientia*, the taste of an object, that which strikes the palate, becomes 'reason'.*

---

* The Greeks seemed to have attached more importance as the sense of sight and the Latins to the sense of taste, as is proved by the following examples:

Greek   *eidos:* aspect, physical form.
        eidolon: image, shade, phantom, idea.
        phantasia: aspect, exterior form, image, idea.
        gnoma: sign, thought.
        gnomon: square, sun-dial, one who knows, scientist.
        noeo: to see, to think.
        saphes: plain, manifest, striking the vision.
        sophia: science, wisdom.

Latin   *sapor:* savour, taste in judging food, reason.
        sapidus: savoury, pleasant to the taste, wise, virtuous.
        sapiens: one with a delicate palate, wise.
        sapio: to have taste, to have reason, to know.

This difference, regarding the sense-sources of ideas, characterize these two nations which played so great a historic role; the one in the evolution of thought and in its poetic and plastic manifestation, and the other in the elaboration of law, in the brutal manipulation of men and nations, and in the unified organization of

Plato, on the contrary, thought that the ideas of the Good, the True, the Beautiful, were innate, unchangeable, universal. 'The soul in its journey in the track of God, disdaining what we improperly call beings, and raising its glances toward the one true Being had contemplated It and remembered what it had seen.' (Phaedrus). Socrates had also placed apart from humanity a Natural Right whose laws, nowhere written, are nevertheless respected by all the world, although men may have never assembled together to enact them by a common agreement.*

Aristotle does not seem to have so robust a faith in Natural Right, which he jests at pleasantly when he assures us that it was inviolable only for the gods, however, the immortals of Olympus were quite at their ease with this Natural Right, and their doings and practices were so grossly shocking to the morals current among mortals, that Pythagoras condemned to the torments of hell the souls of Homer and Hesiod for having ventured to relate them.

Right, Aristotle said, was not universal. According to him it could only exist between equal persons. The father of a family,

---

the ancient world. The very young child and the savage carry to the mouth the object they wish to know; the chemists do the same. The French word *savoir*, to know, and its derivative *savant*, scientist, combine the two meanings. *Voir* indicates the function of the eye; and *sa* the last trace of the verb *sapio*, indicates the function of the palate.

* One of the unwritten laws of Socrates was the universal agreement to forbid sexual relations between the father or mother and their children. Xenophon, who had travelled in Persia and who was not ignorant that the magi practised this incest to honour the divinity and beget the high priests, claimed it was contrary to natural and divine law because the children who were the issue of such matings are puny. He reduced the law from the natural right of his master, Socrates, into nothing more than a physiological law acquired by experience.

Socrates would seem to have forgotten that Hesiod, following the religious legends of his epoch, gives to Uranus for wife his own mother, Gaia, the most ancient goddess, 'the mother of all things', according to Homer; in the religions of India, Scandinavia and Egypt we meet with cases of divine incest. Brahma marries his daughter Saravasty; Odir his daughter Frigga, and Amon in the 'Anastasy Papyrus' in Berlin boasts of being the husband of his mother. These myths, which may be found in all primitive religions. have a historical value: the legends and religious ceremonies preserve the memory of epochs long buried in oblivion. The bible story of the sacrifice of Abraham and the Christian communion — that symbolic repast in which the devout Catholic eats his incarnate God — are the distant echoes of the human sacrifices and the cannibal feasts of the prehistoric Semites.

Man to create his religious legends employs the same process as to elaborate his ideas, he uses as materials events of his daily life; in the course of the centuries, the phenomena which gave birth to them are transformed and vanish, but the

THE ORIGIN OF ABSTRACT IDEAS

for example, could not commit an injustice toward his wife, his children or his slaves, nor toward any person in dependence on him. He could strike them, sell them and kill them without thereby departing from the Right. Aristotle, as is usually done adapted his Right to the manners of his epoch; as he did not conceive of the transformation of the patriarchal family, he found himself obliged to erect its customs into principles of Right. But instead of according to Right a universal and immutable character, he conceded to it only a relative value and limited its action to persons placed on an equal footing.

But, how is it that his teacher Plato, whose mind was so subtle, who had under his eyes the same customs and who had no idea of their abolition, since in his ideal republic he introduced slavery — had not the same opinions regarding the relativity of Justice? A word dropped by Aristotle gives room for the theory that Plato, like the priests of the Sacred Mysteries and a majority of the sophists, had not explained in his writings the whole of his philosophy, but had revealed it only to a small number of trusted disciples. He might have been intimidated by the condemnation of Socrates and the dangers incurred at Athens by Anaxogaras, who had imported thither from Ionia the Philosophy of Nature, and who escaped death only in flight.

This opinion is confirmed by an attentive and comparative reading of the dialogues of Plato, who, as Goethe remarks, often makes game of his readers. In any event, the teacher of Socrates and several of the disciples of the latter had but a slender idea of

---

legendary or ceremonial form, which was their intellectual manifestation, survives; we need only interpret this intelligently to call up the customs of a past which was thought to be lost forever.

The incests practised by the Persian priests, and the religious legends of peoples of such different races would therefore lead us to suppose that at a remote epoch sexual relations between parents and children were a customary thing. On this point Engels remarks that the savage tribes which first arrived at the point of forbidding them, must by this sole fact have acquired an advantage over their rivals, and must consequently either have destroyed them or imposed their customs upon them. It is thus more than probable, that the prohibition of these incestuous marriages, the most universal custom that is known — so universal that Socrates thought it one of the laws of his Natural Right — has not always prevailed, and that on the contrary those sexual relations were naturally practised in the human species emerging from the animal. But experience having demonstrated their bad effects brought about their prohibition, — as Xenophon thought. Breeders have also been obliged to prevent them among the domestic animals in order to get good results.

the immutability of Justice. Archelaus, who merited the surname of 'Naturalist' (Phusikos), and who was the teacher of Socrates, denied Natural Right and maintained that civil laws were the only foundation for the notions of the Just and the Unjust. Aristippus, who, like Plato, was the disciple of Socrates, declared his profound contempt for Natural and Social Right, and professed that the wise man ought to put himself above civil laws and permit himself to do all they forbid when he could do so in safety: the action which they forbid being bad only in the vulgar opinion, invented to keep fools in check.* Plato, without having the boldness to put forth such doctrines, showed by his acknowledged respect for homosexuality, the little importance he attached to the laws of Natural Right. This love against nature, forbidden to slaves, was the privilege of free citizens and virtuous men; in the *Republic* (Book 5) Socrates makes of this one of the rewards for warlike courage.

The quarrel over the origin of ideas was rekindled in the seventeenth and eighteenth centuries in England and France when the bourgeoisie was setting itself in motion and preparing to grasp in the dictatorship of society. There are no innate ideas, declared Diderot and the Encyclopaedists. Man comes into the world as a blank tablet on which the objects of nature engrave their impressions as time passes. The Sensationalist school of Condillac formulated its famous axiom, 'Nothing exists in the understanding which has not originally been in the senses.' Buffon advised the gathering of facts in order to procure ideas, which are nothing but compared sensations, or more accurately, associations of sensations.

Descartes, reviving the method of introspection, and the 'Know Thyself' of Socrates, and bringing again into use the Chinese puzzle of the Alexandrian School, 'Given the Self, to find God,' isolated himself in his ego in order to know the universe, and dated from his ego the beginning of philosophy, for which he

---

* The anarchical opinions of Aristippus and the Cyrenaic School have been reproduced at various times in the course of history. Christian sects during the first centuries and during the middle ages; and political sects during the English Revolution of the seventeenth century and the French Revolution of the eighteenth century have revived them and in our days certain anarchistic sects propagate them. The lack of social equilibrium translates itself in the brain by this cynical rejection of the notions of current and conventional ethics. I shall return to this interesting subject in the study devoted to the crisis of Greek philosophy.

is reproached by Vico. As in his ego purified from beliefs that have been taught, or, so to speak, from the prejudices conceived from infancy by the senses as well as from all truths taught by the sciences, Descartes found the ideas of Substance, of Cause, etc.; he supposed them to be inherent in the intelligence and not acquired by experience. They were, according to Kant's expression, universal and necessary ideas, rational concepts whose objects cannot be furnished by experience, but existing incontestably in our mind; whether we know it or not, we hold at every moment certain necessary and universal judgments; in the simplest propositions are contained the principles of Substance, Cause and Being.

Leibnitz replied to those who with Locke, affirmed that ideas were introduced by way of the senses, that in fact nothing existed in the understanding which had not originally been in the senses, except the understanding itself. Man, according to him, brought with him at birth certain ideas and conceptions concealed in his understanding which the encountering of exterior objects brought to light. The intelligence is pre-formed before individual experience begins. He compared the ideas and conceptions anterior to experience to the different coloured veins which streak a block of marble, and which the skilful sculptor uses to adorn the statues he chisels from it.

Hobbes, who, before Locke, had said in his treatise on *Human Nature*, that there were no ideas which had not previously existed in sensation, and that the sensations are the origins of ideas — reproducing the thesis of Archelaus — maintained in his *De Cive*, that we must turn to the civil laws to know what was just and what was unjust. 'They indicate to us what must be called theft, murder, adultery or injury to a citizen; for it is not a theft simply to take away from some one that which he possesses, but that which belongs to him; now it is for the law to determine what is ours and what is another's. Likewise, not every homicide is murder but rather when one kills one whom the civil law forbids putting to death; nor is it adultery to lie with a woman, but only to have to do with a woman whom the law forbids approaching.'*

* *De Cive*, Sorbière's translation, Amsterdam, 1649. Hobbes in the *Leviathan* takes up the same thesis, which he thought it best to entrust only to the Latin in *De Cive.* The desires and passions of man,' he said, 'are not sins in themselves any more than the actions which result from these passions are faults, until a law forbids them.'

The patricians of Rome and Athens committed no adultery in having connection with the wives of artisans, *in quas stuprum non committitur*, 'against whom a crime is not commited', said the brutal legal formula. They were consecrated to the aristocratic debauch. In our days the husband who in England should kill his wife, taken in the act of adultery, would be summarily hanged as a vulgar assassin; while in France, far from being punished he becomes a hero, who has avenged his honour. The course of a river suffices to transform a crime into a virtuous act, so said, before Pascal, the sceptic Montaigne. (Book 2, Chapter 13.)

Locke maintained that ideas came from two sources, sensation and reflection. Condillac apparently deprived the English philosopher's doctrine of one of its sources, reflection, leaving only sensation — which was transformed into attention, comparison, judgment, reason, and finally into desire and will.

His ex-disciple, Maine de Biran, casting sensation to the winds and restoring to honour the method of Descartes, who drew everything from his ego as from a well, found in the understanding the point of departure of his ideas.* The concepts

---

* The intellectual evolution of M. de Biran is most interesting. It permits us to observe in the most remarkable French philosopher of the beginning of the nineteenth century the sudden and extraordinary veering of bourgeois thought, from the time when from being a revolutionary class, the bourgeoisie became a ruling and conservative class. Biran in the manuscript of 1794, published after his death in 1824, declares that Bacon and Locke founded philosophical science and that Condillac 'assigned its limits and dissipated forever those dreams which are termed "Metaphysics".'

The National Institute, in which the sensationalism of Condillac was dominant, crowned in the month of Nivose of the year IX (1801), a study of Biran on the *Influence of Custom Over the Faculty of Thought,* which he had put up for competition. Biran there laid down as an axiom that the faculty of perception is the origin of all the faculties, and proposed to apply Bacon's method of the study of man and to throw light on metaphysics by transporting physics into it. De Gerando, who also found it necessary to abjure Condillac and his philosophy, in his monograph on the *Influence of Signs on the Faculty of Thought,* crowned by the Institute in 1800, affirmed that the doctrine of Condillac was, as it were, the last word of human reason on the doctrines which interested it the most.

The Institute crowned in 1805 a new monograph by Biran on the *Decomposition of Thought.* The political stage was transformed: the victorious bourgeoisie was occupied in re-introducing and mustering into its service the Catholic religion, which it had ridiculed, despoiled and trampled under its feet when it was the maid-of-all work of the aristocracy, its rival. While the men of politics were reorganizing the power, taking up and reinforcing the repressive forces of the ancient regime, the philosophers were taking up the task of clearing away the intellectual foundation of the 'analytic and inconoclastic' philosophy of the Encyclopaedists. The Institute in

of 'Cause and Substance', he said, 'are antecedent in our mind to the two principles which contain them. We first think these ideas within ourselves, in our knowledge of the Cause and the Substance that we are; once these ideas are acquired, induction

---

crowning this monograph of Biran and he himself in writing it, were conscientiously fulfilling the task imposed by the new social conditions. Biran's monograph points out that there is somewhat of an illusion in the pretended analysis of Condillac and in that sensation which transforms itself into judgment and will without one's having taken the trouble to assign to it a principle of transformation, he makes the method of Bacon — unseasonably applied to the study of the mind — responsible for the aberrations of the eighteenth century philosophy, and takes his stand against any assimilation between the physical phenomena perceived by the senses and internal facts. The Sophists had succeeded to the Philosophers.

Cabanis himself, who was to die in 1808, still had time to make his change of front. In his celebrated work on the Relations of the Physical and the Ethical in Man, which appeared in 1802, he had written: 'Medicine and ethics rest upon one common basis; upon a physical knowledge of human nature. . . . The source of ethics is in the human organization. . . . If Condillac had understood animal economy he would have perceived that the soul is a faculty and not a being. We must consider the brain as a particular organ destined especially to produce thought, just as the stomach and intestines are destined to carry on digestion. Impressions are the food of the brain. . . . They get into the brain and set it at work. . . . They reach it isolated, without coherence, but the brain starts on its activity, acts upon them and soon sends them back metamorphosed into ideas. . . '. Cabanis, who had written these materialistic horrors, proclaimed — in his letter to Fauriel, on 'First Causes', published sixteen years after his deaht — the existence of God; the intelligence governing the world, and the immortality of the soul by the persistence of the ego after death. Fauriel had converted Cabanis, as Fontanes had metamorphosed Chataubriand from the atheistic follower of Rousseau, who wrote the *Essays on Revolutions* in 1797, into the reactionary and mystic Chataubriand who wrote the *Genius of Christianity* in 1802. There existed then a little clique of proselyters influential in the press and departments of government, who had undertaken to bring back the straying literary men and philosophers to sound doctrines.

It is useless to waste any accusations of recanting and treason against the men who had gone through the revolution and come out on the other side. These remarkable men would perhaps have preferred to keep the political and philosophic opinions which at their start in life had brought them to the front, but they were obliged to sacrifice them to retain their means of existence and the positions they had won and to conquer the favours of the bourgeoisie grown wise. They replaced these opinions by the politics and philosophy suitable to its material interests and satisfying its intellectual needs. Besides, they were bourgeois, following the influences of their social environment; they evolved with their class and they could make this change of skin without excessive pains. So it is not a case for moral indignation, but for investigation and analysis of the social causes which imposed upon them certain political changes of front and certain intellectual transformations. There are few moments in history where we can grasp better than in the first years of the nineteenth century, the direct action of social events upon thought. This epoch is all the more characteristic that it is then that almost all the economic, political, philosophical, religious literary and artistic theories were formulated which were thenceforth to form the bulk of the intellectual baggage of the new ruling class.

carries them outside of us and makes us conceive of causes and substances wherever there are phenomena and qualities.' The principle of Cause and of Substance reduces itself to nothing but a phenomenon or rather a fiction of our understanding, to use Hume's phrase. The introspective method of Descartes and Socrates, which the bourgeois spiritualists abused so liberally, leads on one side to scepticism and on the other to impotence, for, 'to pretend to illuminate the depths of psychological activity by means of the individual consciousness is like wishing to light the universe with a match,' says Maudsley.

The final victory of the bourgeoisie in England and in France impressed a complete revolution upon philosophic thought. The theories of Hobbes, Locke and Condillac, after having occupied the centre of the stage, were dethroned. People no longer deigned to discuss them and they were never mentioned unless truncated and falsified, to serve as examples of the wanderings into which the human spirit falls when it abandons the ways of God. The reaction went so far that under Charles X even the philosophy of the sophists of spiritualism fell under suspicion. An attempt was made to forbid their teaching in colleges.* The triumphant bourgeoisie re-established on the altar of its Reason the eternal truths and the most vulgar spiritualism. Justice, which the philosophers of Greece, England and France had reduced to reasonable proportions, which suited it to the conditions of the social environment in which it was manifested, became a necessary, immutable and universal principle. 'Justice', cried one of the most academic sophists of bourgeois philosophy, 'is invariable and always present, although it arrives only by degrees in human thought and in social facts. The limits of its field of action are ever extended and never narrowed; no human power can make it leave ground once acquired.

The Encyclopaedists threw themselves with revolutionary

---

* 'In these last years,' a professor of philosophy writes in 1828, 'authority has almost brought back the study of philosophy to the age of Scholasticism.... It has been ordered that lessons to be given in Latin and under the form of ancient argumentation. This order is carried out in most of our colleges.... They are philosophizing in Latin from one end of France to the other, with the ceremonial and the etiquette of the ancient syllogism; and on what are they philosophizing? On the thesis of the school and on the *objecta* which correspond to them; that is to say that the argument is on logic, metaphysics and ethics.' (Essay on the *History of Philosophy in France in the Nineteenth Century* by Ph. Damiron, Professor of Philosophy in the College of Bourbon, Paris, 1828).

enthusiasm into the quest of the origin of ideas, which they hoped to find by questioning the intelligence of children and savages.* The new philosophy scornfully rejected these inquiries which were of a nature to lead to dangerous results. 'Let us set aside in the first place the question of origin,' exclaimed Victor Cousin, the master sophist, in his argument on the True, the Good and the Beautiful. 'The philosophy of the last century was too complaisant to questions of this sort. To what purpose shall we call on the region of darkness for light, or on a mere hypothesis for the explanation of reality; why go back to a pretended primitive stage in order to account for a present stage which can be studied in itself; why inquire into the germ of that which can be perceived and which needs to be known in its finished and perfect form? We deny absolutely that human nature should be studied in the famous savage of Aveyron or in his peers of the Islands of Oceanica or the American Continent. The true man is man perfect in his type; the true human nature is human nature arrived at its full development, as the true society is also the perfected society. Let us turn away our eyes from the child and the savage to fix them upon the actual man, the real and finished man.' (15th and 16th Lessons.) The ego of Socrates and Descartes could not but inevitably lead to the adoration of the bourgeois, the man perfect in his kind, real, finished — the type of human nature arrived at its complete development and to the consecration of bourgeois society, the finished social order, founded upon the eternal and immutable principles of Goodness and Justice.

It is time to inquire into the value of this Justice and these eternal truths of bourgeois spiritualism and to reopen the debate on the origin of ideas.

---

* *La Sociètè des observateurs de l'homme* (Society of the Observers of Man), of which Cuvier, the alienist Pinel, the philosopher Gerando, the jurist Portalis, etc., were members voted in the month of Prairial VIII. (1800) a prize of 600 francs for the following study: To determine by the daily observation of one or several children in the cradle the order in which the physical intellectual and moral faculties are developed, and to what point this development is helped or hindered by the influence of objects and persons surrounding the child. In the same Session, reported in the Delcade Philosophique of the 30th day of Prairial, Gerando offered certain ideas on the methods to be followed in the observations of savage nations. Another member contributed an essay on the childhood of Massieu, deaf and dumb from birth. The Society was greatly interested in the observation of the young savage from Aveyron brought to Paris about the end of the year VIII. (1800). Three hunters found him in the forest where he lived naked, living on acorns and roots. He was apparently about ten years old.

II

FORMATION OF THE INSTINCT AND OF ABSTRACT IDEAS

We may apply to the instinct of animals what the spiritualist philosophers call innate ideas. Beasts are born with an organic pre-disposition, an intellectual pre-formation, according to Leibnitz's phrase, which permits them to accomplish spontaneously, without going through the school of any experience, the most complicated acts necessary to their individual preservation and the propagation of their species. This pre-formation is nowhere more remarkable than in the insects which go through metamorphoses, like the butterfly and dragon-fly. According to their transformations, they adopt different kinds of life rigorously correlated with each of the new forms which they take on. Sebastien Mercier was altogether right when he declared that 'instinct was an innate idea.'*

---

* On the seventh day of Nivose in the year VIII (1800), S. Mercier delivered in Paris, just emerging from the Revolution, the first lecture on innate ideas, in order to 'dethrone Condillac, Locke and their metaphysics.' To Royer-Collard is attributed the first awakening of spiritualist philosophy, completely out of fashion for half a century. This honour, if honour there be, reverts to this unbalanced intellect, which opposed Kant to the Encyclopaedists and noisily proposed to refute Newton, 'that anatomist of light, who can imagine nothing more ridiculous than to make the earth turn like a turkey before the solar hearth.' Bourgeois spiritualism could not have in France a more worthy godfather. The lectures of Mercier made a sensation: they were largely attended. The *Decade Philosophiaue* of the Tenth Floreal gives an account of the lecture on innate ideas. 'I admit them,' he exclaimed at the start, 'and in this I obey my inmost reason.... Man thinks independently of objects and senses. . . . Innate ideas explain everything. The picture of the ideas of a man would be the picture of celestial truths.... Instinct is an innate idea.' Mercier had a precedent, the celebrated decree of Robespierre, which re-established God like an ordinary police commissioner who had been thrown out: 'Art 1. The French Nation recognizes the existence of the Supreme Being and the immortality of the soul ... Art.4. Feasts shall be instituted to recall to man the thought of divinity and the dignity of his being.' A hymn recited at the feast of the restoration of the Supreme Being after the speech of Robespierre predicted the end of Atheism:

> Where are they who dared threaten Thee
> Who under the mantle of civism
> Vile professors of Atheism
> Hoped to efface Thee from the heart of man
>
> Did they think then
> That in returning to nature
> One would forget the Author of Nature?

The spiritualists, not having the idea that instinct might be the result of the slow adaptation of a species of animals to the conditions of its natural environment, conclude stoutly that instinct is a gift of God. Man has never hesitated to put out of his reach the causes of the phenomena which escape him. But instinct is not like the Justice of the sophists of spiritualism, an immutable faculty, susceptible of no deviation, no modification. Domestic animals have more or less modified the instincts which God in his inexhaustible goodness bestowed on their savage ancestors. The chickens and ducks of our back yards have almost lost their instinct of flight, which became useless in the artificial environment in which man has placed them for centuries. The aquatic instinct has been obliterated in the ducks of Ceylon to such a degree that they have to be pushed to make them go into the water. Different varieties of chickens, Houdans, LaFleche, Campine, etc., have been robbed of the imperative instinct of maternity; although excellent layers they never think of sitting on their eggs. The calves in certain parts of Germany for generations have been taken from their mothers at birth, and among the cows a notable weakening of the maternal instinct has been observed. Giard thinks that one of the prime causes of that instinct in the mammals might be the organic need of relief from the milk, which makes the breasts swollen and painful.*

Another naturalist shows that the nest-building instinct of the stickleback must be attributed not to the Deity, but to a temporary inflammation of the kidneys during the mating season.

No very long time is necessary to reverse the best rooted instinct. Romanes cites the case of a hen which had been made to sit three times on duck's eggs and who conscientiously pushed into the water the true chickens which she had been permitted to hatch. Man has overturned the instincts of the canine race; according to his needs he has given it new instincts and afterwards has suppressed them. The dog in the savage state does

---

* The supplement of *Figaro* for January, 1880, reproduced from the letters of a missionary, the native lamentations of an Indian woman at the equator over the corpse of her new-born child, which illustrates the part played by the milk in the primitive maternal love: 'Oh! my master. Oh! son of my vitals, my little father, my love, why have you left me? For you every day this breast with which you loved to play filled itself with warm milk. Ungrateful one! have I once forgotten you? Oh! woe is me; I have no longer any one to deliver my bosom from the milk which oppresses it.'

not bark. The dogs of the savages are silent; civilized man has given the dog the instinct of barking and has afterwards suppressed it in dogs of certain breeds. When the hound encounters the game, he leaps upon it barking loudly, while the sight of game makes the setter mute and nails him to the spot. If the setter is of a good breed, he needs no individual education to manifest this instinct, which is relatively a new acquisition. The young dogs hunting for the first time stop mute and motionless in their path at the sight of stones, sheep, etc. The tendency is implanted in the brain, but it is blind and requires a special training. Since to modify or suppress the instincts of an animal and to develop new ones in him, it is only necessary to place him in new conditions of existence, the instinct of the wild animals is then only the result of their adaptation to the conditions of the natural invironment in which they live. It is not created all at once; it is developed gradually in the animal species under the action and reaction of external and internal phenomena, which may be unknown but which necessarily have existed.

Man can study in himself the formation of instinct. He can learn nothing mentally or physically without a certain cerebral tension which relaxes in proportion as the object of study becomes more familiar. When, for example, one begins to play the piano, one must watch attentively the movement of the hands and fingers in order to strike exactly the note desired, but with habit one reaches the point of touching it mechanically without looking at the keyboard, and while thinking of other things. Just so when one studies a foreign language one must constantly keep his attention on the choice of words, articles, prepositions, terminations, adjectives, verbs, etc., which come to mind instinctively when one becomes familiar with the new language. The brain and the body of man and the animal have the property of transforming into automatic actions what originally were voluntary and conscious, and the result of a sustained attention. Without this property of automatizing himself, man would be incapable of education, physically or intellectually; if he were obliged to watch over his movements in order to speak, walk, eat, etc., he would remain in everlasting childhood. Education teaches man to dispense with his intelligence. It tends to transform him into a machine more and more complicated. The conclusion is paradoxical.

The brain of an adult is more or less automatized according to the degree of his own education and that of his race. The abstract elementary notions of Cause, Substance, Being, Number, Justice, etc., are as familiar and instinctive to him as eating and drinking, and he has lost all remembrance of the manner in which he acquired them, for civilized man, like the setter, inherits at birth the traditional habit of acquiring them at the first occasion. But this tendency to acquire them is the result of a progressive ancestral experience prolonged through thousands of years. It would be as ridiculous to think that abstract ideas germinated spontaneously in the human head as to think that the bicycle or any other machine of the most improved type had been constructed at the first attempt. Abstract ideas, like the instinct of animals, were gradually formed in the individual and in the race. To seek their origin it is not enough to analyse the manner of thinking of the civilized adult, as Descartes does, but also, as the Encyclopaedists would have had it, to question the intelligence of the child and to retrace the course of the ages to study that of the barbarian and the savage, as we are obliged to do when we wish to find the origins of our political and social institutions, of our arts and our sciences.*

The sensationalists of the eighteenth century in making of the brain a *tabula rasa*, which was a radical way of renewing the 'purification' of Descartes, neglected this fact of capital importance; namely, that the brain of the civilized man is a field worked for centuries and sown with concepts and ideas by thousands of generations, and that, according to the exact expression of Leibnitz, it is pre-formed before individual experience begins. We must admit that it possesses the molecular arrangement destined to give birth to a considerable number of ideas and concepts. Some such admission is required to explain that extraordinary men, like Pascal, have been able to find out for themselves more than one series of abstract ideas, such as the

---

* The ancients were not afraid to go back to the animals in order to discover the beginnings of certain of our sciences: thus while attributing to the gods the origin of medicine, they admitted that several remedies and operations of minor surgery were due to the animals. The elder Pliny reports in his *Natural History* that the wild goats of Crete taught the use of certain healing herbs: the dog taught that of the couchgrass; and that the Egyptians asserted that the discovery of purging was due to the dog, that of bleeding to the hippopotamus and that of injection to the ibis.

theorems of the first book of Euclid, which have only been elaborated by a long procession of thinkers. In any case the brain possesses such an aptitude for acquiring certain concepts and elementary ideas that it does not perceive the fact of their acquisition. The brain is not merely limited to receiving impressions which come from outside, by way of the senses; it, of itself, does a molecular work, which the English physiologists call unconscious cerebration, which enables it to complete its acquisitions and even to make new ones without passing through experience. Students utilize this precious faculty when they learn their lesson imperfectly and go to bed leaving to their slumber the duty of fixing them in memory.

Indeed, the brain is full of mysteries. It is a *terra incognita* which the physiologists have scarcely begun to explore. It certainly possesses faculties which often find no outlet in the environment in which the individual and his race are evolving. These dormant faculties cannot therefore result from the direct action of the exterior environment upon the brain, but rather from its action upon other organs, which in their turn react upon the nervous centres. Goethe and Geoffroy Saint-Hilaire called this phenomenon the balancing of organs. Here are two historical examples.

Savages and barbarians are capable of a far greater number of intellectual operations than they accomplish in their daily life. During hundreds of years the Europeans have transported from the coast of Africa into the colonies thousands of savage and barbarian negroes, removed from civilized men by centuries of culture. Nevertheless at the end of a very short time they assimilated the crafts of civilization. The Guaranys of Paraguay, when the Jesuits undertook their education, were wandering naked in the forests, armed only with a wooden bow and club, with no knowledge, except how to cultivate maize. Their intelligence was so rudimentary that they could not count beyond twenty, using their fingers and toes. Nevertheless the Jesuits made these savages skilful operatives, capable of difficult works — such as complicated organs, geographical spheres, paintings and decorated sculptures. These trades and arts with the ideas corresponding to them did not exist in the inborn state in the hands and brain of the Guaranys. They had been, so to speak, poured into them by the Jesuits as new airs are added to a street organ. The brain of the Guaranys, if it was incapable of discovering them by its own initiative, was at least marvellously 'predisposed' or 'pre-formed', according to Leibnitz's phrase, for acquiring them.

It is equally certain that the savage is as foreign to the abstract concepts of civilized men as to their arts and crafts, which is proved by the absence in their language of terms for general ideas. How then did the abstract ideas and concepts which are so familiar to the civilized man slip into the human brain? To solve this problem, which has to so great an extent preoccupied philosophic thought, we must, like the Encyclopaedists, start on the path opened up by Vico, and question language, the most important if not the first mode of manifestation of sentiments and ideas.* It plays so considerable a role that the Christians of the first centuries, reproducing the idea of primitive men, said, 'The Word is God;' and that the Greeks designated by the same term, *logos*, the word and thought; and that from the verb *phrazo* (to speak), they derived *phrazomai*, to speak to one's self, to think. Indeed the most abstract head cannot think without employing words — without speaking to himself mentally, if he does not do so really, like children and many adults who murmur what they think. Language holds too great a place in the development of the intellect for the etymological formation of words and their successive meanings to fail of reflecting the conditions of life and the mental state of the men who created and used them.

One fact strikes us at the outset; often one and the same word is used to designate an abstract idea and a concrete object. The words which in European languages signify material goods, and the straight line, have also the meaning of the moral Good and Right, Justice:

Ta agatha (Greek) goods, wealth; *to agathon*, the good.
Bona (Latin), goods; *bonum* (Latin) the good.
Les biens (French) goods; *le Bien*, the good.
Orthos (Greek), *rectum* (Latin), *derecho* (Spanish), *droit* (French), etc. have the double meaning of being in a straight line and that of Right, Justice.

---

* Vico, in the preface of his little work on the *Ancient Wisdom of Italy*, says, 'I have resolved to find in the origins of the Latin language the ancient wisdom of Italy. We shall seek its philosophy in the origin of the words themselves.'

Here again are other examples chosen in the Greek language: *kalon*, arrow, javelin, beauty, virtue; *phren*, heart, entrails, reason, will; *kakos*, man of the plebeian origin, base, wicked, ugly; *kakon*, vice, crime. The word *kakos* contributes to the formation of a series of terms, employed for what is vile and evil: *kakke*, execrement; *kakkia*, vice, baseness; *kakotheos*, impious; *kakophonia*, unpleasant sound, etc.

The fact is worth attention, although little noticed. This is the way with daily phenomena; because they fill the eyes they are not seen. Nevertheless, it is worth considering how the vulgar tongue and the philosophic and legal tongue have joined under the same term the material and the ideal, the concrete and the abstract. Two questions are raised at the very outset: first, have the abstract and the ideal been degraded into the concrete and into the material, or have the material and concrete transformed themselves into the ideal and abstract? — and how has this trans-substantiation been accomplished?

The history of successive meanings of words solves the first difficulty; it shows the concrete meaning always preceding the abstract meaning.

Aissa (Greek), used at first for the lot or portion which falls to any one in a division, ends by meaning a decree of destiny:

Moira, at first the portion of a guest at a banquet, the lot of a warrior in the distribution of booty; then one's portion in life and finally the goddess Destiny, to whom 'gods and mortals are equally subject.'

Nomos begins by being used for pasturage and ends by meaning law.

The link which attaches the abstract meaning to the concrete meaning is not always apparent. Thus it is difficult at first glance to perceive how the human mind could have linked pasturage to the abstract idea of law, the straight line to the idea of Justice, the share of a guest at a banquet to immutable destiny. I shall show the links which unite these different meanings in the article on the 'Origins of the ideas, Justice and Goodness.' It is only important at this moment to point out the fact.

The human mind ordinarily employs the same method of work in spite of the difference in the objects on which it operates: for example, the road which it has followed to transform sounds into vowels and consonants is the same as that which is traversed in rising from the concrete to the abstract. The origin of letters appeared so mysterious to the Bishop Mallinkrot, that in his *De Arte Typographica*, to put his mind at rest, he attributed their invention to God, who was already the author of instinct and abstract ideas. But the researches of philologists have torn away one by one the veils enveloping the alphabetical mystery. They have shown that letters did not fall ready-made from heaven, but man arrived only gradually at representing the sounds by consonants and vowels. I shall mention the first steps traversed, which are useful for my demonstration.

Man begins by picture-writing. He represents an object by its image, a dog by a drawing of a dog. He passes then to symbolical writing, and pictures a part for the whole, the head of an animal for the entire animal. Then he rises to metaphorical writing: he portrays an object having some resemblance, real or supposed, with the idea to be expressed — the forepart of a lion to signify the idea of priority, a cubit for Justice and Truth, a vulture for maternity. The first attempt at phonetics was made by rebuses; the sound was represented by the image of an object having the same sound. The Egyptians, calling the pig's tail *deb*, represented the sound *deb* by the picture of the curled tail of a pig. Finally a certain number of pictures are preserved more or less modified, no longer for the phonetic value of several syllables, but for that of the initial syllable, etc., etc.*

Writing had inevitably to pass through the metaphorical stage since primitive man thinks and speaks in metaphors. The Redskin of America to indicate a brave warrior said 'he is like the bear;' the man with piercing glance is like the eagle; to affirm that he forgives an outrage he declares 'he buries it in the earth,' etc. These metaphors are for us sometimes undecipherable; thus, it is difficult to understand how the Egyptians came to represent in their hieroglyphics Justice and Truth by the cubit, and maternity by the vulture. I shall disentangle the metaphor of the vulture. In the next article I will explain that of the cubit.

The matriarchial family had in Egypt an extraordinary longevity, as is shown in its religious myths by numerous traces of the antagonism of the two sexes; struggling, the one to preserve its high position in the family, the other to dispossess it. The Egyptian like Apollo in the Eumenides of Aeschylus,

---

* F. Lenormand's *Essay on the Propagation of the Phoenician Alphabet among the Nations of the Ancient World.*

declares that it is man who fulfils the important function in the act of generation, and that woman, 'like the pistil of a fruit, only receives and nourishes his germ.' The Egyptian woman returns the compliment and boasts that she conceives without the co-operation of man. The statue of Neïth, the mother goddess, the 'Sovereign Lady of the upper regions,' bore at Saïs this arrogant inscription: 'I am all that has been, all that is and all that shall be. No one has lifted my robe. The fruit I have borne is the Sun.' Her name, among other signs, has for its emblem the vulture and the first letter of the word mother (mou).*

Now the hieroglyphics of Horapollon teach us that the Egyptians believed that in the species of vultures there were no males and that the females were fertilized by the wind. They attributed to that bird, everywhere else regarded as ferocious, a motherly tenderness so extreme that it tore its breast to nourish its little ones. So, after having made of it, by reason of its strange generative property, the bird of Neïth, the mother goddess, who herself also propagates without the co-operation of the male, they made of it the symbol of the mother, then of maternity.

This characteristic example gives an idea of the twists and turns through which the human mind passes to picture its abstract ideas through the images of concrete objects.

If in the metaphorical and emblematic writing the image of a material object becomes the symbol of an abstract idea, it is seen that a word created to denote an object or one of its attributes ends by serving to denote an abstract idea.

In the mind of the child and of the savage — 'that child of the human race,' as Vico calls him — there exist only images of definite objects. When the little child says doll, he does not mean to speak of any doll no matter which, but of one certain doll that he has held in his hands and that has already been shown him, and if another is offered him it results in his rejecting it with anger; so, every word is for him a proper name, the symbol of the object with which he has come in contact. His language, like that of the savage, possesses no generic terms embracing a class of objects of the same nature, but one series after another of proper names. Thus the savage languages have no terms for general ideas, such as 'man', 'body', etc., and for the abstract ideas, Time, Cause, etc. There are some which have not the verb 'to be'. The

---

* Champollion le Jeune: *Panthéon Egyptian,* 1825.

Tasmanian had an abundance of words for every tree of the different species, but no term for saying tree in general. The Malay has no word for colour, although he has words for every colour. The Tbiponne has not words for man, body, time, etc. and he does not possess the verb to be. He does not say, 'I am Abiponne,' but, 'Me Abiponne.'*

But by degrees the child and primitive man carry over the name and the idea of the first persons and things they have known to all the persons and things which present real or fictitious resemblances with them. They elaborate after a fashion, by way of analogy and comparison, certain general and abstract ideas embracing groups of objects, more or less extended, and sometimes the proper name of one object becomes the symbolic term of the abstract idea representing the group of objects having analogies with the object for which the word had been coined. Plato maintains that the general ideas thus obtained, which classify objects without taking account of their individual differences, are 'essences of divine origin.' Socrates in the Tenth Book of the *Republic* says that the idea of bed is an essence of divine creation, because it is immutable, always identical with itself, while the beds created by cabinet makers all differ among themselves.

The human mind has often brought together the most dissimilar objects having only a vague point of resemblance among themselves. Thus by a process of anthropomorphism man has taken his own members for terms of comparison, as is proved by the metaphors which persist in civilized languages although they date from the beginning of humanity, such as the 'bowels of the earth', the 'veins of a mine', the 'heart of an oak', 'tooth of a saw', the 'gorge of a mountain', the 'arm of the sea', etc. When the abstract idea of measure takes shape in his brain, he takes for a unit of measure his foot, his hand, his thumb, his arms (*Orygia* a

* The idea of time was long in penetrating into the human brain. Vico remarks that the Florentine peasants of his epoch said so many harvests for so many years. The Latins for so many years said so many ears of corn, (aristas) something still more concrete than harvests. The expression merely indicated their poverty of language (and of thought, he might have added). The grammarians believe they see in it an attempt at art. Before having the concept of the year — that is to say, of the sun's revolution — man had the idea of the seasons and that of the revolutions of the moon. The elder Pliny said that the summer was counted one year, the winter for another. The Arcadians, with whom the year was three months, measured it by the number of seasons, and the Egyptians by the moon. That is why several of them are cited as having lived a thousand years.

Greek measure equal to two arms extended). So every measure is a metaphor. When we speak of an object three feet, two inches in extent, we mean that it is as long as three feet two thumbs. But with the development of civilization, people were forced to resort to other units of measure. Thus the Greeks took the *stadion*, the distance traversed in the foot-race at the Olympic Games; and the Latins *jugerum*, the surface which could be ploughed in one day by a *jugum* (a yoke of oxen).

An abstract word, as Max Muller remarks, is often only an adjective transformed into a substantive — that is to say, the attribute of an object metamorphosed into a personage, into a metaphysical entity, into an imaginary being, and it is by way of metaphor that this metempsychosis is accomplished. The metaphor is one of the principal ways by which the abstract penetrates into the human brain. In the preceding metaphors, they speak of the mouth of a cavern, a tongue of land, because the mouth presents an opening and the tongue an elongated form. The same process has served to procure new terms of comparison in proportion as the need of them has made itself felt, and it is always the most salient property of the object, that which consequently impresses the senses most vividly, which is made the term of comparison.

A great number of savage languages have no words for the abstract ideas of hardness, roundness, warmth, etc., and they are deprived of them because the savage has not yet succeeded in creating the imaginary beings or metaphysical entities which correspond to these terms. Thus, for hard he says 'like stone', for round 'like the moon', for hot, 'like the sun'; because the qualities of hard, round and hot are in his brain inseparable from stone, moon and sun. It is only after a long process of brain work that these qualities are detached, abstracted from these concrete objects to be metamorphosed into imaginary beings. Then the qualifying term becomes a substantive and stands for the abstract idea formed in the brain.

No savage tribes have been found without the idea of number, the abstract idea *par excellence*, although the numeration of certain savages does not go beyond twenty. It is probable that even animals can count up to two. Here is an observation I have made, which is easy to repeat, and which would seem to prove it: the pigeon, although sitting on two eggs — with very rare exceptions — nevertheless has the property of laying eggs at will.

If, after she has laid two eggs one is taken away, the female lays a third and even a fourth and fifth if the eggs are taken as fast as she lays them. She requires two eggs in the nest before she begins to sit. The domestic pigeon, overfed, may sometimes lay three eggs; when that happens she pushes one out of the nest, or else leaves it if she cannot push out the superfluous egg.

It would seem that the abstract idea of number, contrary to Vico's opinion, is one of the first, if not the first, to be formed in the brain of animals and man; for if all objects have not the property of being round, hard or hot, etc., they have nevertheless one quality which is common to them, that of being distinct from one another, by their form and the relative position which they occupy, and this quality is the point of departure of numeration.*

The brain substance must have the idea of number; that is to say, be able to distinguish the objects from each other, in order to carry on its function. This was recognized by the Pythagorian Philolaus, the first who, according to Diogenes of Laercia, affirmed that the motion of the earth described a circle, when he declared that number resides in all that is, and without it nothing can be known and nothing can be thought.

But the extension of numeration beyond the number two was one of the most painful of Herculean labours ever imposed upon the human brain, as is proved by the mystical character attributed to the first ten numbers;† and the mythological and legendary memories attached to certain figures: 10 (Siege of Troy and of Veii, which lasted exactly ten years); 12 (the 12 gods of Olympus, 12 labours of Hercules, 12 apostles, etc.); 50 (the 50 sons of Priam, the 50 Danaides; Endymion, according to Pausanius made Selene the mother of 50 daughters; Acteon hunted with 50 braces

---

* Plato, who in the *Timaeus* represents an astronomer as speaking and who for the moment forgets his essences of divine origin, gives a materialistic origin of Number and Time. 'The observation of day and night, the revolutions of the months and the years have furnished us Number, revealed Time and inspired the desires of knowing Nature and the world.'

† The decade had a sacred character for the Pythagorians and the Cabalists. The Scandinavians regarded the number three and its multiple nine as particularly dear to the gods. Every ninth month they made bloody sacrifices which lasted nine days, during which they sacrificed nine victims, man or animal. The Catholic Neuvaines, which are prayers lasting nine days, preserve the memory of this cult, and their holy trinity preserves the mystical character which all savage nations attach to the number three. It occurs in all primitive religions: three Parcae among the Greeks and the Scandinavians, three goddesses of life among the Iroquois.

of hounds when Diana metamorphosed him; the boat constructed by Danaus according to the instructions of Minerva, had 50 oars, as had that of Hercules at the time of his expedition against Troy.) These numbers are so many stages at which the human mind halted after the efforts made to reach the points, and it has marked them with legends to preserve their memory.

The savage, when he arrives at the end of his numeration, says 'many' to indicate the objects which remain over and which he cannot count for lack of numbers. Vico remarks that for the Romans 60, then 100, then 1,000 were innumerable quantities. The Hovas of Madagascar say for 1,000 'evening', for 10,000 'night', and the word *tapitrisa*, which they use to indicate a million, is literally translated by the end of counting. It was the same for us, but since the war of 1870-1871 it is a billion which marks the limit of our popular numeration.

Language shows us that man has taken his hand, his foot and his arms for units of length. He still uses his fingers and toes for counting. F. Nansen says the Eskimos, with whom he lived more than a year, have no name for any figure beyond five. They count on the fingers of the right hand and then stop when all the fingers have been named and touched. For six they take the left hand and say the first finger of the other hand, for seven, the second finger, thus on to ten. Afterwards they count in the same fashion on the toes and stop at twenty, the limit of their numeration: but the great mathematicians go further and for twenty-one they say the first finger of the other man and begin again, passing over the hands and feet. Twenty is one man, one hundred is five men. The Roman figures which were used until the introduction of the Arabic figures preserve the memory of this primitive mode of numeration; I is one finger, II is two fingers, V is a hand with the three middle fingers folded while the little finger and the thumb are straight; X is two Vs or two hands crossed. But when it was necessary to count beyond the hundred and the thousand, they were obliged to resort to other objects than the human members.

The Romans took pebbles, *calculi*, from which is derived the word calculus in modern languages. The Latin expressions *calculum ponere* (to place the pebble) and *subducere calculum* (to take away the pebble) indicate that it was by adding and taking away pebbles that they added and subtracted. At the Familistere of Guise I saw the first two arithmetical operations taught by a similar process to children of five and six years. Pebbles were the obvious things for this use; they had already served for drawing lots in the distribution of booty and land.

Savages cannot figure in their heads. They must have before their eyes the objects which they are counting. Thus, when they make exchanges they place on the ground the objects which they are giving opposite those they receive. This primitive equation, which in the last analysis is simply a tangible metaphor, is the only thing which can satisfy their minds. Numbers, in their heads, as in those of children, are concrete ideas. When they say two, three or five, they see two, three or five fingers, pebbles or any other objects. In many savage tongues the first five figures bear the names of the fingers; it is only by a process of intellectual distillation that the numbers come to strip themselves in the head of the civilized adult of any form corresponding to a certain object, and to keep only the form of conventional signs.* The most idealistic metaphysician cannot think without words nor calculate without signs — that is to say without concrete objects. The Greek philosophers when they began their inquiries on the properties of numbers, gave them geometrical forms. They divided them into three groups: the group of linear numbers (*mekos*), the group of the numbers of planes, squares (*epipedon*), the group of the numbers of three dimensions, cubes (*trikéauxé*). The modern mathematicians have still preserved the expression 'linear number' for a root number.

The savage, for long, hard, round or hot, says 'like the foot, stone, moon, sun'; but feet are of unequal length, stones are more or less hard, the moon is not always round, the sun is hotter in summer than in winter; so when the human mind felt the need of a higher degree of exactness, it recognized the insufficiency of the

---

* The Greeks employed for figures the letters of the alphabet, preserving the ancient Cadmean letters which carried the numbers up to twenty-seven. The first nine letters were the units, the next nine the tens and the last nine the hundreds. It must have been extremely painful and difficult to calculate with the figures of the Greeks and Romans, who did not possess the zero. The metaphysical abstractors of abstractions of Nirvana were the only ones capable of inventing this marvellous figure — the symbol of nothing, which has no value and which gives value, and which according to the expression of Pascal, is a true indivisible of number as the indivisible is a true zero. The zero plays so considerable a part in modern numeration that its Arabic name *sifr* which the Portuguese transformed into *cifra*, the English into *cipher*. the French into *chiffre* — after having first been employed for zero alone, serves to designate all the signs of number.

terms of comparison which it had till then used. It then imagined types of length, hardness, roundness and heat to be employed as terms of comparison. It is thus that in abstract mechanics, the mathematicians imagined a lever absolutely rigid and without thickness and a wedge absolutely incompressible in order to continue their theoretical investigations, arrested by the imperfections of the levers and wedges of reality. But the wedge and the lever of the mathematicians, like the types of length, roundness, hardness, although derived from real objects whose attributes had been submitted to intellectual distillation, no longer correspond to any real object but to ideas formed in the human head. Because the objects of reality differ among themselves and from the imaginary type, always one and identical with itself, Plato calls the real objects vain and deceptive images and the ideal type an essence of divine creation. In that case, as in a multitude of others, God, the creator, is man thinking.

Artists by an analogous process have given birth to chimeras, whose bodies, although composed of detached organs abstracted from different animals, correspond to nothing real but to a fantasm of the imagination. The chimera is an abstract idea — as abstract as any idea you please of the Beautiful, the Good, the Just, Time or Cause — but Plato, himself, did not dare to class it in the number of his divine essences.

Man, probably when barbarous tribes began to differentiate into classes, separated himself from the animal kingdom and raised himself to the rank of a supernatural being, whose destinies are the constant preoccupation of the gods and the celestial bodies. Later on he isolated the brain from the other organs to make it the seat of the soul. Natural science reintegrates man in the animal series of which he is the sum and crown; the socialist philosophy will restore the brain to the series of organs. The brain has the property of thinking as the stomach has that of digesting. It cannot think but by the aid of ideas, which it fabricates with the materials furnished it by the natural environment and the social or artificial environment in which man evolves.

3

The origin of the idea of justice

I

THE LAW OF RETALIATION — RETRIBUTIVE JUSTICE

JUSTICE as it exists in our civilized societies flows from two sources; one takes its origin in the very nature of the human being and the other in the social environment organized on the basis of private property. The passions and the concepts existing in man before the establishment of property, and the interests, passions and ideas which this engenders, acting and reacting one upon another, have ended by begetting, developing and crystallizing in the brain of civilized man the ideas of the Just and Unjust.

The human sources of the idea of justice are the passion for vengeance and the sentiment of equality.

The passion of vengeance is one of the most ancient in the human mind. It has its root in the instinct of self-preservation — in the necessity which impels animal and man to resist when they receive a blow, and to respond to it mechanically if fear does not put them to flight. It is that blind and unreasoning necessity which leads the child and the savage to strike the inanimate object which has wounded them. Reduced to its simplest and last expression, vengeance is a reflex movement analogous to the involuntary motion which makes the eye wink when it is threatened.

Vengeance with the savage and the barbarian is of an intensity unknown to civilized men. 'The Redskins', says the American historian, Adairs, 'feel their heart burn violently day and night until they have shed blood for blood. They transmit from father to son the memory of the murder of a relative, of a member of their

clan, even though it be an old woman.' There are stories of
Redskins who have committed suicide because they could not
avenge themselves. The Fijian, who has received an insult, places
within the range of his vision an object which he does not take away
until he has assuaged his vengeance. The Slavonic women of
Dalmatia show their child the bloody shirt of the slain father to
incite it to vengeance.

'Vengeance one hundred years old, still has its milk teeth', says
the Afghan proverb. The Semitic god, 'although slow to anger'
visits the 'iniquity of the fathers upon the children and the
children's children unto the third and fourth generation.'
(Exodus, XXXIV., 7.) Four generations do not assuage his thirst
for vengeance. He forbids entrance into the assembly up to the
tenth generation to the Moabites and the Ammonites, 'because
they met you not with bread and with water in the way, when ye
came forth out of Egypt.' (Deut, XXIII., 4.) The Hebrew might
have said, like the Scandinavian, 'The shell of the oyster may fall
into dust by the process of years and a thousand other years may
pass over this dust, but vengeance shall still be warm in my
heart.' The Erinnyes of Greek mythology are the ancient
goddesses 'of vengeance' 'of the inextinguishable thirst for
blood.' The chorus of the sublime trilogy of Aeschylus, palpitating
with the passions that torture the souls of the gods and mortals,
cries out to Orestes, hesitating to avenge his father: 'Let outrage
be punished by outrage, let murder avenge murder.' 'Evil for
evil,' says the maxim of ancient times; 'blood shed upon the earth
demands other blood; the nourishing earth has drunk the blood of
murder; it is dried, but its trace remains ineffaceable and cries for
vengeance.' Achilles to avenge the death of Patroclus, his friend,
forgets the insult of Agamemnon and stifles the wrath which made
him watch unmoved the defeats of the Achaeans. The death of
Hector does not assuage his passion; three times he drags his
corpse around the walls of Troy.

The savage and the barbarian never forgive. They can wait year
after year for the propitious moment of vengeance. Clytemnestra
for ten long years watched patiently for the hour of her
vengeance. When she had assassinated Agamemnon, the
murderer of her daughter, drunk with joy and blood, she cried:
'The dew of murder has fallen on me; as sweet to my heart as is to

the fields the rain of Jupiter in the season when the grain of wheat comes forth from its sheath.'

Man sanctifies and deifies his passions, especially when they are useful for his preservation, private and social. 'The inextinguishable thirst for blood,' vengeance, erected into a sacred duty, becomes the first of duties. The Erinnyes, in number like the curses which come from the mouth of an angered mother, hurl themselves from the shades of Erebus when once the imprecations give them life and motion.* They appear in the light of the sun only to breathe the passion of vengeance and untiringly to pursue the murderer over land and sea. No mortal could escape them. Their rage hunted down the culprit and his family and extended to him who gave him protection — to cities and whole countries. They stirred up civil wars and scattered pestilence and famine. The chorus of the Erinnyes of Aeschylus when Orestes is on the point of escaping them cries:

> And I, dishonoured, wretched, full of wrath,
>   upon this land (Attica), ha! ha!
> Will venom, venom from my heart let fall,
>   In vengeance for my grief
> A dropping which shall smite
>   the earth with barreness!
> And thence shall come, (O Vengeance!) on the plain
> Down-swooping, blight of leaves and murrain dire
> That o'er the land flings taint of pestilence.

(Plumptre's Translation.)

The Semitic god likewise avenged the shedding of blood upon plants, beasts and children. The poetic imagination of the Greeks personified in these terrible goddesses, whose name they feared to pronounce, the terrors inspired in primitive peoples by the unchaining of the passion of vengeance.

Vico, in his *Scienza Nuova*, formulates this axiom of social science:

Legislation takes man as he is to make of him a being adapted for human society. From ferocity, avarice and ambition — these three vices which lead men astray — it derives the army, commerce and the

---

* Curses are not idle words for the barbarian; the word, the verb, is for him endowed with irresistible power. The gods themselves obeyed the imprecations of mortals. The Jews, like the Chinese, condemned to death him who had cursed his father or mother. (Exodus, XXI., 17.) Catholocism in giving the confessor the power of binding and loosing sins on earth and in heaven by the aid of a formula, reproduces the primitive idea of savages on the power of the word.

court; that is to say, the strength, wealth and knowledge of republics; and these great vices, capable of destroying the human race, create social felicity. This axiom proves the existence of a divine providence — the divine legislative thought, which, from the passions of men absorbed completely in their private interests, that would make them live like ferocious beasts in solitude, derives the civil order which permits them to live in human societies.

Inviolable law, to use Aristotle's phrase, arose in fact from the passion of vengeance, furious and ever boiling. But it is not a divine legislative intelligence, which, as Vico thought, creates order out of the disorders of human passions; it is on the contrary these disorders which engender order. I shall try to prove this.

The implacable and furious passion for vengeance which is found in the souls of the savages and barbarians of the old and new world, as is proved by the previous quotations, is imposed upon them by the conditions of the natural and social environment in which they move.

The savage, at perpetual war with man and beast, and his spirit haunted by imaginary dangers, cannot live alone, and gathers himself into herds. He cannot understand existence outside of his clan; to drive him from it is to condemn him to death.* The members of a tribe consider themselves descended from a single ancestor. The same blood flows in their veins. To shed the blood of one member is to shed the blood of the whole tribe. The savage has no individuality; it is the tribe, the clan, and later the family, which possesses an individuality. Solidarity of the narrowest and solidest kind welds together the members of a tribe or clan to the point of making them one single being, like the Briareus of Greek mythology; in the most primitive nations that it has been possible to observe, the women are in common and the children belong to the clan. Individual property has not yet made its appearance. The most personal objects such as arms and ornaments pass from hand to hand with the most startling rapidity, according to Fison and Howitt, those conscientious and intelligent observers of Australian manners. The members of savage tribes and barbarous clans move and act in common like a single man; they change

---

* Cain, driven from his clan after the murder of Abel, laments: 'My punishment is greater than I can bear. Behold, thou hast driven me from this land. I shall be a wanderer and fugitive over the earth and it shall come to pass that whosoever findeth me shall slay me' (Genesis IV., 13, 14.) Exile is one of the most terrible punishments of ancient societies.

their location, hunt, fight and cultivate the land in   common.
When warlike tactics are improved, they range themselves in battle
by tribes, clans and families.

They put offences into the common fund, like everything else;
an injury done to one savage is resented by the whole clan as if it
were personal to every member; to shed the blood of one savage
is to shed the blood of the clan. All its members consider it their
duty to wreak vengeance. Vengeance is collective like marriage
and property. The right of exercising vengeance was among the
barbarous Germans the family bond, *par excellence*. When the
Frankish tribes had established the *wehrgeld*, that is to say, a
monetary compensation for the offence, all the members of the
family shared the price of blood. But the Frank who had gone out
of the family community had no right to the *wehrgeld*. If he was
killed, it was the king who became his avenger and received the
price of his blood.

But, because the clan resents the injury done to one of its
members, the whole clan becomes responsible for the offence
committed by one of its members. The offence is collective like
the injury.* The offended clan takes vengeance by killing any
individual whatever of the offending clan. 'Among the Australian
people a general consternation reigns', writes Sir. G. Grey, 'when
a murder is committed, especially when the guilty one has
escaped, for his relatives consider themselves guilty, and it is
only the persons who have no relation with the family who feel
any safety.' A murder is the declaration of war between two
families, between two clans — a war of ambuscades and
extermination, which lasts for years, since a murder demands a
death to avenge it, which in its turn demands vengeance.
Sometimes two entire clans come to blows. It is only half a
century ago that in Dalmatia 'war extended from the families to
the whole village, and sometimes civil war was let loose over all
the district.'† Even women and children are objects of
vengeance. The Scandinavians did not spare the new-born in the
cradle, for 'A wolf lies in wait in the tender child' says Eddas.
Even in the nineteenth century the Greeks took vengeance upon

---

* Collective responsibility still seems so natural in the Middle Ages that
ordinances of Edward I of England, make the whole Trade Guild responsible for
the crime of one of its members.

† Sir Gardner Wilkinson, *Dalmatia and Montenegro*, 1848.

male children of more than eight years old, and the women and young girls alone were spared.*

It is not only real murders which imperiously demand vengeance, but also the imaginary murders created by the superstitious intelligence of the savage. No death is natural for the Australian; every decease is caused by the mischief of an enemy belonging to a rival clan, and the duty of the relatives is to avenge the deceased by killing; not exactly the presumed author of the mischief, but any member whatever of his clan — several indeed if possible.† Moreover, the dead man avenged himself, his spirit came to torture the guilty. Frazer asserts that one of the causes of the suppression of the cannibal banquets is the fear of posthumous vengeance on the part of the unfortunate who has been eaten. It is not only to avenge himself that the savage kills the murderer, but also to appease the dead, whose spirit would be tormented until human blood be shed. To tranquillize the shade of Achilles, the Greeks sacrificed on his tomb Polyxena, the sister of Paris, his murderer.

The savage, who understands his existence only as an integral part of his clan, transforms the individual offence into a collective offence; and vengeance, which is an act of personal defence and self-preservation, becomes an act of collective defence and self-preservation. The clan protects itself by wreaking vengeance for the murder or wounds of one of its members. But this collective vengeance inevitably involves collective dangers which sometimes compromise the existence of the clan. The collective dangers of these vendettas obliged the savages to stifle their sentiment of solidarity and to sacrifice the member of the clan responsible for the injury and to deliver him up to the clan of his victim. Savages of Australia, arms in their hands, stop and calm themselves, reducing their vengeance to a personal damage exactly equal to that which had been committed, and which had become the cause of the quarrel. Life for life, wound for wound. The law of retaliation was born.

Retaliation, 'life for life, eye for eye, tooth for tooth, hand for

---

* Lord Carnarvon, *Reminiscences of Athens and Morea.*

† Jesus Christ, St. Paul and the Apostles, shared with the savages this opinion; diseases were according to them the work of the demon, the enemy of the human race. (Matthew IX., 33; Luke XI., 14; Acts XIX., 12.) This superstition for centuries kindled in Christian Europe the pyres of sorceresses.

hand, foot for foot, burning for burning, wound for wound, stripe for stripe,' (Exodus, XXI., 23, 25), this alone can give full satisfaction to the sentiment of equality of the primitive communist tribes, whose members are all equal.

The most complete equality follows necessarily from the conditions in which the savage of the communist tribes lives. Darwin in his *Voyage of a Naturalist* relates this characteristic story: He saw a Fuegian, to whom a wool coverlet had been given, tear it into rags equal in breadth, in order that each individual of the tribe might receive a piece, since the savage could not admit that one member of his clan should be better endowed than another in anything whatever. Caesar, when he came in contact with the German tribes, was struck by the equalitarian spirit which governed their division of goods. He attributed it to the desire to create equality among their members. Caesar reasons like a civilized man living in a social environment where unequal conditions of existence inevitably produce inequality among the citizens. The barbarians whom he had under his eyes were living on the contrary in a communist environment producing equality; they therefore did not have to seek for it in their divisions, but to satisfy their equalitarian spirit by distributing equal shares to all without in the least suspecting the social importance of their act. It is in this way that people digest without any knowledge of the chemistry of the stomach, and that the bees construct the cells in their hives according to the most exact geometric and mechanical rules of resistance and economy of space, without suspecting the existence of geometry and mechanics. Equality is not only implanted in the heart and brain of primitive men, but furthermore exists in their physical appearance. Volney relates that a chief of the Redskins expressed to him his astonishment at the great physical differences which existed between the whites whom he saw, while the greatest resemblance was the rule between the members of any one savage tribe.

Old age surrounded with respect is the first privilege which appears in human societies. It is the only one which exists in the savage tribe. Whatever may be the superior qualities of courage, intelligence, endurance of hunger, thirst and pain which distinguish a warrior, they do not give him the right to assert himself. He may be chosen to direct his companions on the hunt, and to command in war, but the expedition ended, he becomes again their equal. 'The greatest chief of the Redskins,' says Volney, 'cannot even in the field strike or punish a warrior, and in the village he is obeyed by no child except his own.'* The Greek chief of Homeric times possessed an authority scarcely more extended. Aristotle remarks that if the power of Agamemnon went as far as the right to kill the run-away when they were marching against the enemy, yet he patiently accepted insults at the time of council. The Greek generals in historic times, when their year of command expired returned to the ranks. Thus according to Plutarch, Aristides and Philopoemen, who had been leaders of armies, and who had won victories, served as simple soldiers.

Retaliation is merely the application of equality in the matter of satisfaction to be awarded for an injury. It is the equalized expiation for the offence. Only a damage exactly equal to the offence committed — a life for a life, a burn for a burn — can satisfy the equalitarian soul of primitive men. The equalitarian instinct, which in the distribution of food and of goods imposed the equal share, created the law of retaliation. The necessity of preventing the disastrous consequences of vendettas introduced it into primitive societies. Justice plays no role, either in its creation or introduction. Thus we find the law of retaliation established among nations, who have so little idea of Justice that they possess no words for crime, fault, justice. The Homeric Greeks, although of a relatively higher civilization, had no word for law, and it is impossible to conceive of Justice without laws.†

Retaliation, invented and introduced to escape the dangers of vendettas and admitted by primitive men because it gave full satisfaction to their passion for vengeance, had to be regulated when once it became a matter of custom. The entire clan originally had a right to vengeance, which it exercised indifferently on any member of the clan which had committed the offence. A beginning was made by limiting the number of persons who could exercise vengeance, and that of the persons upon whom it was permitted to exercise it. The *thar*, the law of blood of the Bedouins and almost all

---

* Volney's *General Observations on the Indians of America*, 1820.

† This absence of the word 'law' had struck the ancients; the historian Josephus observes with astonishment that in the Iliad the word *nomos*, which later was to signify law, is never employed in that sense.

the Arabs, authorizes every individual comprised in the first five degrees of relationship to kill any relative of the murderer comprised in the first five degrees. This custom must have been general, for among the Germans and the Scandinavians the *wehrgeld* was paid and received by the relatives of the first five circles or degrees.

This custom, although limiting the field of vengeance, nevertheless gave up to it too vast a choice of victims; thus among the Hebrews we recognize attempts to restrain it and to limit vengeance to the guilty one. Jehovah, who has no fear of contradicting himself, commands in Deuteronomy (XXIV, 16): 'not to put to death the fathers for the children, nor the children for the fathers, but each to be put to death for his own sin.' It was so difficult to impose this limitation upon fiery vengeance that long afterwards the Eternal protests against the proverb, 'The fathers have eaten sour grapes and the children's teeth are set on edge. As I live, ye shall not have occasion any more to use this proverb in Israel. Behold! all souls are Mine, as the soul of the father, so also the soul of the son is mine, and the soul that sinneth shall die.' (Ezekiel, XVIII, 2, 3, 4.)

But it was still more difficult to limit the number of persons considering themselves authorized to exercise vengeance — and finally to take it away from them. The passion of vengeance could not be assuaged unless the nearest relative of the victim punished the guilty one. Thus, it is Pyrrhus, the son of Achilles, who before the Achaean army had to sacrifice the sister of his father's murderer. Caillaud relates that in certain tribes of the African desert, the guilty one is turned over to the full discretion of the near relatives of the victim — who torture him and kill him at their will. Frazer saw in Persia a woman, to whom they had given up the murderer of her son, pierce him with fifty slashes of a knife, and by a refinement of vengeance, pass the bloody blade over his lips. In the ninth century in Norway, the murderer, led to the edge of the sea by the members of the popular assembly, was put to death by the prosecutor, or on his authority, by the royal provost. As for Athens, the civil power was charged to strike the culprit, the nearest relative assisted at the execution as an avenger of blood. Even though he no longer played an active part, his presence was necessary, not only to assuage his vengeance but also to fulfil the primitive conditions of the law of retaliation.

This law, by regulating and limiting the vendetta, proves that the passion which tortures and blinds primitive man subsides by degrees and can finally be curbed under a yoke; man accustoms himself no longer to exercise vengeance blindly upon a whole clan or upon a whole family, but on the culprit alone, and this vengeance is limited to rendering strictly blow for blow, death for death.* This regulation could not be introduced and maintained but for the collective intervention of the clans and families of the victim and the culprit. The family, always remaining responsible for the actions of its members, is called upon to declare whether it wishes to take the responsibility of the offence, or to give up the offender; in this last case, to determine on an expiation proportionate to the injury, it must also constrain the culprit to submit passively in the event of there being resistance on his part.† Thus they came to establish arbitrating tribunals, whose duties it was to estimate the offence and to award satisfaction.

The members of the tribe assembled together, as was the case with the Scandinavians, constituted this first tribunal of arbitration; but on account of the difficulties presented by the gathering of such assemblies, only cases of murder or serious wounds were submitted to them; as for those of minor importance, like blows and wounds not involving death or the loss of a limb, they had to be settled by the council of elders.

---

* The barbarian does not stop half way. He carries logic to its final consequences: once he had the idea of detaching the culprit from the collectivity of the family to make him carry the responsibility of his action, he pushed this idea to the point of detaching from the collectivity of the body, the organ which had committed the act, to be punished. Diodorus of Sicily reports that the Egyptians punished the violation of a free woman by mutilation. They amputated the nose of an adulterous woman in order to deprive her of the attractions which she had employed for seduction. They cut off the hands of counterfeiters and forgers of public seals, 'in order to chastise the portion of the body with which the crime had been committed.' In almost all countries the hands of thieves have been cut off for petty larceny not involving capital punishment.

† 'When among the Itelmen of Kamchatka,' relates a traveler of the eighteenth century, G. W. Steller, 'a murder is committed, the family of the victim applies to that of the murderer and demands that he be given up. If the latter consents and gives him up he is killed in the same fashion in which he killed his victim; if it refuses, that means that the family approves of the murder. Then war is declared between the two families. That which triumphs, massacres all the males of the vanquished family and carries into slavery the women and girls.' In Polynesia, when the culprit did not submit passively to the vengeance of the offended party, his own family constrained him by force. (Ellis, Polynesian Researches.)

Moses, on the advice of his father-in-law, Jethro, chose `men of truth and placed such over them to be rulers of thousands, rulers of hundreds, rulers of fifty and rulers of tens, to judge the people at all times,` but every grave matter they were to bring to him. (Exodus XVIII.) Moses probably reproduced in the desert what existed in Egypt. A council of Druids was in Gaul charged with looking into the offence and fixing the penalty. If one of the parties refused to submit to its decree, it barred him from sacrifices, which constituted the most terrible punishment, for the interdict was avoided by everyone. (Caesar's Gallic War, 13.) At Athens the Areopagus regulated vengeance. Aeschylus puts in the mouth of the Erinnyes who had just lost their case, these words depicting the evils which had necessitated the institution of such a tribunal:

> For this, too, I will pray,
> That Discord, never satiate with ill.
> May never ravine in this commonwealth
> Nor dust that drinks dark blood
> From veins of citizens,
> Though eager thirst for vengeance, from the State
> Snatch woes as penalty
> For deeds of murderous guilt.

(Plumptre's Translation.)

These ancient goddesses, daughters of Night, who personified primitive vengeance, were pronouncing their funeral oration. After the establishment of the Areopagus, they subsided and lost their savage character along with their function. They then changed their names and were called Eumenides; that is to say, the Good Goddesses.

The Areopagus must have dated back to a remote antiquity. Another legend says it was established to pronounce on the murder committed by Ares. He had killed the son of Poseidon who had violated his daughter. He was acquitted by the twelve gods who formed the tribunal. By the way, the word Areopagus signifies Ares Hill. Another legend has it that the first murder brought before this tribunal was that of Procris, killed accidentally in the chase by her husband, Cephalus. This legend and that of the matricide of Orestes would make the institution of the Areopagus date back to the period of the matriarchate, which at the time of the Trojan war had just been replaced by the patriarchate; in fact, at the moment when woman ceases to be the head of the family, she enters as a slave into the house of her husband, who has the right of life and death over her. Even her son posseses that right. Consequently vengeance could no longer be demanded for her death if the murder was brought about by her husband or her son.* The Areopagus rendered its decrees in the dark, like the Egyptian tribunal corresponding to it. That is why Themis, the goddess emblematic of Justice, has her eyes bandaged. The Athenians no doubt wished this symbolism to recall the fact that the Areopagus had been established as a substitute for the Erinnyes, daughters of Night, who, according to Homer, lived in the shades of Erebus. The Areopagus and the Egyptian tribunal admitted no attorneys. The culprit, himself, was obliged to preserve silence. These two tribunals, replacing the families of the offended and the offender, did not judge; their role was limited to finding the culprit and delivering him to the family of the offended.

If in a commercial city like Athens, the necessity of maintaining order permitted the establishment of a permanent tribunal for regulating vendettas and punishing culprits, almost everywhere else it was necessary to leave to the families the function of satisfying their own vengeance. In England in the tenth century, under King Alfred, custom and law still authorized families to declare private war in case of murder. The civil power in France, not having been able to take vengeance away from the families, tried to attenuate its effects by imposing an interval between the offence and the vengeance. A royal ordinance of the thirteenth century, the *quarantaine-le-roy* (king's forty days), attributed to Philip Augustus or St. Louis, forbade undertaking private war for vengeance until forty days had elapsed since the

---

* Demosthenes in one of his civil pleas cites an article of Draco's laws which gave every Athenian the right of life and death over five women — his wife, his daughter, his mother, his sister and his concubine. The Gragas (gray geese) which are the ancient laws of Iceland, sanctioned this same right, adding to it adopted daughters. Later on in Solon's epoch, customs being transformed, the laws of Draco appeared too blood-thirsty, yet they were never abolished, 'but by the tacit consent of the Athenians,' says Aulus Gellius, 'they were, so to speak, obliterated.' The first laws, precisely because they fix and sanction the customs of ancestors, were never abrogated; they persisted although they were contradicted by new laws. Thus the code of Manu preserves, side by side, the law establishing equal division of goods between brothers and that which established the right of primogeniture. The law of the twelve tables at Rome did not abolish the royal laws. The stone on which the latter were engraved was inviolable; at the very most the least scrupulous believed themselves authorized to turn it over.

commission of the offence. If in this interval a murder was committed upon one of the offenders, the murderer was punished with the death penalty, for having transgressed the royal ordinance. It is only lately that the French Government has been able to suppress vendettas in Corsica.

The passion for vengeance, although subject to the law of retaliation and to arbitrating assemblies, still remained irrepressible. Its claws and its teeth could only be drawn by property. Nevertheless property, which is destined to banish the disorders of private vengeance, makes its appearance surrounded by a train of discords and crimes in the bosom of families. Before the right of primogeniture was recognized and accepted as an established custom, it engendered fratricidal struggles for the possession of the paternal goods, of which Greek mythology has preserved horrible memories in the story of the Atridae.* Since then property has not ceased to be the most efficacious and the most active cause of private dissensions and crimes, and of civil and international wars, which have overwhelmed human societies.

Property enters like a fury into the human heart, overwhelming the most deeply rooted sentiments, instincts and ideas and exciting new passions; nothing less than property would have served to restrain and weaken vengeance, the ancient and dominant passion of the barbaric soul.

Private property once established, blood no longer demands blood; it demands property; the law of retaliation is transformed.

The transformation of retaliation was probably facilitated by slavery and the slave trade, the first international commerce which was regularly established. The exchange of living men for oxen, arms and other objects accustomed the barbarian to giving

---

* If we recall the mythological legends of Greece, it seems that when the father's authority replaced the mother's in the family the order of succession was thrown into serious confusion. All the sons, who in the matriarchal family did not inherit, claimed to have equal rights to take possession of the goods of the deceased father and the management of the household. It is only after many internal struggles that the right of primogeniture succeeded in establishing itself and it could only maintain itself by calling religious superstition to its assistance. The father was accounted to live in his tomb placed in his house or the surrounding garden. He continued to administer his property and gave orders to his successor. Obedience was rendered not to the living heir, but the deceased father. Then by the side of the tribal religion were established the family cults, which Fustel de Coulange supposes to have been primitive.

for blood some other equivalent than blood. A new household phenomenon contributed even more energetically than the slave trade toward modifying the law of retaliation. Woman, so long as the matriarchal family exists, remains in her clan, where she is visited by her husband or husbands; in the patriarchal family the young girl leaves her family to go and live in that of her husband. The father is indemnified for the loss of his daughter, who by marrying ceases to belong to him. The young girl then becomes an object of traffic, a finder of oxen, *alphesiboia* according to the Homeric epithet. It was for oxen that the Greeks exchanged her. The father began by trafficking in his daughters and ended by selling his sons, as is shown by the Greek and Roman laws. The father by selling his own blood breaks the ancient solidarity which united the members of the family and bound them in life and death. The parents, exchanging for beasts and other property their children, their living blood, became for a still stronger reason disposed to accept beasts or other property for blood that had been shed, for a son who was slain. The children, following the example of their parents, came in their turn to satisfy themselves with an indemnity, whatever it might be, for the blood of their father or mother.

Then instead of life for life, tooth for tooth, beasts, iron or gold are demanded for life, tooth and other wounds. The Kaffirs require oxen, the Scandinavians, Germans and barbarians, who by contact with more civilized nations have learned the use of money, demand silver.*

This revolution, one of the most far-reaching ever accomplished in the human soul, was not brought about suddenly

---

* At a time when historians believed that every nation and every race had its own special manners and customs, it was claimed that the *wehrgeld* was of German origin and that the Greeks and Latins had never descended to this barbarous means of compounding for blood by money. Nothing is further from the truth. The Eighth Table of the Roman Law of the Twelve Tables says:

II. Against him who breaks a limb and makes no amends, retaliation
III. For the breaking of a freeman's tooth a penalty of three hundred aces; slave's one hundred and fifty
IV. For an insult a penalty of twenty-five aces.

Ajax having been sent with Ulysses and Phoenix on an embassy to Achilles to influence him to accept Agamemnon's presents and appease his wrath, said to Ulysses: 'Yet doth a man accept recompense of his brother's murderer or for his dead son; and so the man-slayer for a great price abideth in his own land, and the kinsman's heart is appeased, and his proud soul, when he hath taken the recompense.' (Iliad. IX. 632-6).

nor without painful struggles. Not only religion, the preserver of ancient customs, but also the barbarian sentiments of solidarity and dignity opposed themselves to the substitution of money for blood. Superstition attached a curse to blood money. The treasure, which in the Eddas is the cause of the death of Sigurd and the extermination of the family of the Volsungs and the Giukings, is precisely the price of blood which the Scandinavian gods Odin, Loki and Hoenir had to pay for the murder of Balder. Saxo Grammaticus has preserved the song of a Danish bard who is indignant against the customs of his day and against those who carry in their purse the blood of their fathers. The nobles of Turkestan, says Pallas, never consent to receive the price of blood. The Afghan murderer, even if he has committed an involuntary murder, according to Elphinstone, has to beg the family of his victim to accept his money for compensation and has to submit to a humiliating ceremony analogous to that which on a similar occasion was in use among the Slavs of Southern Europe. 'The judges and spectators form a large circle. In the middle, the culprit with a gun and a dagger attached to his neck, crawls on his knees to the feet of the offended party, who, after taking away his arms, raises him and embraces him, saying, 'God forgive you.' The spectators with joyous plaudits congratulate the reconciled enemies. This ceremony, called the ''Circle of Blood'', ends by a feast given at the expense of the murderer, in which all the spectators take part.'* The Bedouin, although accepting blood-money, forces the murderer and his family to recognize their obligations to him.

Retribution for blood was at first left to the award of the offended party, who at his will determined the quantity and quality of the objects to be given to appease him. The Sagas show us the Icelander fixing by himself the price of blood and content with nothing less than all the property of the murderer and his family. To appease his passion for vengeance, complete spoliation was required, that the culprit and his family might be deprived of the joys of life. This excess of compensation made this sort of expiation practically impossible and gave room for endless debates. The barbarians, to obviate this difficulty, saw themselves forced to decide on the price which could be demanded. The barbarian codes fixed minutely the price to be

* Krasinski, Montenegro and the Slavonians of Turkey, 1853.

paid in kind or money for the life of a freeman, according to his
birth and his rank; for wounds on the hand, on the arm, on the leg,
etc.; and for every insult to his honour, and every attempt upon his
domestic peace. The king, as well as the peasant, was protected by
a *wehrgeld*, payable to his relatives. The only difference between
the *wehrgeld* of the king and that of other individuals
in a nation was the scale on which the price of blood was figured.*

The family of the culprit was responsible for the payment of
the price of blood, which the family of the victim shared among its
members, proportionately to the degree of relationship. The
Sagas of Iceland indicate the manner of division: the males of
the family were divided into five circles or degrees of
relationship; the first circle, composed of the father, mother and
the eldest son, received or paid three marks; the second and third
circles two marks; the fourth one mark and the fifth one ore or an
eighth of a mark.

The *wehrgeld* involved the creation of an official body with
the duty of superintending its application. Later, fines were added
to it. The *wehrgeld* continued to be paid to the relatives of the
victim, while the fines accrued to the royal or public funds. It is
almost the same as in our own days in capitalist countries, where
the *werhgeld* has taken the name of damages and interests.

The simple and equalitarian spirit of the savage had led him to
the law of retaliation, life for life, wound for wound, which was
the only way for regulating vengeance that he could imagine; but
when under the operation of property, the law of retaliation was
transformed and the brutal equation of life for life was replaced by
the economic equation, beasts and other goods for life, wound,
insult, etc., the spirit of the barbarian was submitted to a severe
test: he had to solve a problem which obliged him to penetrate
into the domain of abstraction. He had on one side to weigh the
material and moral damage caused a family by the death of one of
its members, and to an individual by the loss of one of his limbs or
by an insult; and on the other hand to measure the advantage
which they derived from the cession of certain material goods —

---

* The establishment of the *wehrgeld* carries with it this curious consequence,
which Mallet observes among the Scandinavians: since the death of a freeman and
wounds on his hand, his foot, etc., are subject to a price schedule, the body of a
debtor may be held responsible for the debt contracted. It is this reasoning which in
all countries has given the creditor the right to mutilate and enslave his debtor.

that is to say, he was obliged to apportion and equilibrate things having no direct material connection between them. The barbarian began brutally in demanding in the case of a murder, the social ruin of the culprit, his economic death, the cession of all his property; and ended after many intellectual efforts by tariffing life, the loss of an eye or a tooth and even insults. This tariffing obliged him to acquire new abstract concepts on the relations of men among themselves and with things, which in their turn engendered in his brain the idea of retributive justice, which has for its mission to proportion as exactly as possible compensation to damage.

II

DISTRIBUTIVE JUSTICE

The instinct of self-preservation, the first and the most imperious of instincts, impels the savage man, like the animal, his ancestor, to take possession of the objects he needs. All that he can seize he grasps to satisfy either his hunger or his fancy. He acts toward material goods in the same way the scientist and the man of letters act toward intellectual goods: he takes his good wherever he finds it, according to Moliere's phrase.* The European travellers who have been the victims of that instinct have given themselves up to fine moral indignation and have belaboured the savage with the epithet of thief, as if it were possible that the idea of theft should enter into the human head before the establishment of property.†

---

* 'Nature,' said Hobbes, 'has given each of us an equal right over all things. In the state of nature each has the right to do and possess all that pleases him; whence comes the common saying that nature has given all things to all men, and from which it is gathered that in the state of nature utility is the rule of Right.' (De Cive, Book I, Chapter I). Hobbes and the philosophers who speak of natural right, natural religion, natural philosophy are lending to Dame Nature their notions of right, religion and philosophy, which are anything but natural. What should we say of the mathematician who should attribute to nature his concepts of the metric system and should philosophize on the natural metre and millimetre? Measures of length, laws, gods and philosophical ideas are of human manufacture; men have invented them, modified them and transformed them, according to their private and social needs.

†|Proudhon, who had taken to himself the proprietorship of Brissot's phrase, committed the same error when he gave for a social axiom his 'property is robbery,' for robbery is the consequence of property and not its determining cause. The historic origin of property, whether personal or real, proves that it never took, at its beginning a character of spoliation; this could not have been otherwise.

To subdue this prehensile* instinct, which is the transformation of one of the essential properties of organized matter, to subject it to the yoke and to compress it to the stifling point, has been one of the tasks of civilization. To subjugate the prehensile instinct humanity has passed through stages more numerous than those required for subduing and extinguishing the passion for vengeance. The subjection of this primordial instinct has contributed to the defining of the idea of justice, rough-hewn by the taming of vengeance.

The savage, while he wanders in little clans over the uninhabited earth, along the seas and the streams, stopping where he finds food in abundance, exercises his prehensile instinct without restrictions of any sort; but from the remotest prehistoric times, the necessity of procuring the means of existence obliges him to restrain that instinct within certain limits. When the population of a country acquires a certain density, the savage tribes inhabiting it divide the land into hunting grounds, or into pastures when they live by the breeding of cattle. In order to preserve their means of subsistence, which are the natural fruits, game, fish and sometimes herds of swine feeding freely in the forests, the savage and barbaric nations of the old and the new world fringe their territories with neutral zones.† Every individual who goes beyond the limit of the territory of his tribe is pursued, trailed and sometimes put to death by the neighbouring tribe. He can within the limit of his territory take freely of what he needs, but beyond that limit he takes only at his risk and peril. The violations of territory, often encouraged to exercise the bravery and the skill of the young warriors, are among the most frequent causes of war between neighbouring tribes. The savages, in order to avoid these wars and to live at peace with their neighbours, were obliged to repress their prehensile instinct and to leave it a free career only within the limit of their own territory, the common property of all the members of their tribe.

* The word prehensile exists in zoological language. Webster defines it, adapted to seizing or grasping.

† The rude savages of Tierra del Fuego define the limits of their territories by broad vacant spaces. Caesar reports that the Suevi took pride in surrounding themselves with vast solitudes. The Germans gave the name of bordering forest and the Slavs the name of protecting forest to the neutral space between two or more tribes. Morgan says that in North America this space was narrower between tribes of the same language, ordinarily allied by marriage, and otherwise, and wider between tribes of different tongues.

But even in the limits of this territory the necessity of preserving the means of existence obliges the savages to put a bridle on their prehensile instinct. The Australians forbid the consumption of chickens and pigs when there is a scarcity, and that of bananas and yams when the crop of the bread-fruit trees promises ill. They prohibit fishing in certain bays when fish are scarce. The Redskins of Canada for other reasons do not kill the female beavers. The savages, even when dying of hunger, do not touch the plants and animals which are the totems of their tribes, that is the ancestors from which they claim to be descended. These prohibitions, to be more effective, often take on a religious character. The forbidden object is tabooed, and the gods take it upon themselves to punish those who violate the prohibition.

These restrictions to the prehensile instinct are communistic; they are imposed only in the interest of all the members of the tribe and it is only for this reason that the savage and the barbarian submit to them voluntarily. But there exist even among savages other restrictions which have not this character of common interest.

The sexes in savage tribes are distinctly separated by their functions. The man fights and hunts, the woman feeds and watches over the child, which belongs to her and not to the father, who is generally unknown or uncertain. She takes charge of the preservation of the provisions, the preparation and the distribution of food, the making of clothes, household utensils, etc., and she attends to agriculture at its beginning. This separation — based upon organic differences, introduced to prevent promiscuous sexual relations and maintained by the functions devolving upon each sex — is reinforced by religious ceremonies and mysterious practices peculiar to each sex and forbidden on pain of death to the persons of the other sex and by the creation of a language which is understood only by the initiated of one sex. The separation of the sexes inevitably brought on their antagonism, which translated itself by prohibitions imposed upon the prehensile instinct, which no longer have a general character, but which take on a special sex character — we might say a class character; for, as Marx observes, the class struggle first shows itself under the form of a struggle between the sexes. Here are a few of these sex prohibitions: the savage tribes ordinarily forbid women to participate in their cannibal feasts; certain choice meats such as

the flesh of the beaver and emu are in Australia especially reserved
for the warriors; it is from a sentiment of the same kind that the
Greeks and Romans of historic times forbade women the use of
wine.

The restrictions imposed upon the prehensile instinct continued
to become more numerous with the establishment of the
collective family property. As long as the terriority of the clan
remains the undivided property of all its members, who cultivate
it in common just as they hunt and fish in common, the provisions
entrusted to the keeping of the married women, according to
Morgan, remain common property. Also within the limit of the
territory of his clan a savage takes freely the food he needs. 'In a
village of Redskins,' says Catlin, 'every individual, man, woman
or child, has the right to enter into any cabin, no matter what,
even into that of the military chief of the nation, and eat all he
requires.' The Spartans, according to Aristotle, had preserved
these communistic manners, but the division of the arable lands
of the clan introduces other manners. The division of lands could
only take place on condition of its giving full satisfaction to the
sentiment of jealous equality which filled the soul of primitive
man. This sentiment demands imperatively that *all have the same
things*, according to the formula which Theseus, the mythical
law-giver of Athens, had given for the foundation of
justice. Every distribution of food or of the booty of war among
primitive men was made in the most equalitarian manner; they
could not conceive that it should be otherwise. The equal
partition is for them the inevitable, so in the Greek language,
moira, which signifies at first the part coming to each guest at a
banquet, ends by indicating the supreme goddess of Destiny, to
whom men and gods are subject; and the word *dike* used at
first for equal division, custom, ends by being the name of the
goddess Justice.*

If the most perfect equality must rule in the distribution of food,

---

* A fragment of Heraclides of Pontus, a disciple of Plato, contains a description of
the communistic banquets of the Dorians. Every person at the andreias (the common
repast of the men) received an equal share, except the archon, the member of the
council of the elders; he had a right to a quadruple portion — one in his quality of
citizen, a second in his quality of president of the table and two others for the support
of the hall; these probably must have been reserved for his servants. Each table was
under the special supervision of a matriarch, who distributed food to the guests. This
function of distributor, reserved to woman, impressed so forcibly the prehistoric
Greeks that they personified destiny and the fates by the goddesses Moira, Aisa and

so much more the egalitarian spirit will be awakened when it comes to distributing the lands which provide the support for the whole family, for the division of lands was made by families proportionately to the number of their male members.

It has been rightly said that the inundations of the Nile forced the Egyptians to invent the first elements of geometry that they might redistribute the fields when the stream, bursting its banks, had effaced their landmarks. The custom of holding ploughed lands in common after the harvest, and their annual redistribution, imposed upon other nations the same necessity as the overflowing of the Nile. The primitive men were obliged in all countries to discover for themselves the elements of surveying without going through the Egyptian school. Measuring follows naturally from counting. Probably the flock fortified the idea of number and developed numeration, while the division of land engendered the idea of measurement, and the vessel that of capacity.

Rectilinear geometry was naturally the first to be discovered. It required year after year to learn how to decompose a curve into an infinity of straight lines and the area of a circle into an infinity of isoceles triangles. The arable lands were then divided by straight lines into parallelograms, very long and very narrow. But before they knew how to measure the surface of parallelograms by multiplying the base by the altitude and consequently before they had the power of making them equal, the primitive men could not be satisfied until the pieces of ground falling to each family were enclosed in straight lines of equal length. They arrived at these lines by carrying over the ground the same stick the same number of times. The stick which was used for measuring the length of the lines was sacred. The Egyptian hieroglyphics take for the symbol of Justice and Truth, the cubit, that is to say, the unit of measure. What the cubit had measured was just and true.*

Ceres, whose names signify the part which is received in the distribution of food or of booty.

* Haxthausen relates in his curious journey in Russia that he saw in the State House of Yaroslav certain rods which were revered as the sacred units of land measurement. The length of the rods was in inverse ratio to the quality of the lands: the shortest served to measure the best lands and the longest for lands of inferior quality. 'All the portions are in this way unequal in size and equal in value.'

The portions comprised between the straight lines of equal length set at rest their egalitarian spirit and gave no room for contests. The straight line was thus the important part of the operation. The straight lines once traced, the fathers of families were content. They gave full satisfaction to their egalitarian sentiments. For this reason the Greek word *orthos*, which at first means what is in a straight line, has the further meaning of that which is true, equitable and just.*

The straight line, because it acquired the power of subduing their savage passions, must of necessity have taken on in their eyes an august character. It is by a like phenomenon that the Pythagorians, dazzled by the properties of the numbers they were studying, attributed to the decade a fatalistic character, and that all nations have given mystical qualities to the first numbers. We may thus conceive that the straight line represented in the minds of the men of the first agrarian allotments all they could conceive of Justice.

The egalitarian spirit of primitive men was so fierce, that to prevent the division of lands divided into narrow strips of equal lengths from exciting quarrels, they were distributed by lot, with the aid of pebbles, before the invention of writing. Thus the Greek *kleros*, which means pebble, takes on the added significance of portion assigned by lot; then that of patrimony, fortune, condition, country.

---

* The root *or* in the Greek language contributes to the formation of three series of words, which seem contradictory, but which are complimentary and connect themselves with the division of land:
  1. The idea of going in a straight line.
     or-thos, straight, erect, vertical, true, equitable, just;
     or-me, movement upward, soaring, leaping, passion;
     or-numi and *or-ino*, to set in motion, to excite;
     or-ugma, ditch, subterranean gallery;
     or-ux, pick-axe;
     or-thoo, to make straight, to redress;
     ot-thosios, Zeus — Jupiter, who redresses wrongs.
  2. The idea of bounding, of limiting:
     oros, boundary, frontier;
     or-izo, to bound, to limit, to define, to enact;
     or-ios, that which serves as a limit;
     Zeus or-ios, the god of boundaries.
  3. The idea of vigilance:
     our-os, guard, guardian;
     pul-or-os, guardian of gates;
     tima-or-os, he who punishes, who avenges;
     or-omai, to watch over, to guard.

The idea of justice was originally so closely linked to the division of lands, that in Greek, the word *nomos*, which means usage, custom, law, has for its root *nem*, which gives birth to a numerous family of words containing the idea of pasturage and of sharing.*

Nomos, at first exclusively used for pasturage, took on in the course of time numerous different meanings (sojourn, habitation, usage, custom, laws), which are so many historical sediments deposited by human evolution. If we unroll the chronological series of these meanings, we pass in review the principal stages traversed by pre-historic peoples. *Nomos*, pasturage, recalls the pastoral and vagabond epoch: from the time the nomad (*nomas*) pauses, *nomos* is used for sojourn, habitation: but when once the pastoral peoples pause and choose their homes in a country, they must inevitably divide up the lands: then *nomos* akes on the meaning of division. When once the agrarian divisions have passed into popular customs, *nomos* takes on its last meaning, custom, law, — law being originally the codification of custom. In the Greek of the Byzantine period and of the modern epoch, *nomos* no longer preserves any other meaning than law. From *nomos* are derived *nomisma*, that which is established by custom, religious practice: *nomizo*, to observe the custom, to think, to judge: *nomisis*, worship, religion: *Nemesis*, the goddess of distributive justice, etc. — which are so many witnesses of the effect of agrarian divisions upon human thought.

The division of the common lands of a clan reveals a new world to the imagination of prehistoric man. It revolutionizes the instincts, the passions, the ideas and the customs in a more energetic and more profound fashion than would be done in our days by the return of capitalist property to the community. The

---

* *Nemo*, to share, to distribute, then to treat someone according to law.
nome, pasturage, portion, lot;
nomas, nomad, vagabond, who wanders feeding a herd;
nomos, originally pasturage — then sojourn dwelling, portion — and finally usage, custom, law;
nomizo, to observe the custom, the law; to think, to believe, to judge;
nomisma, a thing established by custom, by law, religious practice, money;
nomisis, worship, religion, belief;
nemisis, wrath of the gods against those who infringe on the rights of another, the goddess of distributive justice;
epi-nomia, right to pasturage;
pro-nomia, privilege.

primitive men, to familiarize their brains with the strange idea that they must no longer touch the fruits and the harvests of the neighbouring fields within reach of their hands, were obliged to resort to all the witchcraft that they were capable of imagining.

Every field assigned by lot to a family was surrounded by a neutral zone like the territory of the tribe. The Roman law of the Twelve Tables fixed it at five feet. Boundaries marked its limits. At first they were only heaps of stone or trunks of trees. It was not until later that they were given the form of pillars with human heads to which arms were sometimes added. These heaps of stone and pieces of wood were gods for the Greeks and Latins. Oaths were made not to displace them;* the ploughman was not allowed to approach it, 'for fear that the god, feeling himself struck by the ploughshare, should cry to him, 'Stop, this is my field, there is thine.''' (Ovid, *Fasti*.) 'Cursed be he who removeth his neighbour's landmark,' thunders Jehovah, 'and all the people shall say Amen!' (Deuteronomy, XXVII, 17). The Etruscans called down all manner of curses on the head of the culprit. 'He who shall have removed the boundary,' says one of their sacred anathemas, 'shall be condemned by the gods, his house shall disappear, his race shall be extinguished, his land shall produce no more fruits; hail, blight and the fires of the dog-star shall destroy his harvests, his limbs shall be covered with ulcers, and shall fall into corruption.' If property brought justice to humanity, it drove away brotherhood.

Every year at the Terminalia, the neighboring proprietors of Latium decorated the landmarks with garlands, made offerings of honey, wheat and wine, and sacrificed a lamb on an altar built for the occasion, for it was a crime to stain with blood the sacred landmark.

If it is true, according to the word of the Latin poet, that fear gave birth to the gods, it is still more true that the gods were invented to inspire terror. The Greeks created terrible goddesses to subdue the prehensile instinct and to horrify the violators of the property of others. Dike and Nemesis belonged to this class of divinities. Their birth was subsequent to the introduction of

---

* Plato in his Laws says: 'Our first law should be this — that no one touch the boundary which separates a field from that of his neighbour, for it should remain unmoved, that no one should think of shaking the stone, which he has bound himself by an oath to leave in its place.'

agrarian divisions, as their names indicate. They were charged
with maintaining the new customs and punishing those who
infringed them. Dike, terrible as the Erinnyes, with whom she is
allied to terrify and punish, is appeased in proportion as men
acquire the habit of respecting the new agrarian customs; she
loses little by little her forbidding aspect. Nemesis presided over
the divisions and took care that the distribution of the land was
accomplished in an equitable manner. Nemesis on the bas-relief
which represents the death of Meleager, is represented with a roll
in her hand; doubtless the roll on which were inscribed the lots
that fell to each family. Her foot rests on the wheel of fortune. To
understand this symbolism it must be remembered that the
portions of land were drawn by lot. *

The Greeks were so thoroughly convinced that the culture and
sharing of lands had given birth to law and justice, that out of
Demeter, the goddess of the shepherds of Arcadia, where she
bore the name of Erinnys,† and who plays no part in the two

---

* Agriculture had a decisive influence over the development of the mentality of
primitive men. Thus, for example it was this which modified their opinions on the
division of time. The hours, which in Greek mythology designated not the
divisions of the day, but those of the year, were originally two in number; the hour
of spring-time, Thallo, whose name signifies to be verdant, to bloom; and the hour
of autumn, Karpus, which means fruit. Spring and autumn are the important
seasons for the savage, who does not cultivate the land, but who lives on the fruits
which it bears spontaneously. After the division of the lands, the number of hours
is increased to three — Dike, Eunomia, whose name signifies good pasturage,
equity, observation of custom, and Eirene, which means peace. Hesiod describes
them in his Theogouy as giving customs to men and establishing among them
peace and justice, like Demeter Thesmophora. As long as men live by hunting,
fishing and gathering wild fruits, it is a matter of indifference to them to be at war
during one season rather than another, but when they have fields to sow and to
reap, they are obliged to suspend during certain seasons of the year the wars of
tribe against tribe, and to establish truces for the sowing times, the harvests and
other agricultural labours. They then created the hour of peace, Eirene, and put
these truces under her protection. The Catholics of the Middle Ages placed them
under that of God and called them 'Truces of God.' Eirene is derived from the
word eiro, to speak. At Lacedaemon they gave the name eiren to the young man
more than twenty years of age who had a right to speak in public assemblies.
During the periods consecrated to the labours of the fields, the disputes between
tribes and villages were settled no longer by arms, but by speech — whence is
derived Eirene, the goddess who speaks. The cultivation of the land might have
had an influence over writing, as would seem to be proved by the ancient manner
of writing employed by the Greeks, Chinese, Scandinavians, etc., which consists
in writing alternately from left to right and right to left — returning to one's steps
like the oxen which plough.

† Erinnys might have come from Erion, wool, from which is derived eriole, wool
stealer.

Homeric poems, they made the godess of the fruitful earth, who initiated men into the mysteries of agriculture and established peace among them, giving them customs and laws. Demeter, on the monuments of the more ancient type, is represented with her head crowned with ears of wheat, holding in her hand implements of husbandry and poppies, which by reason of their innumerable grains are the symbol of fruitfulness; but in the more recent representations, which show her as law-giver, *Thesmophora,* Demeter replaces her ancient attributes by the stylet, which serves to engrave the customs and laws regulating the divisions of land; and by the roll on which are inscribed the titles of property.*

But the most formidable goddesses and the most horrible curses and anathemas, however deeply they disturbed the fantastical and artless imagination of the child-nations, failed utterly in curbing the prehensile instinct and the people's inveterate habit of taking the things they needed. So there was nothing for it, but to resort to corporal punishment of a ferocity never before heard of and totally opposed to the sentiments and customs of savages and barbarians, who, if they do inflict blows to prepare themselves for their life of incessant struggles, never give to them the character of punishment. The savage does not strike his child. It is the proprietor fathers who invented the horrible precept, 'He who loves well punishes well.' Attempts against property were punished more fiercely than crimes against persons. The abominable codes of iniquitous justice made their entrance into history in the train, and as the consequence, of private appropriation of land.

Property marks its appearance by teaching the barbarians to trample underfoot their noble sentiments of equality and brotherhood. Laws inflicting the death penalty are enacted against those who menace property. 'He, who at night shall secretly have cut or pastured his flocks on harvests produced by the plough.' commands the law of the Twelve Tables, 'if he is of age, shall be sacrificed to Ceres and put to death; if he is under age, he shall be beaten by rods at the will of the magistrate and condemned to make amends for double the damage. The open robber (that is to say, taken *in flagrante delicto*), if he is a

---

* The mythological gallery of Millin (Paris 1811) reproduces numerous medallions, vases, cameos, bas-reliefs, etc., on which Demeter is pictured with her various attributes.

freeman shall be beaten with rods and delivered up into slavery. The incendiary of a hay stack shall be flogged and put to death by burning.' (Table VIII, 9, 10, 14.) The law of Burgundy goes beyond the ferocious Roman law. It condemned to slavery the wife and the children of more than fourteen years who did not immediately denounce the husband and father guilty of theft of horses or oxen. (XLVII, 1,2). Property introduced espionage into the bosom of the family.

Private property in real and personal goods, from its appearance, gives birth to instincts, sentiments, passions and ideas which under its action have been developing in proportion to its transformations, and which will persist as long as private property shall survive.

The law of retaliation introduced into the human brain the germ of the idea of justice, which the division of lands, laying the foundations of private property and real estate, was to fertilize and make fruitful. The law of retaliation taught man to subdue his passion for vengeance and subject it to regulation; property curbed, under the yoke of religion and law, his prehensile instinct. The role of property in the elaboration of justice was so preponderant that it obscured the earlier working of the law of retaliation to the point that a nation as subtle as the Greeks, and minds as keen as those of Hobbes and Locke, did not perceive it. In fact Greek poetry attributed the invention of laws only to the goddesses who preside over the partition and culture of lands. Hobbes thinks that before the establishment of property in a state of nature there is no injustice in whatever a man might do against another. Locke affirms that 'where there is no property, there is no injustice, is a proposition as certain as any demonstration of Euclid: the idea of property being a right to a thing, and the idea to which the word injustice corresponds being the invasion or the violation of the right.'* The Greeks and these profound thinkers, hypnotized by property and forgetting the human being and his instincts and passions, suppressed the first and principal factor of history. The evolution of man and his societies cannot be understood and explained if we do not take account of the actions and reactions, one upon another, of human energies and economic and social forces.

---

* Hobbes: *De Cive*, remark added to the French translation of Sorbières. Locke: *Essay on Human Understanding*.

The egalitarian spirit of primitive men, to overcome the passion of vengeance, had not and could not have found anything but the law of retaliation. On the occasions of the divisions of food, booty and lands, this same egalitarian spirit required imperatively equal parts for all, 'that all might have the same things,' according to the formula of Theseus. Blow for blow, equal compensation for the wrong caused, and equal parts in the distribution of food and of lands were the only ideas of justice that primitive men could conceive. An idea of justice, which the Pythagorians expressed by the axiom 'Not to over-pass the equilibrium of the balance,' which as soon as it was invented became the attribute of justice.

But the idea of justice, which at its origin is but a manifestation of the egalitarian spirit, goes on, under the action of the property which it helps establish, to sanction the inequalities which property engenders among men.

Property, in fact, can only be consolidated by acquiring the right to set aside the prehensile instinct, and this right once acquired becomes an independent and automatic social force, which dominates man and turns against him.

The right of property conquers such a legitimacy, that Aristotle identifies justice with respect for the laws which protect it, and injustice with the violation of these same laws; that the *Declaration of the Rights of Man and the Citizen*, of the bourgeois revolutionists of 1789 erect it into a 'natural and inalienable right of man' (Article II); and that Pope Leo XIII in his famous encyclical on the condition of the labourers transforms it into a dogma of the Catholic Church. Matter leads the spirit.

The barbarian had substituted property for the shedding of blood. Property substituted itself for man, who in civilized societies possesses no rights but those conferred upon him by his property. Justice, like those insects which as soon as born devour their mother, destroys the egalitarian spirit which engendered it, and sanctions the enslavement of man.

The communist revolution, by suppressing private property and giving 'to all the same things,' will emancipate man and will bring to life the equalitarian spirit. Then the ideas of justice, which have haunted human heads since the establishment of private property will vanish — the most frightful nightmare which ever tortured sad civilized humanity.

4

The origin of the idea of good

FORMATION OF THE HEROIC IDEAL

ONE and the same word is used in the principal European languages to indicate material goods and moral Good. We may without suspicion of rashness conclude that the fact must be the same in the idioms of all nations which have arrived at a certain degree of civilization, since we know today that all traverse the same phases of material and intellectual evolution. Vico, who had set forth this historic law, affirms in his *Scienza Nuova* that ˙there must necessarily exist in the nature of human affairs a mental language common to all nations, which language designates uniformly the substance of things which are the moving causes of social life. This language bends into different forms, as numerous as the different aspects which the things may assume. We have proof of this in the fact that proverbs, these maxims of popular wisdom, are alike in substance among all nations, ancient and modern, though they may be expressed in the most different forms.˙

I pointed out in the preceding articles on the origin of abstract ideas and the idea of justice, the twists and turns through which the human spirit passed to represent in Egyptian hieroglyphics the abstract idea of motherhood by the image of the vulture and that of justice by the cubit. In this study I shall try to follow it in the tortuous road which it has traversed to arrive at confusing under the same word material goods and moral Good.

The words which in the Latin and Greek languages serve for

material goods and moral Good were originally adjectives applied
to the human being.

Agathos (Greek), strong, courageous, generous, virtuous, etc.
Ta agatha, goods, riches.
To agathon, good, *to adron agathon*, the Supreme Good.
Bonus * (Latin), strong, courageous, etc.
Bona, goods, *bona patria*, patrimony.
Bonum, Good.

Agathos and *bonus* are generic adjectives. The Greeks and
the Romans of barbarous times to whom they were applied
possessed all the physical and moral qualities required by the
heroic ideal; so their irregular and superlatives, *aristos, esthlos,
beltistos*, etc., and *optimus*, are in the plural used substantively to
indicate the best and the foremost citizens. The historian
Velleius Paterculus gives the name of *optimates* to the patricians
and the rich plebeians who leagued themselves against the
Gracchi.

Strength and courage are the first and most necessary virtues of
primitive men in perpetual war among themselves and against

---

* The same phenomenon may be observed in our own language: *bon* (good) in the
old French signifies courageous. The song of Roland implies it always in this
sense:

> *Francis sunt bon, si ferrunt vassalement.*
> (The French are brave, they will strike bravely, XCI)

Speaking of the archbishop Turpin, Roland says:

> *Li arcevesque est mult bons chevaliers:*
> *Nen ad meillur en terre desuz ciel,*
> *Bien set ferir e de lance e d'espiet.*
> (The archbishop is a brave knight, none better on earth under heaven, he
> knows how to strike well with the lance and the spear, CXLV)

King John had been surnamed 'Good' on account of his courage. Commines, who
wrote in the fifteenth century, said good men for brave men. Goodman, after
having been in English the epithet for the soldier and after having indicated the
head of the family, the master of the house, ends like the French *bonhomme* in
being applied to the peasant, — *goodman* Hodge. Hodge is a contemptuous term
for peasant. It is no doubt when *bonhomme* came to be generally applied to
peasants, whom the nobles and soldiers pillaged (to live on the goodman, was a
current expression), that the word took on the ridiculous meaning which it has
kept. According to Ducange, it has had at times the significance of cuckold. The
addition of a suffix makes good and *bon* grotesque, *goodi, bonasse. Agathos* and
bonus could not in ancient times acquire such a meaning. It is only in the Latin of
the Middle Ages that we meet with, *bonatus, goodie.* The writers of the Byzantine
period used *agathos* especially in the sense of gentle, mild, and it seems that the
street urchins of modern Athens use it for imbecile.

nature.* The savage and the barbarian, strong and courageous possess in addition the other moral virtues of their ideal. Thus they comprise all physical and moral qualities under the same adjective. Strength and courage were then so near to the sum total of virtue that the Latins, after using the word *virtus* for physical strength and courage, came to employ it for virtue, while the Greeks gave the same successive meanings to the word *areté;* and that the word *pavelin*, the primitive weapon, which in Greek is called *kalon* serves later for the beautiful, while the Latin word for it, *quiris*, indicates the Roman citizen. Varro tells us that originally the Romans represented the god Mars by a javelin.

It was inevitable that strength and courage should make up the whole of virtue at that time, since to prepare for war, to acquire bravery in order to meet its perils, to develop physical strength so as to endure its fatigues and privations; and moral strength in order not to fall under the tortures inflicted upon prisoners, was the whole physical and moral education of the savages and barbarians. From childhood their bodies were suppled and tempered by gymnastic exercises and hardened by fasts and blows, under which they sometimes succumbed. Pericles, in his Funeral Oration over the first victims of the Peloponnesian War, contrasts this heroic education still in force at Sparta, which preserved its primitive customs, with that of the young men of Athens, which had entered into the democratic bourgeois phase. 'Our enemies,' said he, 'from the earliest childhood train themselves to courage with the severest discipline, and we, brought up with mildness, have no less ardour for running the same risks.' Livingstone, who found among the African tribes these heroic customs, drew a similar contrast for certain black chieftains between the English soldiers and the negro warriors.

Since courage in ancient times was the whole of virtue, cowardice must necessarily have been vice; thus the words which

---

* Physical force was so prized that in the Third Book of the Iliad, when Helen points out to the old men of Troy the Greek chieftains, it is not by their age, their physiognomy or their character, but by their strength that she distinguishes Ulysses from Menelaus and Ajax, both of whom he surpasses in the breadth of his shoulders. Diodorus Siculus, in summing up the qualities of Epaminondas, mentions first the vigour of his body, then the strength of his eloquence, his bravery, his generosity and his skill as general.

in Greek and Latin mean cowardly, *kakos* and *malus*, have the meaning of evil, vice.*

When the barbarian society became differentiated into classes, the patricians monopolized courage and the defence of the country. This monopoly was 'natural' (if I may apply the expression of bourgeois economics), although nothing appears more natural to the capitalists than to send in their place on colonial expeditions working men and peasants, and even, when they can, to entrust the defence of their country to proletarians, who possess neither an inch of land, nor a cog of a machine. The patricians reserved to themselves, as a privilege, the defence of their country, because they alone had a country, for, then, one had a country only on condition of possessing a corner of its soil. The foreigners who for reasons of commerce and industry resided in an ancient city, could not even possess the house in which they trafficked from father to son, and they remained foreigners although living in the city for generations. It required three centuries of struggles for the Roman plebeians who lived on the Aventine Hill to obtain property in the lands on which they had built their dwellings. The foreigners, the proletarians, the artisans, the merchants, the serfs and the slaves were relieved of military service and had no right to bear arms, nor even to have courage which was the privilege of the patrician class.†
Thucydides relates that the magistrates of Sparta massacred treacherously two thousand Helots, who by their bravery had just saved the republic. From the moment that it was forbidden to the plebeians to take part in the defence of their native country, and consequently to possess courage, cowardice must necessarily have been the sovereign virtue of the plebeians, as courage was that of the aristocracy. Thus the Greek adjective, *akos*, (cowardly, ugly, bad), indicates a man of the plebeians; while

---

* *Imbellis, imbecillis*, which signify unsuited for war, are especially used by the Latin writers for cowardly, weak in body and mind: *malus* has a more general sense, it is the epithet applied to one who physically and morally does not possess the requisite virtues.

† Even in democratic Athens in the time of Aristophanes, the merchants were not drafted for military service. The sycophant of his Plutos declares that he has become a merchant so as not to go to war. Plutarch says that Marius, 'to fight against the Cimbri and the Teutons, enrolled, in spite of the customs and laws, slaves and vagrants. All the generals before him excluded such from their armies. Arms, like other honours of the Republic, were only for men who were worthy and whose well known fortune answered for their fidelity.'

aristos, superlative of *agathos*, indicates a member of the patrician class — and the Latin *malus* indicates ugly, deformed, as were in the patrician eyes the slave and the artisan — deformed according to Xenophon, by their trades, while the gymnastic exercises developed harmoniously the body of the aristocrat.*

The patrician of ancient Rome was *bonus*, and the nobleman of Homeric Greece was *agathos*, because both possessed the physical and moral virtues of the heroic ideal — the only ideal that could have been engendered by the social environment in which they moved. They were brave, generous, strong of body, and stoical of soul, and moreover landed proprietors — that is to say, members of a tribe and of a clan possessing the territory on which they resided.†

The barbarians, who practise only the raising of cattle and agriculture of the rudest kind, give themselves up passionately to brigandage and piracy, as an outlet for their surplus physical and moral energy and to produce goods which they know no other way of procuring. In the Greek poem, of which only one strophe remains (the skolion of Hybrias), a barbaric hero sings, 'I have for wealth my great lance, my sword and my buckler; ramparts of my flesh, with them I plough, with them I harvest; with them I gather the sweet juice of the vine, with them I am called Master of the Mnoia (troop of slaves of the community).‡ Caesar relates that the Suevi every year sent half of their male population on pillaging expeditions. The Scandinavians, when their planting was finished, boarded their vessels and went out to pillage the coasts of Europe. The Greeks, during the Trojan War, left the siege to give themselves up to brigandage. 'The trade of piracy then had nothing shameful about it; it led to glory,' said Thucydides. The capitalists hold it in high esteem. Colonial expeditions of civilized nations are nothing but wars of brigandage; but while the

---

* 'Work at a trade deforms the body and degrades the mind. It is for this reason that those who engage in these labours are never called upon for public services.' (Xenophon's Economics.)

† The epithet stoical applied to the barbaric heroes is an anachronism, but merely a verbal one: the word was manufactured to indicate the disciples of Zeno, who taught under the portico, *stoa;* the barbarians possessed the moral force, which the stoics forced themselves to acquire.

‡ The cavaliers at the end of the Middle Ages, who had been ruined by the Crusades and dispossessed of their lands, by their internal dissensions, lived only by war, and like the Greek hero gave the name of the 'Harvest of the Sword' to the booty gained in combat.

capitalists have their piracies committed by proletarians, the
barbaric heroes paid in their own person. The only honourable
way of gaining riches was then by war. Thus the savings of the
son of a Roman family were called *peculium castrense* (money
gathered in the camps). Later on when the dowry of the wife
came to increase them they took on the name of *peculium quasi
castrense*. This general state of brigandage made the Middle Age
proverb literally true: 'Who has land, has war.' The proprietors of
flocks and crops never laid aside their arms. They accomplished
with their arms in their hands the functions of every day life. The
life of the heroes was one long combat. They died young, like
Achilles, like Hector. In the Achaean army there were but two
old men, Nestor and Phoenix. To grow old was then a thing so
exceptional that age became a privilege — the first that slipped
into human societies.

The patricians, assuming the defence of the city, naturally
reserved to themselves its government. This was confided to
fathers of families; but when the development of commerce and
industry had formed in the cities a numerous class of rich
plebeians, they were obliged after many civil struggles to make
for them a place in the government. Servius Tullius created at
Rome the Order of Knights with plebeians possessing a fortune of
at least 100,000 sesterces (about 1,000 dollars) as estimated by the
census. Every five years, they revised the roll of the equestrian
order, and the knights whose fortune had fallen below the census
figure, or had incurred a censorial stigma, lost their dignity.
Solon, who had grown rich through commerce, opened the
Senate and tribunals of Athens to those who possessed the means
of maintaining a war-horse and a yoke of oxen. In all cities, of
which historical records have been preserved, we find traces of a
similar revolution, and everywhere wealth, which comports with
the support of a war-horse, gives political rights. This new
aristocracy, which took its origin in wealth amassed by industry
and especially usury, could only gain acceptance and maintain
itself in its social supremacy by adapting itself to the heroic ideal
of the patricians and by assuming a part in the defence of the city,
in whose government it shared.*

---

* Aristophanes, an advocate of the aristocratic party and an adversary of the
Athenian democracy, opposes the ancient manners to the new, and by a strange
inconsistency, overwhelms with the most envenomed arrows of his satire

There was a time in antiquity when it was as impossible to conceive of a proprietor without warlike virtues as in our days to imagine a superintendent of mines or of a factory of chemical products without some administrative capacity and scientific knowledge. Property was then exacting; it imposed physical and moral qualities upon the possessor. The very fact of being a proprietor presupposed the possession of the virtues of the heroic ideal, since property could be conquered and preserved only on condition of having these. The physical and moral virtues of the heroic ideal were in some fashion incorporated into the material goods which communicated them to their proprietors. It is thus that in the feudal epoch the title of nobility was welded to the land. The baron, dispossessed of his manor, lost his title of nobility, which was added to those of his conqueror. It was the same with the dues and services; they were regulated according to the conditions of land and not according to the persons occupying it. Thus nothing was more natural than the barbaric anthropomorphism which endowed material goods with moral virtues.*

The role of defender of the nation, which the proprietors reserved to themselves, was not a sinecure. Aristotle remarks in his *Politics* that during the Pelopponnesian Wars the defeats on land and sea decimated the rich classes of Athens; that in the war against the Iapyges the upper classes of Tarentum lost so many of

---

Lamachus, Cleon and the demagogues, demanding that obtaining in spite of the opposition of the aristocrats, the continuance of the war against Sparta. The times had changed, the ancient aristocracy of blood and the new aristocracy of wealth had lost a great part of their warlike sentiments and preserved in its integrity only the proprietor sentiment. War no longer enriched them. It carried off their cattle, ravaged their fields, uprooted their olives and their vines, destroyed their crops and burned their houses. Aristophanes, himself, had estates in Emboea, which was one of the battle fields of the Peloponnesian war. Plato, who in his quality of idealist is an ardent defender of property, demands in his Republic that the Greeks decide that in every war among themselves, houses and crops should not be burned. These warrior pastimes should be permitted only in barbarous countries.

* An inverted phenomenon of hippomorphism was produced in the Middle Ages The nobles, having reserved to themselves the right of bearing arms on horseback, had by this fact such superiority in combats that the horse appeared to communicate to the feudal baron certain warlike virtues; so he took, like the rich men of ancient republics, the name of his mounts and called himself *chevalier, caballero,* etc. His most highly prized virtues were those of the horse as *chevaleresques, caballerescos, chivalrous.* Don Quixote judged the horse so important a personage in errant chivalry that it required all his casuistry to permit Sancho Panza to follow him mounted on an ass.

their members that it was possible to establish a democracy and that thirty years before, following certain unhappy combats, the number of citizens had fallen so low at Argos that they were obliged to grant the right of citizenship to the *perioeeci* (colonists living outside of the city walls). War made such ravages in its ranks that the warlike Spartan aristocracy feared to engage in it. The fortune of the rich, as well as their persons, was at the absolute disposition of the state. The Greeks designated among them the Liturgists, the Trierarchists, etc., who were obliged to defray the expenses of the public feasts and of the armament of the ships of the fleet. When after the Persian Wars it was necessary to reconstruct the walls of Athens destroyed by the Persians, public and private edifices were demolished in order to procure the materials to reconstruct them.

Since it was permitted only to the proprietors of real and personal property to be brave and to possess the virtues of the heroic ideal; since without the possession of material goods, these moral qualities were useless and even hurtful to their possessors, as is proved by the massacre of the 2,000 Helots, related above; since the possession of material goods was the justification of the moral virtues — nothing was then more logical and natural than to identify moral qualities with material goods and to confuse them under the same word.

II

THE DECOMPOSITION OF THE HEROIC IDEAL

Economic phenomena and the political events which they engendered took it upon themselves to ruin the heroic ideal and to dissolve the primitive union of moral virtues and material goods, which language records in so artless a manner.

The division of the arable lands, possessed in common by all the members of the clan began to introduce inequality among them. The lands under the action of multiple causes became concentrated into the hands of a few families of the clan and ended by falling into the possession of strangers, to such an extent that increasing numbers of patricians found themselves dispossessed of their goods. They took refuge in the cities, where they lived as parasites, hornets, Socrates calls them. It could not be otherwise; for in ancient societies, and in fact every society based on slavery, manual and even intellectual labour, being performed only by slaves and foreigners, is poorly paid and is considered as degrading, except indeed for agriculture and the care of flocks.

The political situation created by the economic phenomena is explained by Plato in the Eighth Book of the _Republic_, with a strength and clearness of vision which cannot be too much admired. A violent class struggle was troubling the cities of Greece. The oligarchical state, that is to say the one based on the census, says Socrates, 'is not one in its nature, it necessarily contains two states; one composed of the rich, the other of the poor, who inhabit the same ground, and conspire one against the other.' Socrates does not include among the poor the artisans and still less the slaves, but simply the ruined patricians.

'The greatest vice of the oligarchical state is that under it a man may sell all that he has, and another may acquire it, yet after the sale he may dwell in the city of which he is no longer a part, being neither trader, nor artisan, nor horseman nor hoplite, but only a poor, helpless creature.* It is impossible to prevent this disorder, for if it were prevented, a part would not possess excessive wealth, while others are reduced to extreme misery. The members of the ruling class, owing their authority only to the great property they possess, refrain from repressing by severe laws the libertinism of the dissipated young men and preventing them from ruining themselves by excessive expenditures, for they have the intention of buying their goods and appropriating them through usury, to increase their own wealth and power.'

The concentration of property creates in the state a class of 'people — armed with stings like hornets, some overwhelmed with debt, others marked with infamy, others who have at the same time lost their property and their honours — in a state of hostility and constant conspiracy against those who have enriched themselves with the wreck of their fortunes and against the rest of the citizens; and loving but one thing, revolution. Nevertheless, the greedy usurers, with their heads down and without seeming to perceive those whom they had ruined, since others keep coming, inflict large wounds upon them by means of

---

* Socrates means that not being able to maintain a warhorse and not having the means to buy a complete armour, they could not serve either as a horseman or as a hoplite, that is to say, a fully armed warrior.

the money which they loaned them at high interest; and while multiplying their own revenues, they multiply in the state the breed of hornets and mendicants.'

When the hornets became by their number and their turbulence a menace to the security of the governing class, they were sent out to found colonies, and when this resource failed, the wealthy citizens and the state tried to calm them by distributions of food and money. Pericles could maintain himself in power only by exporting and feeding the hornets. He sent one thousand citizens of Athens to colonize the Chersonesus, five hundred to Naxos, two hundred fifty to Andros, one thousand to Thrace, as many to Sicily and to Thurium. He distributed to them by lot the lands of the Island of Aegina, whose in habitants had been massacred or banished. He paid the hornets, of whom he could not relieve Athens. He gave them money, even for going to the theatre. It was he who introduced the custom of paying six thousand citizens, that is to say nearly half the population enjoying political rights, for exercising the function of judges (*dikasts*).* The pay of the judges, which at first was one obol per day was raised to three by the demagogue Cleon. The annual sum amounted to 5,560 talents, or 180,000 dollars, which was a considerable sum even for a city like Athens. So when Peisander abolished the democratic government, he decreed that the judges should no longer be paid, that the soldiers alone should receive wages, and that the management of the public affairs should be entrusted to but five thousand citizens, capable of serving the state with their fortune and their person. Pericles, to restrain and satisfy the artisans, who made common cause with the hornets, had been obliged to undertake great public works.

The economic phenomena, which, by dispossessing a part of the patrician class, created a class of unclassed, ruined revolutionaries, developed more rapidly in the cities, which by their maritime position became centres of commercial and industrial activity. The class of plebeians enriched by commerce, industry and usury, increased in proportion as the number of ruined patricians and parasites increased. These enriched plebeians, to snatch political rights from the rulers, leagued

---

* The number of citizens of Athens having political rights was 14,040, as is proved by the census made by Pericles, for the distribution of the grain which was sent to them as a present from Egypt.

themselves with the dispossessed nobles and when they had obtained political rights, they united with the rulers to combat the impoverished patricians and the plebeians with little or no fortune; and these latter, when they became masters of the city, abolished debts, banished the wealthy and divided up their property. The banished rich implored the assistance of foreigners to return to their city, and in their turn massacred their conquerors. These class struggles ensanguined all the cities of Greece and prepared them for the dominance of Macedonia and Rome.

The economic phenomena and the class struggles which they engendered had overthrown the conditions of life, in the midst of which the heroic ideal had been elaborated.

The manner of making war had been profoundly transformed by the economic phenomena. Piracy and brigandage, those favourite industries of barbaric heroes, had been rendered difficult, since the improved fortifications of the cities sheltered them from surprises. Solon, although at the head of a commercial city and himself a merchant, had been obliged out of complaisance for inveterate habits, to found at Athens a college of pirates, but the establishment of numerous colonies along the shores of the Mediterranean, and the commercial development resulting from this, had forced the maritime cities to police the seas and give chase to the pirates, whose industry lost prestige in proportion as its profits diminished.

Changes of great importance had been made in the military organization on sea and land. The Homeric heroes, like the Scandinavians who later on were to ravage the European shores of the Atlantic, when they started on a maritime expedition took no rowers and sailors with them. Their flat-bottomed ships, which they built themselves and which according to Homer could not have carried more than from fifty to one hundred and twenty men, were manned only by warriors who rowed and fought. The battles were on land only. The Iliad mentions no engagement on the sea. The improvements which the Corinthians introduced into ship building and the increase of naval strength made necessary the use of mercenary sailors, who took no part in the battles in which the hoplites and other less heavily armed warriors engaged on sea and land. The mercenary once established in the fleet pushed himself into the land armies. These were at first composed

only of citizens taking the field with three or four days' rations,
which they furnished themselves, as well as their horses and
arms. They foraged on the enemy when their provisions gave out
and returned to their firesides when the expedition, always of
short duration, was ended. But when the war, carried on at a
distance, required a long attendance of the army, the state was
obliged to provide for the support of the warrior. Pericles at the
beginning of the Peloponnesian War gave for the first time at
Athens pay to the warriors, who then became soldiers — that is to
say, wage-workers, mercenaries. The pay amounted to two
drachmas (about forty cents) a day, for the hoplites. Diodorus
Siculus says that it was at the siege of Veii that the Romans
introduced pay into their armies. From the moment when pay was
given for fighting, war became a lucrative profession, as in the
Homeric times; corps of soldiers were formed in which the poor
citizens and the unclassed and ruined patricians enrolled
themselves, just as there existed already bands of mercenary
rowers and sailors, selling their services to the highest bidder.*

Socrates said that an oligarchical state — that is to say, one
governed by the rich — 'is powerless to make war, because it is
obliged to arm the multitude and consequently to have more to
fear from it than from the enemy; or else not to use it and go into
battle with an army truly oligarchical' — that is to say reduced to
the rich citizens. But the new necessities of war forced the rich to
repress their fears and to violate the ancient customs. They were
obliged to arm the poor and even the slaves. The Athenians
enrolled slaves in their fleet, promising them liberty, and they

---

* Thucydides relates that the ambassadors of Corinth, in order to influence the
Spartans, intimidated by the naval forces of Athens, to join them in declaring war,
said to them: 'We need only make a loan to entice away with higher wage the
rowers of Athens.' Nicias, in the letter which he addresses from Sicily to the
Athenian assembly, complains of the desertion of the mercenaries. Some years
later the sailors left the Athenian fleet in Asia Minor to pass over to that of
Lysander, who gave them higher pay. The Carthaginians, to fight the Greek army
in Sciily, enrolled Greek soldiers who were working at the trade of fighting for pay.
Alexander found in the service of Darius Greek mercenaries whom he
incorporated in his own army after having pardoned them for fighting on the side of
the barbarians against the Greeks. Fighting for pay abolished the patriotic
sentiment so savage and deep-rooted in the barbarian. Greek mercenaries were
found fighting in all armies. When the stoics and cynics, long before the
Christians, spoke of human brotherhood arising above the narrow walls of the
ancient city, they were merely giving a humanitarian and philosophical expression
to the fact accomplished by economic and political events.

liberated those who had fought valiantly at Arginousae (B.C. 406). The Spartans themselves were obliged to arm and liberate Helots. They sent to the relief of the Syracusans, besieged by the Athenians, a corps of 600 hoplites composed of Helots and Neodamodes (newly admitted to citizenship); while the government of the Spartan Republic branded with infamy the Spartans who had laid down their arms at Sphacteria, although several of them had occupied high political positions, it granted liberty to the Helots who had smuggled provisions through to them while they were besieged by the Athenians. The wage which transformed the warrior into a mercenary, into a soldier,* becomes in a short time an instrument of social dissolution. The Greeks had sworn at Platea, that 'they would bequeath to their children's children hatred against the Persians, that this hatred might last as long as the rivers should flow to the sea.' Nevertheless half a century after this proud oath Athenians, Spartans and Peloponnesians paid eager court to the king of Persia in order to obtain subsidies to pay their sailors and their soldiers. The Peloponnesian War hastened the fall of the aristocratic parties and brought out into broad daylight the ruin of heroic customs, which the economic phenomena had silently prepared.

The rich who had reserved to themselves as the first of their privileges the right to bear arms and to defend their country rapidly acquired the custom of replacing themselves in the army by mercenaries. A century after the innovation of Pericles the bulk of the Athenian armies was composed of paid soldiers. Demosthenes says in one of his Olynthiacs that in the army sent against Olynthus there were 4,000 citizens and 10,000 mercenaries; that in that which Philip defeated at Chaeronea there were 2,000 Athenians and Thebans and 15,000 mercenaries. The rich, although not fighting, reaped the benefits of war. 'The rich are excellent for keeping riches,' said Athenagoras, the Syracusan demagogue, 'they leave dangers to the multitude, and not content with seizing the greater part of the advantages of war, they usurped them all.'

---

* The word *soldat*, which in European languages has replaced warrior (*soldier*, English; *soldat*, German; *soldado*, Spanish; *soldato*, Italian, etc.) comes from *solidus*, a small coin, from which is derived *solde*, pay. It is from the wage he receives that the soldier derives his name. Historically the soldier is the first wage worker.

The barbarian patricians, trained from childhood to all the labours of war, were warriors who defied all comparison. The newly rich, on the contrary, could endure war with difficulty, as Socrates states: 'When the rich and the poor find themselves together in the army on land or sea and observe each othei mutually in circumstances of danger, the rich then have no reason to despise the poor; on the contrary, when the poor man, wiry and sunburned, posted on the battlefield by the side of a rich man, brought up in the shade and weighed down with superfluous flesh, sees him all out of breath and troubled with his body — what thought do you think comes to him at that moment? Does he not say to himself that these people owe their riches only to the cowardice of the poor, and when they are by themselves, do they not say to each other, 'Of a truth, these rich are not good for much''.'

The rich, deserting the military service and putting mercenaries in their place to defend their country, lost the physical and moral qualities of the heroic ideal while preserving the material property which justified their existence. It happened then, as Aristotle observes, that wealth, far from being the reward of virtue, excused men from being virtuous.*

But the heroic virtues, no longer cultivated by the rich, became the appanage of mercenaries, freedmen and slaves, who possessed no material goods; and these virtues, which led the barbaric heroes to property, sufficed only to enable the soldiers to live miserably on their pay. Economic phenomena had thus decreed the divorce of the material goods and the moral qualities, formerly so intimately united.†

Among these mercenaries with heroic virtues were found a

---

* A similar phenomenon reappeared toward the end of the Middle Ages. The feudal lord had no right to the rents in kind or the personal service of his serfs and vassals, except on condition of defending them against the numerous enemies which surrounded them; but when in the course of economic and political events there was a general pacification within the country, the lord no longer had to fulfill his role of protector, yet this did not prevent him from preserving and even aggravating the services and the rents in kind, which had lost their justification.

† The capitalist epoch has seen an analogous divorce, quite as brutal and quite as fertile in revolutionary consequences. At the beginning of the capitalist epoch, during the first years of the nineteenth century, the ideal of the small trader and the artisan acquired a certain consistency in public opinion: labour, order and economy were considered as closely bound to property. These moral virtues then

considerable number of patricians who had lost their property through usury and civil wars, while the rich included in their ranks many people enriched by commerce, usury, and even by war, carried on by others. Thus at the beginning of the Peloponnesian War, when Corinth prepared its expedition against Corcyra, Thucydides relates that the state promised its citizens, who should enroll themselves a share in the conquered lands and offered the same advantages to those who, without taking part in the campaign, should give 50 drachmas.

The heroic ideal had fallen to pieces, sowing disorder and confusion in moral ideas, and this confusion was reflected in the religious ideas. The grossest superstition continued to flourish even at Athens: which condemned to death Anaxagoras, Diagoras and Socrates; which burned the works of Protagoras for impiety against the gods. Nevertheless the comic authors launched against the gods and the priests, which was still bolder, the most audacious and the most cynical attacks. The demagogues and tyrants profaned their temples and pillaged their sacred treasures; and debauchees defiled and overturned by night the statues of the gods placed in the streets. The religious legends, handed down from the most remote antiquity and accepted naively as long as they agreed with current customs, had become shocking by their grossness. Pythagoras and Socrates demanded their suppression, even though it were necessary to mutilate Homer and Hesiod, or to forbid the reading of their poems. Epicurus declared that to believe in the legends about the gods and to repeat them were the acts of atheism. The Christians of the first centuries did nothing but generalize and systematize the criticisms which the pagans had made in the midst of paganism.

The hour had sounded for the bourgeois society, then springing up — for the society based on individual property and commercial production — to formulate a moral ideal and a religion corresponding to the new social conditions fashioned by economic phenomena; and it is the eternal honour of the sophistical philosophy of Greece to have traced the principal lines

---

led to the possession of material goods. The economists and the bourgeois moralists may still, like parrots, repeat that property is the fruit of labour, but it is no longer its reward. The virtues of the ideal artisan and the small trader no longer lead the wage-worker anywhere but to the bureau of charities and the hospital.

of the new religion and the new moral ideal. The ethical work of
Socrates and Plato has not yet been surpassed.*

III!

THE BOURGEOIS MORAL IDEAL

The heroic ideal, simple and logical, reflected in thought the
surrounding reality without disguises and without distortions. It
erected into primary virtues of the human soul the physical and
moral qualities which the barbarian heroes had to possess in order
to conquer and preserve the material goods which classed them
among the first citizens and the happy men of earth.

The reality of the rising democratic bourgeois society no longer
corresponded to this ideal. Riches, honours and enjoyments were
no longer the prize of valour and of the other heroic virtues any
more than in our capitalistic society property is the recompense
of labour, method and economy. Nevertheless, riches continued
always to be the end of human activity and even became more
and more its sole and supreme end. To reach this end, so ardently
desired, it was no longer necessary to put in action the heroic
qualities formerly so prized; but as human nature was not
despoiled of these qualities, while in the new social conditions
they had become useless and even hurtful for making one's way
in life, and as they became in the ancient republics causes of
trouble and civil war, there was urgent need of subduing and
domesticating them by giving them a platonic satisfaction in order
to utilize them for the prosperity and preservation of the new social
order.

The sophists undertook the task. Some, like the Cyrenaics, not
trying to disguise the reality, recognized squarely and proclaimed
loudly that the possession of wealth was 'the sovereign good' and

---

* We must understand by commodity production the form of production in which
the labourer produces not for his consumption or that of his family, but for sale.
This form of production, which characterizes bourgeois society, is distinguished
absolutely from the forms which preceded it, in which production was for one's
own consumption, whether employing slaves, serfs or wage-workers. The
patrician families of antiquity, like the lords of the Middle Ages, had produced on
their estates and in their workshop, food, clothing, arms, etc.; in a word, almost
everything they had need of, and they exchanged only the surplus above their
consumption at certain periods of the year.

that the physical and intellectual enjoyments which it procures
were 'the chief end of man'. They professed boldly the art of
gaining wealth by all means, lawful and unlawful, and of escaping
the disagreeable consequences which might ensue from the
unskilful violation of laws and customs. Other sophists, like the
cynics and many of the stoics, in open revolt against the laws and
customs, wished to return to the pre-social state and to 'live
according to nature'. They affected contempt of wealth: 'The
wise man alone is rich,' they shouted ostentatiously. But this
disdain for the wealth beyond their reach, was too violently
opposed to the trend of the day and the general sentiment, and
was often too declamatory to be taken seriously. Moreover,
neither group gave any tendency of social utility to their moral
theories, and it was precisely this that bourgeois democracy
demanded. Other sophists, like Socrates, Plato and a great number
of stoics faced the moral problem squarely. They did not erect
contempt for riches into a dogma, but on the contrary they
recognized they were one of the conditions of happiness, and
even of virtue, though they had ceased to be its recompense. The
just man ought no longer to call on the outside world for the
reward of his virtues but to seek for it within his inner sanctuary,
in his conscience, which should be guided by eternal principles
placed outside the world of reality, and he could hope to obtain
this reward only in another life.*

---

* The soul, a metaphysical entity, existing by itself, independently of the body,
which it animates during life and abandons after death, is an invention of the
savages. They had found nothing simpler to explain the phenomena of the dream
than to divide man in two; the body buried in sleep, remained in its place deprived
of life, while the soul, which they called the double, set off on a journey, hunted,
fought, avenged itself and acted; then returned to reanimate its corporal envelope,
which came to life. The double after death continued to live. Thus at funerals they
sacrificed animals and broke weapons in order that their doubles might continue to
serve the dead. The souls of savages and barbarians living the communal life of the
clan, those of women as well as those of men, betook themselves after death to an
extra-terrestial dwelling where they lived again an existence analogous to that
which they had lived on earth. The soul of the Eskimo hunted the seal: that of the
Redskin chased the bison; that of the Scandinavian fought by day and banqueted
by night in Valhalla with the Valkyries. Following and resulting from the
transformation of primitive communism, the notion of the extra-terrestial dwelling
slipped away from the human mind, and that of the soul became obscured — to
the point that during the patriarchal period, the head of the family was the only one
who was thought to live after death; but his soul instead of betaking itself to
paradise, led a supremely sad life in his tomb. The head of the family, who in his
quality of administrator of the property had centralized in his person the rights of

They did not revolt against the laws and customs like the cynics; on the contrary they advised conformity to them and counselled each to remain in his place and to adjust himself to his social station. It is thus that St. Augustine and the fathers of the church imposed as a duty upon Christian slaves to redouble their zeal for their earthly master in order to merit the favours of their heavenly master.*

Socrates, who had lived in intimacy with Pericles, and Plato, who had frequented the courts of the Tyrants of Syracuse, were profound politicans, seeing in ethics and religions nothing but instruments for governing men and maintaining social order.

These two subtle geniuses of sophistical philosophy are the founders of the individualistic ethics of the bourgeoisie — of the ethics which can only end by putting words and acts into contradiction, and by giving a philosophical sanction to the division of life into two parts; the ideal life, pure, and the practical life, impure — one being the antithesis of the other. It is thus, that 'very noble and very honourable ladies' of the seventeenth century had succeeded in making love in a double fashion, consoling themselves for their intellectual love with platonic lovers by solid enjoyment of physical love with their husbands, completed according to their need by one or several lovers for good measure.

---

the members of his family, equally concentrated in himself their immortal souls. Then another explanation of the dream was discovered. Dreams were communications from the divinity, which had to be interpreted to understand one's destiny. I spoke above of the role played by the immortality of the soul of the head of the family in the establishment of the right of primogeniture. The new explanation of the dream gave birth to a new order of exploiters of human stupidity, practising the trade of dream-interpreter. They flourished in the time of Socrates. At the time of the dissolution of the patriarchate, all members of the family, women excepted, in regaining their independence, found again, at the same time with their rights, their immortal souls, which had been confiscated by the head of the family. But as most of those who had re-entered into the possession of their souls had on the contrary lost their house and terrestial goods, they were greatly embarrassed to know where they should lodge after death. They were obliged to reinvent the extra-terrestial dwelling of the savages. Socrates and Plato were ardent in utilizing the immortality of the soul as an instrument for governing men, disengaging it from the ruins of the patriarchal family. They had been preceded on this path by the Pythagorians. But it was Christianity which carried the exploitation of the soul to its highest perfection.

* The cynics, and after them the first Christians, could demand the abolition of slavery. They were revolutionaries, but Socrates and the fathers of the church undertook rather the mission of propping up the existing social institutions by the aid of morals and religion.

It is impossible for the ethics of any society based on commodity production to escape this contradiction, which is the consequence of the conflicts in which the capitalist struggles: if to succeed in his commercial and industrial enterprises, he must capture the good opinion of the public by adorning himself with virtues, he cannot put them into practice if he wishes to prosper. But he understands that these virtues of parade are for others imperious — 'categorical imperatives', as Kant says. It is thus that if he unloads worthless merchandise, he demands payment in good money.* The bourgeoisie, if it maintains its class dictatorship only by brutal strength, has need of sapping the revolutionary energy of the oppressed classes by making them believe that its social order is the realization as nearly as possible of the eternal principles which adorn the liberal philosophy, and which Socrates and Plato had partially formulated more than four centuries before Jesus Christ.

Religious ethics does not escape this fatal contradiction. If the highest formula of Christianity is 'love one another', the Christian churches, to draw customers to their shops, think only of converting the heretics by fire and sword, in order to save them, as they assure us, from the eternal fires of hell.

The barbarian social environment, engendered by war and the communism of the clan, resulted in stretching to their extreme limit the noble qualities of the human being — physical strength and courage and moral stoicism, the devotion of body and goods to the community, to the city. The bourgeois social environment,

---

* The pagans did not try to disguise the truth and they put commerce under the patronage of Mercury, the god of thieves. The Catholics are more Jesuitical. The religious orders, which are not exclusively consecrated to the capture of inheritances, make of commerce and industry their principal and even their only occupation, although they pretend to worship a God pure of all falsehood and innocent of all fraud. The first act of the capitalistic bourgeoisie on coming into power in 1789 was to proclaim the liberty of theft, by relieving commerce and industry from all control. The guild masters of the Middle Ages, working only for the local market, for their neighbours, had established a severe control over production. The syndics of the guilds were authorized to enter workshops at any hour in order to examine the material and the manner in which it was worked. To facilitate their inspection the doors and the windows of the workshop remained open while the work was going on. The artisans of the Middle Ages worked literally under the eyes of the public. The goods before being put on sale were controlled by the syndics and marked with a seal or some other sign attesting that the guild guaranteed their good quality. This incessant control, which hampered and repressed the fight of the thieving genius of the capitalistic bourgeoisie, was one of its most serious grievances against the guilds.

based on individual property and commodity production, erects on the contrary into cardinal virtues the worst qualities of the human soul, egotism, hypocrisy, intrigue, profligacy and pilfering.*

Bourgeois ethics, although Plato claims that it descends from the heavens and that it is on a plane above vile interests, reflects so modestly the vulgar reality, that the sophists instead of elaborating a new word to designate this principle, which according to Victor Cousin, who is a good judge of it, is 'ethics in its entirety', took the current word and called it the Good — *to agathon*. When the Christian ideal was formulated by the side of and in the train of the philosophical ideal, it underwent the same necessity. The fathers of the church impressed upon it the seal of vulgar reality.

Beatus, which the pagans employed for rich, and which Varro defines as 'he who possesses much goods', *qui multa bona possidet*, becomes in ecclesiastic Latin, 'he who possesses the grace of God'; *beatitudo*, which Petronius and the writers of the Decadence employ for riches, means under the pen of St. Jerome, heavenly felicity; *beatissimus*, the epithet given by the authors of paganism to the opulent man, becomes that of the patriarchs, of the fathers of the church and the saints.

Language has revealed to us that the barbarians, by their

---

* The bourgeois writers are accustomed to heaping all the vices of civilization upon the savages and barbarians, whom the capitalists rob, exploit and exterminate under pretext of civilizing them, and it is they who corrupt them physically and morally with alcoholism, syphilis, the Bible, obligatory labour and commerce. The travellers who come in contact with savage nations not contaminated by civilization, are struck by their moral virtues; and Leibnitz, who alone is worth all the philosophers of liberalism, could not refrain from paying homage to them: 'I know beyond doubt,' he wrote, 'that the savages of Canada live together in peace, although there is no sort of magistrate among them. We never, or scarcely ever, see in that part of the world quarrels, hatreds or wars, if not between men of different nations and different languages. I should almost dare call this a political miracle unknown to Aristotle, and which Hobbes has not observed. Even the children playing together rarely come to blows, and when they begin to warm up a little too much, they are soon restrained by their comrades. Do not imagine that the peace in which they live is the effect of a sluggish and insensible character, for nothing equals their activity against the enemy, and the sentiment of honour among them is active to the last degree, as is testified by the ardour which they show for vengeance and the fortitude with which they die in the midst of torments. If these people, with such great natural qualities, could some day add to them our arts and science we should by the side of them be mere abortions.'

habitual anthropomorphic way of proceeding, had incorporated their moral virtues into material goods. But the economic phenomena and the political events which prepared the ground for the mode of production and exchange of the bourgeoisie, dissolved the primitive union of the moral and the material. The barbarian did not blush for this union, since it was the physical and moral qualities of which he was the proudest which were set in action for the conquest and the preservation of material goods. The bourgeois, on the contrary, is ashamed of the low virtues which he is forced to put in play to arrive at his fortune, so he wishes to make believe, and he ends by believing, that his soul wanders above matter and feeds on eternal truths and immutable principles; but language, the incorrigible tell-tale, unveils to us that under the thick clouds of the most purified ethics hides the sovereign idol of the capitalists, the Good, the Property-god.

Ethics, like the other phenomena of human activity, is subject to the law of economic materialism formulated by Marx: the mode of production of the material life dominates in general the development of the social, political and intellectual life.